Reader Meets Author/ Bridging the Gap

A Psycholinguistic and Sociolinguistic Perspective

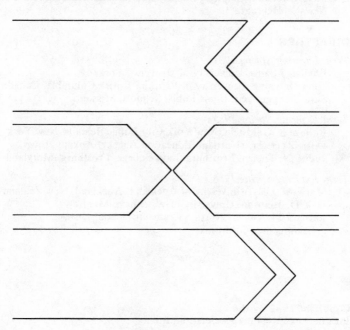

Edited by

Judith A. Langer
University of California at Berkeley
and
M. Trika Smith-Burke
New York University

INTERNATIONAL READING ASSOCIATION
800 Barksdale Road   Newark, Delaware 19711

INTERNATIONAL READING ASSOCIATION

Copyright 1982 by the
International Reading Association, Inc.

Library of Congress Cataloging in Publication Data
Main entry under title:

Reader meets author/bridging the gap.

Includes bibliographies.

1. Reading comprehension—Addresses, essays, lectures. 2. Reading research—Addresses, essays, lectures. I. Langer, Judith A. II. Smith-Burke, M. Trika.
LB1050.45.R399   428.4'3   81-20769
ISBN 0-87207-529-X   AACR2
Second Printing, December 1983

Contents

iii

Foreword

The International Reading Association is a worldwide organization consisting mostly of professionals from a wide range of backgrounds united by a common interest in written language. In our meetings and our publications we provide a platform for a full range of ideas from a full range of perspectives. In this, our goal is to advance literacy and understanding of literacy by providing for communication, and bridging the gap among people with different perspectives.

In this publication, Trika Smith-Burke and Judith Langer have sought to explore how the gap is bridged between reader and author. To do this, they have brought together a group of scholars, researchers, theoreticians, and teacher educators from a range of disciplines: linguistics, psychology, and education, with a range of approaches to the establishment of knowledge. The objective is to create an interdisciplinary exchange among contributors and to make available to teachers the frontier knowledge on comprehension. Thus, the creators of this volume seek to bridge a gap between those who convey knowledge and those who make practical application of that knowledge.

Nothing is more important to the central mission of IRA than transforming current knowledge into current practice. That is the ultimate bridge that concerns us all.

Kenneth S. Goodman, President
International Reading Association
1981-1982

Preface

Both researchers and reading teachers agree that a major question in reading instruction is how to help students learn to comprehend what they read. This question has been asked for years, and although diverse groups of educators and researchers have contributed significantly to our growing body of knowledge, the question remains only partially answered.

One complicating factor is that, in trying to further our understanding of reading comprehension, we need to examine more closely how readers derive meaning from texts. And when meaning is the focus, it becomes necessary to view reading as a language process involving flexible interactions among the reader, the text, and the context in which the meaning is derived. The *reader* brings an entire lifetime of experiences, knowledge, and abilities to each reading situation, and each of these substantially affects comprehension. The *text* represents an author's attempt to convey a message, for a reason, to an anticipated audience, and each of these factors will affect the style, format, language, and structure of the text, and these in turn will affect the comprehending process. The *context* represents all those environmental cues which are present in any communication situation and which help to shape comprehension. It is not the physical environment alone, but the specific reading task as well as the physical, psychological, and affective conditions of the reader which determine the emotional and cognitive responses which influence the meaning derived by each reader.

Within this view of reading for meaning, it becomes necessary to consider comprehension as somewhat idiosyncratic, to consider the consequences or effects which the communication act has on the particular hearer or reader. A range of meanings may be derived from a particular text based upon all the personal, environmental, and cognitive influences which shape every moment of reading.

From this brief introduction it becomes evident that an extremely broad view of reader-text interaction must be taken by teachers who wish to help students improve their comprehension. Readability formulae are insufficient in predicting a successful reader-text match, and a subskills approach to reading performance neglects important dimensions of the process in teaching reading comprehension.

This book examines how comprehension is affected by: 1) what the reader brings to the text; 2) the manner in which the text is structured by the author; and 3) the contextual variables which shape the meaning a reader derives. In order to examine these issues, we have commissioned a series of articles presenting current research about a variety of aspects of comprehension. Because of the diversity of the issues addressed, it has been necessary to choose examples of research which are based on diverse paradigms, utilizing many different techniques to collect, analyze, and interpret data. These theoretical articles are presented in Part 1 of this book.

In order to understand how the research findings in Part 1 relate to the realities of the classroom, we also commissioned a series of articles which describe some of the implications for instructional environments. We feel it is important for us, as practitioners, to continually reflect on existing practice in light of new theories and research findings. In some cases this may lead to a validation of current practice, in others to a restructuring or combining of existing practices, and in still others to the development of new types of instructional activities. Articles which link theory to implications for classroom practice appear in Part 2 of this book.

Background

During the past twenty years reading researchers have turned to the research findings and methodological approaches of related disciplines in order to find answers to their multidimensional questions. The primary focus has been on the processes involved in deriving meaning from text. Cognitive psychologists have provided us with insights as to how people take in, organize, store, and retrieve information. Advances in the field of linguistics have focused on language acquisition, linguistic development, and the structure of texts. Sociologists and anthropologists have made us aware of the influence of cultural and situational variables on the use of oral and written language.

The task for the reading specialist is to consolidate and integrate this knowledge to further our understanding of reading comprehension. In order to provide both a conceptual and a methodological background for the articles included in this volume, an overview of some of the major questions and research techniques follows.

The early work in reading research (Gates, 1921; Gray, 1919) tended to focus on the identification of specific factors which were presumed to comprise reading. Tests were developed to assess proficiency in component skill areas such as vocabulary, word recognition, structural analysis, and literal and interpretive comprehension. Diagnostic and prescriptive teaching as well as classroom management systems were designed and implemented based on this model. Although many important insights were gained from the early reading research findings, the area of reading comprehension as a communication activity and how reading comprehension is related to the other language arts remained elusive.

More recent theoretical perspectives have been based on aspects of the communication triangle which presupposes that interactions among the reader, the text, and the larger context all contribute to aspects of comprehension. The act of communication involves a sender and a receiver. A message may be conveyed by the sender in a variety of modes: written, oral or nonverbal. As the message travels from sender to receiver, it may be affected by factors in the environment or by the communicators themselves. Those aspects of sender-message-receiver interaction which facilitate or impede comprehension have received greatest scholarly attention in recent years.

The Text Variable

Linguistic inquiry in the late 1950s (Chomsky, 1957) focused on describing language patterns and their underlying syntactic rules. The units of study were primarily the word and the sentence. During this period there was also great emphasis, through observational case study, on how children acquire language (Brown & Bellugi, 1964; Weir, 1962) and the relationship of oral language to written language (Chomsky, 1969; Ruddell, 1965). Subsequently, the focus of linguistic inquiry shifted from syntax to semantics—how meaning is conveyed. New linguistic models were developed for text characteristics including case grammar at the sentence level (Fillmore, 1968; Grimes, 1972), discourse analysis at both the propositional and rhetorical levels (Applebee, 1978; Frederickson, 1975; Halliday & Hasan, 1976; Kintsch, 1972; Meyer, 1975; Van Dijk, 1977) and story grammars at the level of larger structural units within narratives (Mandler & Johnson, 1977; Stein & Glenn, 1978; Thorndyke, 1977). These advances permitted reading professionals to better identify those aspects of the written message which affect text processing and comprehension.

Reader-Text Interaction

In their interactive views of reading first presented in the late 1960s, Goodman (1970) and Smith (1971) both emphasized how the reader's past experiences influence word identification and text recall. They pointed out that when cultural, experiential, or linguistic differences exist between author and reader, text processing and comprehension are affected. Although comprehension may or may not be adversely affected, some idiosyncratic interpretation of the text might result from these personal experiential and knowledge bases.

Some years later, psychologists such as Anderson and Ortony (1975) and Rumelhart (1975), frustrated by the limitations of the behaviorist and verbal learning research paradigms, returned to the more global works of Bartlett (1932) and Kant (1781) for inspiration. They began to ask questions about cognition and the processing of larger chunks of text: questions such as how knowledge is organized, stored, and retrieved from memory. Developmental psychologists such as Flavell (1976) began to examine the metacognitive or executive monitoring processes by which learners become aware of what they know and what they need to know, and are able to utilize decision-making strategies to monitor and facilitate successful comprehension.

In spite of their differing traditions, psychologists, reading researchers, and reading educators commonly recognize that knowledge, based on past experiences, affects the processing, comprehension, and interpretation of texts. As a result, many classroom practices have become more integrative during the past few years.

Examining the Context

As research findings began to affirm the strong influence of prior knowledge or comprehension, questions concerning the influence of contextual and cultural factors arose. The large number of urban children who were failing to learn to read led a number of researchers to study the effects of contextual and cultural variables on learning. First attempts by researchers such as Labov (1970) and Shuy (1969) were sociolinguistic in nature, detailing the systematic features of specific dialects and the interaction of these features with school tasks. Next, the influence of anthropologists such as Gumperz and Hymes (1971), Hymes (1967), and McDermott (1976) led to a broadened definition of cultural influences. These researchers focused on how the differences between home and school language and goals affect personal interactions and academic achievement. Currently, investigations in this area of inquiry are focusing on the interaction between cultural variables and specific linguistic phenomena. It has been demonstrated that readers tend to impose their own cultural perspectives in their comprehension of culturally discrepant material (Steffensen, Jogdeo, & Anderson, 1978). In addition, researchers have begun to describe the influence of culture on the educational experiences of minority children (Gumperz, 1981; Heath, in press). Many eduators now view print and story awareness, home language, and the functional uses of language as aspects of the total language background drawn upon by each reader during each reading event.

In this overview, we have briefly outlined the underlying linguistic, psychological, sociological, and anthropological based movements which have led to the issues discussed in this book. We are fully aware that some of the ideas will not be new to many of our readers, but hope the variety of views presented in the following pages will help our readers to reflect on the broad spectrum of factors which may assist or impede students in comprehending the texts they read.

JUDITH LANGER AND TRIKA SMITH-BURKE

References

ANDERSON, R.C., & ORTONY, A. On putting apples into bottles, a problem of polysemy. *Cognitive Psychology*, 1975, 7, 167-180.

APPLEBEE, A.N. *The child's concept of story*. Chicago: University of Chicago Press, 1978.

BARTLETT, F.C. *Remembering: A study in experimental and social psychology*. Cambridge University Press, 1932.

BROWN, R., & BELLUGI, U. The acquisition of language. *Monographs of the Society of Research in Child Development*, 1964, 29.

CHOMSKY, C. *Acquisition of syntax in children from 5 to 10*. Cambridge, Massachusetts: MIT Press, 1969.

CHOMSKY, N. *Syntactic structures*. The Hague: Mouton, 1957.

DAVIS, F.B. Fundamental factors of comprehension in reading. *Psycometrika*, 1944, 9, 185-197.

FILLMORE, C.J. The case for case. In E. Bach & R.T. Harms (Eds.), *Universals in linguistic theory*. New York: Holt, Rinehart & Winston, 1968.

FLAVELL, J.H. Related properties of cognitive development. *Cognitive Psychology*, 1971, 2, 421-453.

FREDRICKSON, C.H. Representing logical and semantic structures of knowledge acquired from discourse. *Cognitive Psychology*, 1975, 7, 371-458.

GATES, A.I. An experimental and statistical study of reading tests. *Journal of Educational Psychology*, 1921, 12, 303-314.

GOODMAN, K.S. Behind the eye: What happens in reading. In K.S. Goodman & O. Niles (Eds.), *Reading: Process and program*. Urbana, Illinois: National Council of Teachers of English, 1970, 3-38.

GRAY, W.S. Principles of method in teaching reading as derived from scientific investigations. *National Society for the Study of Education yearbook*, 18, part 2. Bloomington, Illinois: Public School Book Company, 1919.

GRIMES, J.E. *The thread of discourse*. Ithaca, New York: Cornell University, 1972.

GUMPERZ, J. Conversational inference and classroom learning. In J. Green & C. Wallatt (Eds.), *Ethnography and language in educational settings*. Norwood, New Jersey: Ablex, 1981.

GUMPERZ, J., & HYMES, D. *Directions in sociolinguistics*, New York: Holt, Rinehart & Winston, 1971.

HALLIDAY, M.A.K., & HASAN, R. *Cohesion in English*. London: Longman, 1976.

HEATH, S.B. Protean shapes in literacy events. In D. Tannen (Ed.), *Spoken and written language*. Norwood, New Jersey: Ablex (in press).

HYMES, D. Models of the interaction of language and social settings. *Journal of Social Issues*, 1967, 23, 8-28.

KANT, E. *Critique of pure reason* (1st ed., 1781). London: Macmillan, 1963.

KINTSCH, W. Notes on the structure of semantic memory. In E. Tulving & W. Donaldson (Eds.), *Organization of memory*. New York: Academic Press, 1972.

LABOV, W. *Language in the inner city: Studies in the black English vernacular*. Philadelphia: University of Pennsylvania Press, 1972.

MANDLER, J.M., & JOHNSON, N.S. Remembrance of things parsed: Story structure and recall. *Cognitive Psychology*, 1977, *9*, 111-151.

McDERMOTT, R. Achieving school failure. In H. Singer & R. Ruddell (Eds.), *Theoretical models and processes of reading*. Newark, Delaware: International Reading Association, 1976, 389-447.

MEYER, B. *The organization of prose and its effect on memory*. Amsterdam: North Holland Press, 1975.

RUDDELL, R.B. Effect of the similarity of oral and written patterns of language structure on reading comprehension. *Elementary English*, 1965, *42*, 403-410.

RUMELHART, D.E. Notes on a schema for stories. In D.G. Bobrow & A.M. Collins (Eds.), *Representation and understanding: Studies in cognitive science*. New York: Academic Press, 1975.

SHUY, R. Some language and cultural differences in a theory of reading. In K. Goodman and J. Fleming (Eds.), *Psycholinguistics and the teaching of reading*. Newark, Delaware: International Reading Association, 1969.

SMITH, F. *Understanding reading*. New York: Holt, Rinehart & Winston, 1971.

STEFFENSEN, M.S., JOGDEO, C., & ANDERSON, R.C. A cross-cultural perspective on reading comprehension (Technical Report No. 97), July 1978. (ED 159 660)

STEIN, N., & GLENN, C.G. An analysis of story comprehension in elementary school children. In R.O. Freedle (Ed.), *Discourse processing: New directions*. Norwood, New Jersey: Ablex, 1978.

THORNDYKE, P.W. Cognitive structures in comprehension and memory of narrative discourse. *Cognitive Psychology*, 1977, *9*, 77-110.

VAN DIJK, T.A. *Text and context*. London: Longman, 1977.

WEIR, R. *Language in the crib*. The Hague: Mouton, 1962.

Part 1 Theory and Research
Introduction

The articles in the first section of this book present current theory and research and are organized according to three aspects of comprehension: reader/text interaction, text structure, and the context for reading. The first two articles describe different facets of reader/text interaction. Adams and Bruce discuss how the reader's prior knowledge or schemata is used to interpret text, while Brown explores the role of metacognitive processes in learning how to learn from reading. The third article, by Tierney and Mosenthal, examines the second aspect of reading comprehension—text structure. The authors summarize and critique recent methods of text analysis for researchers and teachers. The last two articles in this section focus on contextual factors which can influence comprehension. Using a case study approach, Harste, Burke, and Woodward document the development of oral and written langauge, based on experiences in the natural environment before children enter school. They discuss the possible mismatch between naturally developing strategies and instructional strategies utilized in classrooms. In the final article, Hall and Guthrie examine cultural variations in the use and function of vocabulary as they affect communication and the acquisition of school skills.

Background Knowledge and Reading Comprehension

Marilyn Adams
Bertram Bruce
Bolt Beranek and Newman Incorporated*

So very much of what we learn, we learn through language. Certainly most of our formal education is acquired through language. These observations seem almost too common to set in print. Yet they turn from banal to deeply paradoxical with the realization that we can only learn through language that which we, in some sense, already know. That is, through language, novel concepts can only be communicated in the form of novel combinations of familiar concepts.

As an example, we can directly access the meanings of only the words we already know. New words are interpretable only if they are explained in terms of old words. This can be done either explicitly, by presenting their definitions, or implicitly, by setting them in a context of old words that effectively constrains their meanings. The analogous situation holds for objects, events, and ideas. If familiar, they may be brought to mind by the slightest and most oblique reference; if unfamiliar, however, they can be communicated through language only by comparing and contrasting them with familiar concepts, by decomposing them into familiar concepts and then piecing together the whole, or by setting them in or against a familiar context.

An upshot of these considerations is that it is misleading to speak of language as a means of expressing one's thoughts.

* The authors would like to thank Elizabeth Collins for her analysis of several fables; Allan Collins for collaboration in gathering protocols; Ed Smith and Kathy Starr for comments on the chapter; and Cynthia Hunt and Brenda Starr for their help in preparing the manuscript. This research was supported by the National Institute of Education under Contract No. US NIE C 400-76-0116.

Language is, at best, a means of directing others to construct similar thoughts from their own prior knowledge. The purpose of this chapter is to discuss some of the aspects of the author/ reader relationship that make communication possible under these conditions. We begin by describing what we believe to be the most important components of this relationship. Then, through the analysis of two readings of one of Aesop's fables, we illustrate the way the author and the reader must depend on these components. We focus on three kinds of knowledge that the author and the reader must use in order for successful communication to take place: conceptual knowledge, social knowledge, and story knowledge. Finally, we discuss implications of this work for reading education.

The Author-Reader Relationship

The initial responsibility for a text's comprehensibility belongs to the author, as it is the author who composes it. The author's first task is that of deciding what she/he wishes to communicate. The second and more difficult task is that of determining how to communicate it. (Of course, these tasks are not easily separated in practice.) The task of constructing an effective linguistic message consists of 1) correctly guessing what sorts of related knowledge the intended readers already have, 2) producing expressions that will evoke appropriate subsets of that knowledge, and 3) presenting those expressions in a way that will induce the readers to interrelate the evoked knowledge into a structure that most nearly captures the meaning intended.

With the task broken down in this way, it is clear that a major determinant of a text's comprehensibility is the goodness of the match between the knowledge the author has presumed of the reader and that actually possessed by the reader. This requirement is not unique to written text; it applies equally to all forms of linguistic communication. However, it is especially difficult to fulfill with formal written text. For example, in the typical conversational exchange, the speaker and the listener may know each other very well and, in any case, can exploit the fact that they share a spatial and temporal setting. In addition, conversations are interactive and thus provide ample opportunity for misunderstandings to be detected and corrected when they do arise. In contrast, the author and reader of a formal text are typically strangers, removed from each other in space and time (Rubin, 1980).

Our analysis of the author's task points out a second condition for comprehensibility: the goodness of the match between the interpretive or inferential tendencies presumed of and possessed by the reader. As we shall see, an author may explicitly present very little of the information critical to the story; much may be left for the reader to infer. At the same time, not everything presented in the text requires elaboration by the reader. Moreover, any given piece of information could lead to an infinite variety and range of inferences. The reader is *not* to generate all possible inferences: to do so would be to lose the author's message entirely. Rather, the reader must have some system for deciding when and what to infer. We argue that this system is based on the concept of good structure. This concept governs what the author may omit from the text and what the reader must add. For written text to be an effective means of communication, both the author and the reader must have a sound grip on this concept and trust that the other does as well.

These points can be illustrated by considering what is involved in comprehension of the following fable.

The Rabbits and the Frogs

A group of rabbits was very unhappy because it had so many enemies. So they decided to end their troubles by killing themselves. To do this, they went to a lake nearby to jump in and drown.

There were a number of frogs on the edge of the lake, and they were so frightened by the rabbits that they all jumped into the lake. Seeing this, one of the rabbits said, "Life is not so hopeless after all since these frogs are even more unhappy than we are." So the rabbits all went back to their homes. —Aesop

Adults who have read this fable for us have uniformly come up with some version of the following interpretation: the rabbits believed that the frogs had drowned themselves; the sight of creatures so pathetic as to feel threatened even by rabbits made the rabbits reevaluate their own lot in life; with this new perspective, the rabbits abandoned their own plans of suicide and returned to the forest to live stoically ever after; comfort is a question of perspective.

Adams and Bruce

It came as a surprise then to discover that other interpretations were not only possible, but were quite defensible. A six year old girl, Elizabeth, gave this account when interviewed about the fable:

> *Interviewer:* Why did the rabbits go back home?
>
> *Elizabeth:* Because they thought the frogs were trying to kill themselves.
>
> *Interviewer:* And why did that make them go back home?
>
> *Elizabeth:* Because then they wouldn't have any more enemies and they could live in peace. But really, they [the frogs] *weren't* going to die. Right?

Elizabeth showed by these and other comments that she thought that the frogs were the enemies who had worried the rabbits and that the rabbits believed the frogs had drowned themselves. This meant that the *source* of the rabbits' unhappiness [". . . so many enemies"] had been removed. The rabbits abandoned their suicide plans and returned to what they mistakenly believed was an improved life situation.

What is happening here? Did Elizabeth simply miss the point of the story and fabricate her own without adequate basis? We would argue to the contrary that, in view of the information presented by the author, Elizabeth's interpretation is as rich and well founded as that of the adults. To defend this argument, let us examine some of the types of knowledge the reader must bring to bear on the story. Each type of knowledge must be considered as a potential culprit in the production of the conflicting interpretations. In order to expose the real culprit we need to examine, in detail, the story and the two interpretations. Our analysis suggests that the difference between the two interpretations is a difference in the knowledge or application of a single facet of the background information presumed by the author.

Conceptual Knowledge

Because even novel concepts and events can be communicated only through terms that are already familiar to a reader, an author must make certain presumptions about what the reader already knows. In particular, the author must presume the reader has sufficient knowledge that the words from which the text is built will evoke concepts necessary for building the story. To the extent that any concept can be made comprehensible to anyone by providing enough information in a clear and simple manner, the author's problem is essentially one of finding the right words for the projected readers. However, the problem is only partly one of *vocabulary*, at least in the strict sense of that term. Even a word that is well within the reader's vocabulary may fail to elicit the meaning intended by the author. As described below, such breakdowns are liable to arise whenever the author has made erroneous assumptions about either the *intensional* or the *extensional* elaborations the reader will make of the concepts named. These three types of mismatches in the conceptual knowledge presumed of and possessed by the reader may be best understood by way of example.

Vocabulary

First, consider a straightforward vocabulary problem:
a. The discovery of a number of fossilized porbeagles in Kansas is intriguing.

Intriguing for whom? Surely none but the unusual reader who happens to know what a porbeagle is. In contrast, the author might capture the imagination of many readers if the description were reworded:
b. The discovery of a number of fossilized mackerel sharks in Kansas is intriguing.

Or, depending on how much the author believes the projected audience knows about sharks, an even better wording might be:
c. The discovery in Kansas of the fossilized bones of a number of large, ocean-dwelling fish is intriguing.

The comprehension difficulties that may be engendered by the use of esoteric words are obvious. If any idea can be expressed in common words, one wonders why an author would ever risk such an impasse. The answer is that less common words are, in general, more informative than more common ones (Finn, 1977–1978); their meanings are more specific. The rhetorical impact of this difference in information is well illustrated in examples (a), (b), and (c). As our hypothetical author has tried to find increasingly simple words to communicate what has been discovered in Kansas, she/he has been obliged to use an increasing number of words to do so. At the same time, the author has relinquished a large amount of the meaning carried by the original word, porbeagle. Rather than trying to explain the exact nature of a porbeagle, the author has tried to convey only as much of its meaning as would allow the reader to understand why the discovery was mysterious.

Intensional Meaning

This brings us to the second kind of mismatch that may occur between the conceptual knowledge presumed of and possessed by a reader. The intensional meaning of a word consists of the total set of characteristics or properties associated with that class of objects or events to which the word refers (Copi, 1961). Typically, when an author uses a particular word, she/he is not equally interested in all aspects of its intensional meaning. In the examples above, the author's interest in porbeagles was only in those characteristics that made it unlikely for them to be in Kansas. Similarly, the author was not the least interested in the facts that Kansas produces corn, is enjoying an industrial boom, or even that it is one of the United States; she or he cared only that Kansas is many miles from the nearest present-day ocean.

The relevant aspects of a term's intensional meaning should be clear to the reader from the context (Barclay, Bransford, Franks, McCarrell, & Nitsch, 1974); the relevant aspects are those which can be interrelated with the meanings of the other concepts present such that the message as a whole coheres (attains good structure). However, this is true only if the reader possesses the relevant aspects of the word's intensional meaning. If not, the stage is set for an especially insidious type of comprehension difficulty.

To see this, let us return to our fable. Both the adults' and Elizabeth's interpretations pivoted on the information that frogs can swim. This information was provided by the author only in the sense that it is part of the intensional meaning of frogs. Imagine a reader who was comfortably familiar with the word "frogs," except that all of his knowledge about frogs had to do with tree frogs. Since the ability to swim would not be an element of this reader's intensional knowledge of frogs, he could not generate the same interpretation of the fable as either Elizabeth or the adults. Moreover, if told that he had misunderstood the fable, he might never locate the source of his misunderstanding. He might never suspect the word "frog" since he believed he understood the relevant aspects of its meaning.

Extensional Meaning

The extensional meaning of a term consists of all the objects or events to which it refers (Copi, 1961). For a given reader, the extensional meaning of the word "frog" would consist of all the frogs she or he had seen or otherwise learned about, be they bullfrogs, tree frogs, fairy tale frogs, or toy frogs. To the extent that these instances differ from one another, the meaning of the word "frog" would depend on which of them is brought to mind (Anderson, Pichert, Goetz, Schallert, Stevens, & Trollip, 1976). This is not a problem for readers whose distribution of experiences with frogs has been fairly typical. The natural tendency is to assume the most typical instance permitted within context (Anderson & McGaw, 1973), and researchers have demonstrated that there is a high degree of concurrence among adult Americans as to what constitutes the most typical instance of various categories (Bower, Black, & Turner, 1979; Rosch, 1973; Smith, 1978). However, a reader who has had limited or atypical experience with a particular concept may well instantiate it inappropriately. Several investigators have demonstrated that such comprehension problems arise where there are differences in the cultural backgrounds of the author and the reader (e.g., Bartlett, 1932; Kintsch & Greene, 1978; Steffensen, Jogdeo, & Anderson, 1978). Our hypothetical reader, who knows only of tree frogs, is a case in point. Conversely, the fact that none of our adult readers believed the fable to be about tree frogs, though many of them were undoubtedly familiar with tree frogs, illustrates the typicality assumption.

Elizabeth vs. the Adults

There is no indication that any of the words in the fable were beyond Elizabeth's vocabulary. Both Elizabeth and the adults seemed to select the same extensional meaning for "frogs": typical pond frogs. Similarly, both seemed to appreciate the relevant intensional characteristics of "frogs": it is normal for them to be at the edge of a lake, and to jump in and swim away when disturbed. Similarly, the extension of "rabbits" seemed, for both, to be the typical storybook rabbits. In terms of intension, storybook rabbits are much like prototypical real rabbits, except that they can talk and plan and tend to be frivolous. Both Elizabeth and the adults seemed to accept all of these qualities. In short, even though subtle differences in conceptual knowledge may result in different understandings of a text, there is no evidence that the difference in the interpretations given by Elizabeth and the adults in this case arose from differences in their knowledge about the concepts presented by the author.

Social Knowledge

Language has traditionally been viewed as a code for packaging and transmitting information from one individual to another. Under this view, the meaning of a linguistic message is fully represented by the words and sentences it comprises. Although this view has led to a rich body of theoretical work on the semantics of natural languages (e.g., Wittgenstein, 1961; Katz, 1966), it has limitations.

In recent years, there has been a shift in our conception of what language is all about. In particular, it is increasingly accepted (see Wittgenstein, 1953; Austin, 1962; Searle, 1969) that language, like most other human activities, is primarily instrumental in nature; its primary function for the speaker or writer is as a tool for producing desired effects on the listener or reader.

This shift in perspective has two important and closely associated ramifications for the study of communication. The first is that the meaning of a linguistic message is only partly represented by its content. Its full meaning depends additionally on the purpose that the speaker or writer had for producing it. The second is that the imputation of intentions to a speaker or writer must be an integral component of the listener's or reader's comprehension process.

The way the meaning of a message is shaped by its producer's beliefs and goals is most obvious in the case of blatant propaganda, sarcasm, or tact. But beliefs and goals are no less critical in cases where their role is less apparent. Suppose someone said to you, "I brought two egg salad sandwiches today." Although the referential meaning of this statement might be straightforward, its full meaning depends on whether the speaker's intention was to offer one of the sandwiches to you, to decline a luncheon invitation, or to explain why the office smelled bad. Whatever the speaker's goal in producing this statement, she/he would, in some sense, have wasted breath if it were not achieved. Thus the meaning conveyed by the statement depends not only on the speaker's beliefs and goals, but on your realizing that and correctly inferring what they are. Note that if you attributed the wrong intention to the speaker, the result would be confusion and possibly some embarrassment; if you could intuit no plausible motive for the speaker, your response probably would be, "So what?"

Because of the integral relationship between intention and meaning, the task of engaging in an ordinary conversation can be seen to require an impressive degree of social sophistication. However, the task of comprehending stories brings with it new dimensions of social complexities (Bruce & Newman, 1978; Bruce, in press). To interpret the significance of anything a character says or does, one must consider both that character's intentions and the impact of the action or utterance on other characters in the story. The impact of an action or utterance on another character depends, in turn, not only on its actual effect or meaning but on how that other character perceives the intentions of its perpetrator *and* on how both the actual effect and the intended effect, as she/he perceives it, fit with her/his own beliefs and goals. Thus, the reader must understand not just the actual event, but what its perpetrator believes and is trying to do, what the second character believes and is trying to do, and what the second character believes the perpetrator believes and is trying to do. Moreover, characters in stories, as well as real people, know that the significance of their actions or utterances to another depends on the other's beliefs and

Adams and Bruce

goals and on the way the other perceives the intention behind the act. Therefore, to understand what one character is doing when she/he plans an action or utterance with the purpose of exerting a specific effect on another, the reader must additionally understand what the perpetrator believes about what the other character believes about the world and what the perpetrator believes about what the other character believes or would be willing to believe about the motive underlying the event.

If this sounds impossibly complicated, our only rejoinder is that what we have just described corresponds to the most simple level of social interaction that may underlie a story. For example, either character may genuinely misunderstand the beliefs and intentions of the other, thereby setting the scene for a tragedy or a comedy of errors. Alternatively, speakers or actors may try to conceal or falsely portray their intentions. The other characters in turn may or may not perceive the true motivation for the event; and, if they do, they may or may not let on, and they may or may not object; and whether or not they object, they may conceal, reveal, or believe their true feelings. It is in this way, by creating layers upon layers of true beliefs, projected beliefs, and beliefs about beliefs, that an author develops romance, deception, collusion, treachery, and foils. Nor are such social intricacies relegated to the domain of adult literature. The interested reader is referred to Bruce and Newman's 1978 analysis of the social structure underlying the first episode of "Hansel and Gretel."

The reader's appreciation of a story depends critically on the recognition of the social relations among its characters. It is often only in terms of the interacting beliefs, plans, and goals of the characters, that events and activities of a story can be related to one another. Further, it is by creating and relieving tensions among the beliefs, plans, and goals of the characters that the author produces such rhetorical effects as conflict, suspense, surprise, and happy endings. The catch is that these aspects of the story structure are typically not fully or explicitly described by the text; nor, inasmuch as they correspond to psychological dimensions of the characters, could they be, except in the case of a fully omniscient and trustworthy author (Bruce, in press). To be sure, the text will provide clues with respect to the beliefs, plans, and goals of its characters, but their elaboration and their relationship to the event structure and message of the story as a whole must be left largely to inferential processes of the reader.

What factors influence the reader's tendency to infer the underlying social structure of stories? An absolute prerequisite for the reader is that she/he approach the text with firmly established and well articulated models of the social situations on which the narration pivots. As with conceptual knowledge, deficiencies on this dimension may often explain comprehension difficulties for readers who are very young or otherwise culturally different from the author of the story. In other cases, however, comprehension difficulties may arise, not because of any lack of the appropriate social knowledge, but because of a failure to apply, develop, and draw inferences from that knowledge in the way intended by the author of the story. Beyond directly depending on the reader's empathy, authors use a variety of rhetorical devices to shape the social structure of their stories. Examples include: stereotyped characters (princesses, wicked witches, foxes, owls); peripetia (a sudden or unexpected reversal of a situation); and inconsistencies with real world knowledge. To illustrate better the way in which the social dimensions of a narrative may be communicated, let us return to our fable.

The fable begins with a rather direct statement of the rabbits' initial beliefs, plans, and goals. They feel so threatened by their enemies that they decide to end their lives by drowning themselves. The rabbits' proposed solution provides additional information about the state of their feelings and beliefs; within Western culture, suicide can be contemplated only when one believes that a situation is both intolerable and otherwise inescapable. The rabbits then troop to the lake with the intention of carrying out their plan.

There are some frogs sitting at the edge of the lake. Because they are frightened by the rabbits' approach, they jump in. The account given, combined with the reader's real world knowledge, should yield a completely ordinary and acceptable explanation for both the frogs' presence at the pond and their response to the rabbits. Yet, it is odd that the rabbits should have reacted so strongly to such mundane behavior on the part of the frogs, and this inconsistency is the reader's only clue that the rabbits misapprehended the frogs' situation. To make social sense of the rabbits' response, the reader is obliged to generate a different hypothesis as to what the rabbits believed that the frogs believed and were trying to do. Within the fable, the only motive given for jumping into lakes is that of drowning and thereby escaping from one's enemies. Since this was the rabbits' own motive, the reader knows it is familiar to them. Further, the imputation of one's own motives to others is a commonplace social occurrence. Finally, both the nature and intensity of the rabbits' reaction can be fit with the notion that they thought the frogs were drowning themselves. In short, it is not only plausible, with respect to our knowledge of social behavior, that the rabbits might come up with such a motive for the frogs, but the assumption that they did so gives the story good social structure—it coheres with the social information given both before and after the frogs' plunge.

The fable ends as the rabbits abandon their own plans of suicide and return to their homes in the forest. Once again, in the interest of good structure, the reader is forced to make an inference about the rabbits' beliefs. Plans arise from the need to reduce discrepancies between existing and acceptable states of the world. They thus reflect an underlying tension which, in a well structured story, must somehow be resolved. Either the plan must be carried through or its initiating conditions must be altered. In this case the reader is left with only the latter possibility.

The initiating condition for the rabbits' plan was that they felt intolerably and inescapably plagued by their enemies. In what way can it be inferred that these conditions had changed by the end of the story? The adults focused on the intolerability of the initial situation: the rabbits, having "realized" that they were not nearly as bad off as they could be, found renewed strength to cope. Elizabeth, on the other hand, focused on the inescapable aspect of the rabbits' initial situation. She assumed that the frogs were the enemies in question. (Note that nothing in the text violates this assumption.) From this, it follows that if the rabbits believed the frogs had drowned themselves, they must have believed, in effect, that they had permanently escaped from their enemies.

Elizabeth vs. the Adults

Elizabeth's interpretation of the social events in the fable differed significantly from the adults'. Perhaps this was because the social schema of gaining solace through another's misery was unfamiliar to her. Alternatively, as we shall see in the next section, the difference between Elizabeth's and the adults' interpretations might have been due to differences in the knowledge about stories which they brought to bear on the text. It is interesting to note that Elizabeth's interpretation, in that it assumed planned behavior on the part of the frogs, was socially more complex than that of the adults. In particular, Elizabeth had to infer that the frogs intended to trick the rabbits with the goal of waging a surprise attack later. Further, for that to be a reasonable plan, she must have inferred that the frogs believed both that the rabbits would consequently relax and go home. In contrast, the adults' interpretation requires virtually no inferential elaboration on the frogs' belief structure. Under their interpretation, the information given in the text together with common knowledge about frogs provides sufficient support for the frogs' actions.

Story Knowledge

Knowing characteristics of rabbits and frogs is crucial to one's understanding of our example fable. Furthermore, one needs to know characteristics of rabbits-in-stories and frogs-in-stories, e.g., that they can talk, plan, and have emotions. The reader's acceptance of concepts like talking rabbits was described by Coleridge as the "willing suspension of disbelief." However, the acceptance of the rabbits' human qualities does not involve a suspension of the disbelief that real rabbits can talk, but an invocation of the belief that fantasy rabbits often do. Moreover, what the good readers will imagine in the real rabbits' stead is not an idiosyncratically fantastic rabbit but, a definite, well formed and conventional concept in and of itself.

The willing suspension of disbelief or invocation of fantasy beliefs is a central aspect of the contract that a good story presupposes between the author and the reader. The reader, in collaboration with the author, replaces real-world concepts and events with stylized constructs built upon abstractions of the real-world phenomena that are thematic to the story.

Thus, to understand a story, the reader must not only understand the relevant words, real-world concepts, and social interactions, but must additionally draw on knowledge that pertains to stories in general. The reader must be familiar with the kinds of story-world conventions that the author employs and be sensitive to the devices by which they are signalled. In this section we discuss three of the most important classes of rhetorical conventions: stereotypes, genre characteristics, and story structure.

Stereotypes

In the section on social knowledge we argued that the imputation of beliefs and motives to characters in stories is essential to understanding their actions and reactions. However, one can soundly impute beliefs and motives to a person only to the extent that one knows that person. In the case of fictional characters which are inventions of an author, the reader knows only what the author provides. In a long story, an author might devote considerable space to the development of major characters. Yet, for lesser characters and characters in shorter stories, the author generally does not have the rhetorical freedom to present complete descriptions; to do so would be to detract from the story itself.

Stereotypes or "stock" characters are the solution to this problem. Instead of wholly developing a character through the text, the author can communicate the character's essence by identifying it with a stereotype and then elaborating to whatever extent is appropriate. Aesop exploited this technique to its fullest. He typically used different types of animals as characters, and to each type of animal he systematically attached a specific stereotype: foxes are cunning and self-serving; ants are industrious; rabbits are frivolous; and frogs are a little stupid. The reader who is familiar with Aesop's system need know only the character's species in order to understand its essential qualities.

Different kinds of stories use different kinds of stereotypes. In classical mythology there are jealous gods and heroes with hubris; in Western European fairy tales there are valiant princes, wicked stepmothers, and powerful but stupid giants. Where stereotypes are less pat, their identification on the reader's behalf may be no less crucial to the meaning of the story. The extent to which authors expect and, in fact, depend on a reader to draw on knowledge of stereotypes to flesh out their characters is evidenced by the causal obliqueness with which they are often signalled. For example, the Brothers Grimm tell us that "Rose-Red would run and jump about the meadows, seeking flowers and catching butterflies" (Grimm, 1945, p. 289). Obviously, what the authors stated about Rose-Red is not all they intended to communicate about her. But the rest is up to the reader. Communication will break down if the reader generates an incomplete or inappropriate image for the character in reference. An inappropriate image is a particular hazard for the reader whose cultural experiences do not match the author's expectations.

Genre Characteristics

Imagine that you, as a tenth grade English student, are given the assignment to discuss the following poem:

SYSTEMS

Aristotle (seems to me)

    to approach   Poetry

As a

Biologist

    would approach   a system of organisms

P
 i
  c
   k
    i
     n
      g
       O
        u
         t

Its genera and species

Formulating the broad laws of literary experience

You might not *like* the poem, but you would know what is expected of you; you are to view the sequence of words as a poem, not as a newspaper story, a joke, a personal letter, or a science text. This means that you should invoke a set of expectations about the purpose of the author, and relationships between the form and the content of the text. Some of these expectations apply to other types of texts, but some seem appropriate only for poems.

In your discussion, you might, for instance, point out the parallelism that the poet shows between "poetry" and "a system of organisms," and then elaborate on the way the arrangement of the words on the page emphasizes this parallelism. You might discuss other word arrangement effects as well, for example, the spreading of "Picking Out." You could also mention that "literary" and "experience" can be viewed as "broad" words.

Turning more to the content of the poem, you might note the tension that exists between the abstract, almost mechanistic concepts such as "systems," "picking out," "genera and species," or "broad laws" and the incongruous personal connotations of "seems to me," "experience," or even "poetry." This would call into question the author's intended meanings: Is he merely describing Aristotle's approach, or is he suggesting its ultimate inadequacy? In short, your strategies for reading the poem depend on your beliefs that it is a poem and that it is to be read as a poem.

In fact, the "poem" above was not originally written as a poem at all. We have recast it as such only to make a point. The passage was actually taken from Frye's *Anatomy of Criticism* (1957). It is part of the introduction to his essays on literary criticism in which he puts forth a program of analysis that can be traced back to Aristotle's *Poetics*. Reading his sentence in the manner of our unfortunate tenth grader gives it a meaning quite different from the one obtained by reading it as part of an analytical prose work, and, we suspect, from the one intended by the author.

In a similar way, one might present a newspaper story with the content of its dateline incorporated into the text and its short paragraphs combined into longer ones. Such a presentation could make the story seem disorganized and undirected, even for a text that would be viewed as well-written in the newspaper genre (Green, 1979). The problem lies in the reader's expectations about how the information should be organized. The more typical nonfictional account of an event typically begins by summarizing the event at issue and then the events that preceded or led up to it. Where such a text departs from the temporal order, it is usually for the purpose of clarifying causal relationships among a family of events. In contrast, the typical newspaper article is written in a "pyramid" form, which gives successively more elaborate summaries of events, following neither a temporal nor a causal order. This facilitates the task of the page editor who may have to cut a story at the last minute to fit the available space. It can also be a convenience for the reader, as long as she/he is expecting it. An unexpected pyramid form, however, is likely to cause trouble.

In general, each type of text calls forth a set of expectations and suggests specific strategies to be applied in reading (see Olson, Duffy, & Mack, in press). In our example, the story can be viewed as a fable or as a simple narrative about some rabbits and frogs. The view the reader takes will entail specific assumptions about how an interpretation for the story is to be constructed.

For example, viewing the story as a fable suggests that the reader should look for a moral, and interpret the characters' actions to support that moral (see Adams & Collins, 1979). Viewing it as simple narrative, on the other hand, suggests that general comments such as "life is not so hopeless after all" are ornamental and that one should simply construct a satisfying explanation for the actions based on one's social knowledge (as outlined in the previous section). Thus Elizabeth, viewing the story as a simple narrative, looks for an interpretation that simultaneously accounts for all the loose ends and captures that dimension of intrigue or excitement that is expected in a good, basic story. The adults, reading the story as a fable, must ensure that the interpretation they construct for the rabbits' actions will lead to a lesson or moral. For them, it is better to assume that the rabbits acted on the basis of their judgment of the frogs' misery than to assume that they thought

Adams and Bruce

their problems were really solved. The attribution of fable-hood to the story, then, becomes a critical factor that leads to an interpretation radically different from the one Elizabeth constructed.

Story Structure

Stories also have structural characteristics (see Propp's 1958 discussion of Russian folk tales). Some of these reflect conventions of the culture in which the stories were written. Others, as discussed above, pertain only to particular genres or kinds of stories. Most, however, arise from the simple fact that stories relate conflicts and their resolutions, planning, and goal-seeking. A story typically presents a problem or a conflict followed by its resolution. When the resolution is ill-defined, the story tells us so. In other words, a story has a beginning, a middle, and an end. Work on story grammars (Mandler & Johnson, 1977; Rumelhart, 1975; Stein & Glenn, 1979; Sutton-Smith, Rotvin, & Mahoney, 1976; and Thorndyke, 1977) has shown that readers develop and use a concept of good story structure when reading.

We have already discussed many of the constraints that help the reader to discover the meaning of a story: genre characteristics, stereotypes, patterns of social interaction and tension resolution, and semantic coherence. However, the most important constraint, one that supersedes and, indeed, shapes each of the aforementioned, is that a story is a story. No description, character, event, or outcome is random. Every detail has been contrived by the author. Knowledge of contrivance is then a powerful heuristic for the reader. It says: When in doubt, assume that the author of the text had a purpose, for example, events that are mentioned are meant to be noticed. More generally, the rule tells the reader to posit a conscious author, who, in turn, has imagined a conscious reader. The author and the reader may then interact in a social relationship easily as complex as that between the characters in a story.

Elizabeth's interpretation of the fable indicates full appreciation of both the basic structure of stories and the contrivance heuristic. Reading that the rabbits abandoned their plan of suicide, she searched for an explanation. She evidently was not sufficiently familiar with the social schema of "feeling better just because you know of someone who feels worse" or with the nature of fables (or both) to come up with the adults' interpretation. Yet, she evidently was sufficiently familiar with the nature of social schemata and story structure to be biased toward an explanation that would cancel the rabbits' initial motive for suicide and its accompanying tension. She turned to the only "loose" concept in the fable: the rabbits' enemies. Since the enemies were explicitly cited in the setting of our fable, one should, under the contrivance heuristic, expect them to play an important role in the story. But they are never mentioned again. Thus, Elizabeth, in assuming that the frogs and the enemies were one and the same, has constructed an interpretation which not only provides a sound explanation for the rabbits' retreat, but further, results in a story structure that is *more* refined than the one the author presumably had in mind.

Elizabeth vs. the Adults

Considerations in this section lead us to suspect that Elizabeth's misinterpretation of the fable arose primarily from a failure to appreciate that it was indeed a fable. Had she known that the story was one of Aesop's fables, she would not have been satisfied with an interpretation that did not entail some lesson of conduct. Further, she probably would not have ascribed that devious quality of the frogs that enabled her own interpretation. We cannot tell whether Elizabeth's failure to interpret our story as a fable resulted from a lack of knowledge of fables and their properties, a failure to recognize the cues that the story was a fable, or simply an inappropriate bias towards a more exciting interpretation—but then that is part of the point of this chapter.

Discussion

Our analysis of Elizabeth's reading of the fable uncovers a possible explanation for the differences between her interpretation and the adults'. First, there are two ways of resolving the tension created when the rabbits change their plan, one focused

Adams and Bruce

on the intolerableness of their life situation and the other focused on its inescapableness. Adults appeared to choose the former because of their recognition of the characteristics of the genre, i.e., a fable must have a lesson or a moral. This one can easily be interpreted as an account of how an intolerable situation can become tolerable through nothing more than a change in perspective. Elizabeth, on the other hand, chose the latter focus, since she apparently viewed the story as a simple narrative in which finding an escape from a bad situation seemed a tighter, more satisfying ending.

This analysis suggests that problems with story understanding arise not only when the reader lacks certain knowledge but also when the reader has selected the wrong knowledge to apply. Knowing that they can choose from conceptual knowledge, social knowledge, and story knowledge, readers may give too much credence to one fact and too little to another. Is there a general rule that will enable readers to search among the vast network of potentially relevant items of information?

A candidate for such a rule follows from the discussion in the section on story knowledge (though it applies equally well to the understanding of texts other than stories). The social interaction between the author and the reader depends on the knowledge they trust they share, and, regardless of the specifics of the text, a crucial component of that shared knowledge is that the reader is looking for good structures. The good structure heuristic is essential for understanding not only stories, but all texts. Indeed, the good structure heuristic is a central determinant of all of our perceptions of the world (Bateson, 1978; Bransford & McCarrell, 1974; Bregman, 1977; Plato, 347 B.C.).

Current research in psychology and artificial intelligence has begun to show some of the characteristics of structural knowledge and its use in comprehension (Adams & Collins, 1979; Anderson, 1977; Gentner, 1979; Rumelhart & Ortony, 1977). We can also see the beginnings of a model of the process a person might engage in during comprehension, i.e., during the search for a satisfying account of complex phenomena (Collins, Brown, & Larkin, 1980; Cohen & Perrault, 1979; Spiro & Tirre, 1979; Woods, 1980). These theories, however, are still far from providing a general and detailed explanation of what we observe in the protocols of children's reading and listening to fables. Future research may well give us more insight into the process of searching for good structures.

Meanwhile, a practical implication of the view presented in this chapter is that misunderstandings can often be viewed most productively as clues to a reader's expectations or prior beliefs rather than as a measure of competence alone. For example, we found in work with some nonnativeborn children that they had special difficulties with Amelia Bedelia (e.g., Parish, 1976) stories. These stories depend for their humorous effect upon misinterpretations of idioms, such as, "draw the drapes" or "dust the furniture." The children, who could read other stories reasonably well, missed the jokes because they were less familiar with the idioms, which are more a part of spoken than of written language and more culture-specific. In a similar way, Elizabeth's misunderstanding of the fable reflects specific assumptions she had made about the text and about the knowledge that was appropriate to apply in understanding it.

A related consequence is that reading comprehension must be placed in a context of experiencing, thinking about, and talking about the world. Moffett (1979) and others have argued that reading and writing are hardly "basic skills" in that they rely on the more fundamental skills of conceptualizing, verbalizing, and perhaps, just pondering. This suggests that the widely approved activities of reading to children, talking about books, and so on, serve more than just a motivational purpose. In an important sense they exercise the basic skills needed for comprehension.

Conclusion

To say that background knowledge is often used, or is useful, in comprehending a story is misleading. It suggests that a reader has the option of drawing on background knowledge to enhance the comprehension process, but that she/he might just as well do without such frills—as if there were a reading process separate from the drawing-on-background-knowledge process.

In fact, reading comprehension involves the construction of ideas out of preexisting concepts. A more correct statement

of the role of background knowledge would be that comprehension is the use of prior knowledge to create new knowledge.
Without prior knowledge, a complex object, such as a text, is
not just difficult to interpret; strictly speaking, it is meaningless.
We have seen in the discussion of the "The Rabbits and
the Frogs" a hint at the complexities of background knowledge
that are needed to understand an apparently simple story
and also the problems that can arise when there is a mismatch
between the author's expectations of the reader and the reader's
actual knowledge. These problems are not restricted to story
understanding. Instead, we might say that the application
of background knowledge in "The Rabbits and the Frogs"
is merely illustrative of the role prior knowledge plays in
understanding texts or, for that matter, life in general.

References

ADAMS, M.J., & COLLINS, A. A schema-theoretic view of reading. In R.
Freedle (Ed.), *New directions in discourse processing*. Norwood,
New Jersey: Ablex, 1979.
ANDERSON, R.C., & McGAW, B. On the representation of the meanings of
general terms. *Journal of Experimental Psychology*. 1973, *101*,
301–306.
ANDERSON, R.C., PICHERT, J.W., GOETZ, E.T., SCHALLERT, D.L., STEVENS,
K.V., & TROLLIP, S.R. Instantiation of general terms. *Journal of
Verbal Learning and Verbal Behavior*, 1976, *15*, 667–679.
AUSTIN, J.L. *How to do things with words*. London: Oxford University
Press, 1962.
BARCLAY, J.R., BRANSFORD, J.D., FRANKS, J.J., McCARRELL, N.S., &
NITSCH, K. Comprehension and semantic flexibility. *Journal of
Verbal Learning and Verbal Behavior*, 1974, *13*, 471–481.
BARTLETT, F.C. *Remembering*. Cambridge: Cambridge University Press,
1932.
BATESON, G. *Mind and nature: A necessary unity*. New York: Dutton,
1978.
BOWER, G.H., BLACK, J.B., & TURNER, T.J. Scripts in memory for text.
Cognitive Psychology, 1979, *11*, 177–220.
BRANSFORD, J.D., & McCARRELL, N.S. A sketch of a cognitive approach
to comprehension. In W. B. Weimer & D. S. Palermo (Eds.), *Cognition and the symbolic processes*. Hillsdale, New Jersey: Erlbaum,
1974.
BREGMAN, A.S. Perception and behavior as compositions of ideals. *Cognitive Psychology*, 1977, *9*, 250–292.
BRUCE, B.C. *Analysis of interacting plans as a guide to the understanding
of story structure* (Technical Report No. 130). Urbana: University
of Illinois, Center for the Study of Reading, June 1979. (ED 174 951)

BRUCE, B.C. Asocial interaction model of reading. *Discourse Processes,* in press.

BRUCE, B.C., & NEWMAN, D. Interacting plans. *Cognitive Science,* 1978, *2,* 195-233.

COHEN, P.R., & PERRAULT, C.R. Elements of a plan-based theory of speech acts. *Cognitive Science,* 1979, *3,* 177-212.

COLLINS, A., BROWN, J.S., & LARKIN, K.M. Inference in text understanding. In R.J. Spiro, B.C. Bruce, & W.F. Brewer (Eds.), *Theoretical issues in reading comprehension.* Hillsdale, New Jersey: Erlbaum, 1980.

COPI, I.M. *Introduction to logic.* New York: Macmillan, 1961.

FINN, P.J. Word frequency, information theory, and cloze performance: A transfer feature theory of processing in reading. *Reading Research Quarterly,* 1977-1978, *13,* 508-537.

FRYE, N. *Anatomy of criticism.* New York: Atheneum, 1965. (Originally published, 1957.)

GENTNER, D. Integrating verb meanings into context. *Discourse Processes.*

GREEN, G.M. *Organization, goals, and comprehensibility in narratives: Newswriting, a case study* (Technical Report No. 132). Urbana: University of Illinois, Center for the Study of Reading, July 1979. (ED 174 949)

GRIMM'S fairy tales. E. V. Lucas, L. Crane, & M. Edwards, Eds. and Trans. New York: Grosset & Dunlap, 1945.

KATZ, J. *The philosophy of language.* New York: Harper & Row, 1966.

KINTSCH, W., & GREENE, E. The role of culture-specific schematics in the comprehension and recall of stories. *Discourse Processes,* 1978, *1,* 1-13.

MANDLER, J.M., & JOHNSON, N.S. Remembrance of things parsed: Story structure and recall. *Cognitive Psychology,* 1977, *9,* 111-151.

MOFFETT, J. Commentary: The word and the world. *Language Arts,* 1979, *56,* 115-116.

OLSON, G.M., DUFFY, S.A., & MACK, R.L. Knowledge of writing conventions in prose comprehension. In W.J. McKeachie & K. Eble (Eds.), *New directions in learning and teaching.* San Francisco: Jossey-Bass, in press.

PARISH, P. *Good work, Amelia Bedelia.* New York: William Morrow, 1976.

PLATO. The republic. H.D.P. Lee, Ed. and Trans. Toronto: Penguin Books, 1955.

PROPP, V.I. *Morphology of the folktale.* Austin: University of Texas Press, 1958.

ROSCH, E. On the internal structure of perceptual and semantic categories. In T. E. Moore (Ed.), *Cognitive development and the acquisition of language.* New York: Academic Press, 1973.

RUBIN, A.D. Comprehension processes in oral and written language. In R. Spiro, B. Bruce, & W. Brewer (Eds.), *Theoretical issues in reading comprehension.* Hillsdale, New Jersey: Erlbaum, 1980.

RUMELHART, D.E. Notes on a schema for stories. In D. Bobrow & A. Collins (Eds.), *Representation and understanding: Studies in cognitive science.* New York: Academic Press, 1975.

RUMELHART, D.E., & ORTONY, A. The representation of knowledge in memory. In R.C. Anderson, R.J. Spiro, & W.E. Montague (Eds.), *Schooling and the acquisition of knowledge.* Hillsdale, New Jersey: Erlbaum, 1977.

SEARLE, J.R. *Speech acts: An Essay in the philosophy of language.* Cambridge: Cambridge University Press, 1969.

SMITH, E.E. Theories of semantic memory. In W. K. Estes (Ed.), *Handbook of learning and cognitive processes* (Volume 5). Hillsdale, New Jersey: Erlbaum, 1978.

SPIRO, R.J., & TIRRE, W.C. *Individual differences in schema utilization during discourse processing* (Technical Report No. 111). Urbana: University of Illinois, Center for the Study of Reading, January 1979. (ED 166 651)

STEFFENSEN, M.S., JOGDEO, C., & ANDERSON, R.C. *A cross-cultural perspective on reading comprehension* (Technical Report No. 97). Urbana: University of Illinois, Center for the Study of Reading, July 1978. ERIC Document Reproduction Service No. ED 159 660. July 1978. (ED 159 660)

STEIN, N., & GLENN, C.G. An analysis of story comprehension in elementary school children. In R. Freedle (Ed.), *New directions in discourse processing.* Norwood, New Jersey: Ablex, 1979.

SUTTON-SMITH, B., BOTVIN, G., & MAHONEY, D. Developmental structures in fantasy narratives. *Human Development,* 1976, *19,* 1-13.

THORNDYKE, P.W. Cognitive structures in comprehension and memory of narrative discourse. *Cognitive Psychology,* 1977, *9,* 77-110.

WITTGENSTEIN, L. *Philosophical investigations.* New York: Macmillan, 1953.

WITTGENSTEIN, L. *Tractatus logico-philosophicus.* London: Routledge & Kegan Paul, 1961. (Originally published, 1921.)

WOODS, W.A. Multiple theory formation in high level perception. In R.J. Spiro, B.C. Bruce, & W.F. Brewer (Eds.), *Theoretical issues in reading comprehension.* Hillsdale, New Jersey: Erlbaum, 1980.

Learning How to Learn from Reading

Ann L. Brown
University of Illinois

Introduction

The major academic achievement expected during school years is that students not only learn how to read but learn how to learn from reading. In order to develop the necessary skills of reading and studying, students must come to structure their own cognitive activities in such a way that learning can occur. This demands some understanding of the learning process in general and the concomitant development of self-regulatory (Brown, 1978, 1980) or autocritical (Binet, 1909) strategies; students need to design, monitor, evaluate, and revise their own plans for learning. Formal schooling not only fosters such skills, it demands them, and a consideration of the difference between formal and informal instruction illustrates why.

As Bruner (1972) pointed out, schools as institutions in western society are separated from both the early play activities thought suitable for childhood and often from most vocational activities demanded of adults. By contrast, in primitive societies, children learn by imitating adult models, initially in the context of play (mock hunting, weaving, cooking, ritualistic practices). The transition from play activities to real adult occupations is gradual (i.e., play hunting to hunting): there is no sharp division between the early exploratory play of childhood and the vocational pursuits of the adult. In our society, schools intercede between the two worlds of the young child and the adult, but they often fail to forge a meaningful link between them. Entering school can be a difficult transition; play activities are discouraged, while learning by listening or reading rather than acting is encouraged. Similarly, the relationship between schooling and many adult occupations is less than clear and, perhaps, only directly relevant if the student wishes to pursue an academic career. If schools do not relate to the real-life experiences of play or work activities children encounter daily, it is not surprising the enterprises valued in the classroom do not make sense to many children. If lessons are not meant to make sense, why should children check their performance against criteria of the plausible or sensible?

Consider in this light how traditional apprenticeship training differs from formal schooling. In apprenticeship training, the interaction of teacher and student is often one-to-one and the teacher, an expert, is more interested in directly transmitting the essential information or skills than in engaging the learner in a Socratic dialogue. In this situation, the expert closely monitors the learner's performance and can notice and correct any misunderstandings, often without there being any need for the learner to become aware that she/he has failed to understand.

I consider formal schooling to be quite different, in that the aim (if not the end result) is to inculcate general skills of flexible thinking (Brown, 1978, 1980; Brown & Campione, in press). It is a common stricture that schools should teach children how to think rather than to deluge them with specific content which may soon become outdated. One way in which schooling may foster the ability to learn new information and solve novel problems is by instilling an awareness of whether information being presented is understood. If we "know we don't know," this knowledge can lead to self-questioning routines such as, "What do I know that might help me figure it out?" "What specifically do I not understand?" "Where can I go to find out?" In schools, instruction is carried out in groups and it is essential that students learn to monitor their own comprehension because the teacher in a large classroom cannot perform this function for them all the time. To receive assistance, students must realize they need it and know how to request it. Generally, after several years of formal education, students are asked to acquire much of their information from books. Learning through reading makes it even more crucial that students be able to monitor their own comprehension, because there is no chance that a book will notice that a student has failed to understand (Brown & French, 1979).

In this chapter, I will describe some of the comprehension and study monitoring skills necessary for effective reading, trace some difficulties young and poorer readers have in employing such tactics, indicate how successful students develop more effective learning techniques, and discuss methods to help students who fail to spontaneously develop necessary skills.

Metacognitive Skills

Recently, there has been a revival of interest in the skills of meaningful reading and studying, a revival spurred primarily by general interest in the development of metacognition, i.e. knowledge and control of one's own thinking and learning activities (Brown, 1975, 1978, 1980; Flavell & Wellman, 1977). Two forms of metacognition have been examined extensively. First, there is the knowledge that learners have about various aspects of the learning situation, including their own capabilities as learners. The ability to reflect on one's own cognitive processes (to be aware of one's own activities while reading, solving problems, and studying) is a late-developing skill with important implications for children's effectiveness as active learners. If students are aware of what is needed to perform effectively, it is possible for them to take steps to more adequately meet the demands of a learning situation. If students are not aware of their own limitations, or the complexity of the task at hand, they can hardly be expected to take preventative actions in order to anticipate or recover from problems.

The second cluster of activities studied under the heading of metacognition consists of the self-regulatory mechanisms used by active learners during an ongoing attempt to read, solve problems, listen, or learn in general. These indices of metacognition include attempts to relate a new problem to a similar class of problems and to imbue the unfamiliar with the familiar, engaging in *means end analysis* to identify effective strategies; checking the outcome of any attempt to solve the problem; planning one's next move; monitoring the effectiveness of any attempted action; testing, revising, and evaluating one's strategies for learning and other strategic activities that facilitate learning.

Given that students have at least some rudimentary awareness of their own cognitive processes, and can monitor their progress sufficiently well to detect a problem if one occurs, are they also capable of introducing some remedial strategy to overcome the detected problem? The appropriate strategy to deploy will vary depending on the goal of the activity; for example, reading for meaning demands different skills than reading for remembering (studying). The type of strategies available to a learner and the efficiency with which they can be orchestrated are important developmental questions with obvious implications for the study of reading.

Effective readers, then, are those who can have some awareness and control of the cognitive activities they engage in as they read. Most characterizations of effective reading include skills and activities that involve metacognition: 1) clarifying the purposes of reading (understanding both the explicit and implicit task demand); 2) identifying the important aspects of a message; 3) focusing attention on the major content rather than trivia; 4) monitoring ongoing activities to determine whether comprehension is occurring; 5) engaging in self-questioning to determine whether goals are being achieved; and 6) taking corrective action when failures in comprehension are detected (Baker & Brown, in press; Brown, in press). Effective readers are those who monitor their own understanding while reading, being constantly alert to comprehension failure. Whimbey's characterization (1975) of a good reader illustrates this point well.

> A good reader proceeds smoothly and quickly as long as his understanding of the material is complete. But as soon as he senses that he has missed an idea, that the track has been lost, he brings smooth progress to a grinding halt. Advancing more slowly, he seeks clarification in the subsequent material, examining it for the light it can throw on the earlier trouble spot. If still dissatisfied with his grasp, he returns to the point where the difficulty began and rereads the section more carefully. He probes and analyzes phrases and sentences for their exact meaning; he tries to visualize abstruse descriptions; and through a series of approximations, deductions, and corrections he translates scientific and technical terms into concrete examples (p. 91).

With mature readers such constant monitoring is so well practiced that is has become automated and unconscious, the reader is not constantly aware of these monitoring activities (Adams, 1980; Brown, in press; Collins, Brown, Morgan, & Brewer, 1977). Less efficient readers may rarely monitor their own activities and when they do such monitoring may be time consuming and painful.

The importance of self-awareness and self-control while learning were recognized well before current metacognitive theories became popular. Binet and Spearman describe similar factors as central to intellectual functioning in general. For example, Binet (1909) identified four general factors of intelligence, "Comprehension, invention, direction, and criticism— intelligence is constrained in these four words." Three of Binet's four general factors, "direction of thought, autocriticism, and invention," are very similar to current metacognitive features of learning (Brown, 1978; Brown & Campione, in press). Note particularly the concepts of direction and autocriticism. In describing the characteristic learning mode of slow children, Binet claims that:

> the child is unreflective and inconstant; he forgets what he is doing. . . he lets himself be carried away by fantasy and caprice. . .he lacks direction (Binet, 1909, pp. 119–120).

Similarly on autocriticism:

> The power of criticism is as limited as the rest. . .*he does not know what he does not understand* [italics mine]. The whys with which his curiosity hounds us are scarcely embarrassing, for he will be contented naively with the most absurd becauses (Binet, 1909, p. 122).

Spearman, another early intelligence theorist, also pinpointed a few general skills central to thinking and reasoning. Spearman's general factors were not unlike Binet's and even more like contemporary theories of metacognition. The three principle components were 1) educing relations, 2) educing correlates, and 3) self-recognition or the "apprehension of one's own experience." Spearman claims that people "more or less" have the power to observe what goes on in their own minds.

> A person cannot only feel, but also know that he can feel; not only strive, but know that he strives; *not only know but know that he knows* [italics mine] (Spearman, 1923, p. 342).

Spearman does not claim scientific priority with such notions of metacognition. Indeed he points out that:

Such a cognizing of cognition itself was already announced by Plato. Aristotle likewise posited a separate power whereby, over and above actually seeing and hearing, the psyche becomes aware of doing so. Later authors, as Strato, Galen, Alexander of Aphrodisias, and in particular Plotinus, amplified the doctrine, designating the processes of cognizing one's own cognition by several specific names. Much later, especial stress was laid on this power of "reflection," as it was now called by Locke (Spearman, 1923, pp. 52–53).

What Spearman did contribute was the identification of such metacognitive elements as essential elements of intelligence, agreeing with Binet that self-awareness and autocritical skills are fundamental learning processes.

Educational psychologists since the turn of the century (Dewey, 1910; Huey, 1968; Thorndike, 1917) also have been quite aware that reading involves planning, checking, and evaluating activities now called metacognitive skills. For example, Dewey's system of inducing reflective thinking is essentially a call for metacognitive training. The aim was to induce active monitoring, critical evaluation, and deliberate "seeking after meaning and relationships." To Dewey, "learning is learning to think":

Everything which has been said in the discussion of thinking has emphasized that passivity is the opposite of thought. . . .The mind is not a piece of blotting paper that absorbs and retains automatically. It is rather a living organism that has to search for its food, that selects, rejects and evaluates (Dewey, 1916, 1933 edition, p. 261).

Thorndike, another early advocate of learning to learn processes, directly claimed that reading *was* reasoning.

Understanding a paragraph is like solving a math problem. It consists of selecting the right elements of the situation and putting them together in the right relations, and also with the right amount of weight or influence or force for each. The mind is assailed as it were by every word in the paragraph. It must select, repress, soften, emphasize, correlate, and organize, all under the influence of the right mental set or purpose or demand (Thorndike, 1917, p. 329).

Given the considerable agreement that reading involves metacognitive skills of self-awareness and self-control, let us turn to the evidence that suggests children might have difficulty in this arena.

Metacognition and Reading

One of the earliest experimental examinations of metacognitive problems in children was conducted by Thorndike (1917) who suggested that comprehension problems arise if the reader "is not treating the ideas produced by the reading as provisional [so that he can] inspect and welcome them or reject them as they appear." Moreover, he argued that "The vice of the poor reader is to say the words to himself without actively making judgments concerning what they reveal." In his reserach, Thorndike found that many sixth graders did not spontaneously test their understanding as they read though they often felt they understood when in fact they did not. Such behavior reflects poor comprehension monitoring. A considerable body of contemporary research is now available to substantiate Thorndike's early diagnosis that immature readers have a variety of metacognitive problems. Full reviews of this literature are available elsewhere (Baker & Brown, in press; Brown, in press). Here I will give only a few prime examples of the types of difficulties that seem to beset the novice reader.

One way of finding out what children know about reading is simply to ask them. There are nontrivial problems associated with this approach, for children may not prove the most reliable witnesses of their own cognitive processes. But questioning children does reveal interesting differences between good and poor readers. In general, younger and poorer readers are unaware that they must attempt to make sense of texts; they focus on reading as a decoding process rather than as a meaning-getting process (Clay, 1973; Denney & Weintraub, 1963, 1966; Johns & Ellis, 1976; Myers & Paris, 1978; Reid, 1966). They do not seem to be aware that they must expend additional effort to make sense of the words they have decoded or of appropriate strategies for coping with words or sentences they do not understand. Older children, more sensitive to the fact that reading is an effort after meaning, are more likely to say that they would use a dictionary, ask for help, or reread a paragraph to try and figure out the meaning of an unknown word from context (Myers & Paris, 1978).

Are younger students reflective while reading? Several self-report studies have been conducted in an effort to identify differences in strategy used between good and poor readers in high school (Olshavsky, 1976-1977, 1978; Smith, 1977; Strang & Rogers, 1965). In general, good readers try to describe their methods for reading while poor readers seem almost unaware of deliberate strategies that could be employed. Not surprisingly, poor readers are less likely to take remedial actions when they encounter ideas and words they do not understand (Strang & Rogers, 1965).

Although it is difficult to obtain reliable self-report measures from young readers there are other methods that are quite revealing concerning the extent of poor readers' passivity in reading contexts. For example, younger and poorer readers tend to tolerate inconsistencies and contradictions quite happily, a fact described graphically by Holt (1964) in *How Children Fail*. Markman (1977) has confirmed this diagnosis of inadequate comprehension monitoring. Children in first and third grades were asked to listen to simple instructions on how to play a game or perform a magic trick; crucial information was omitted. For example, the instructions for the card game were as follows:

> We each put our cards in a pile. We both turn over the top card in our pile. We look at cards to see who has the special card. Then we turn over the next card in our pile to see who has the special card this time. In the end the person with the most cards wins the game.

The instructions were incomplete because, among other things, there was no mention of what the "special card" might be. Third graders realized the instructions were incomplete more readily than did the younger children. Often, it was not until the first graders actually tried to carry out the instructions that they realized they did not understand. It seems clear the first graders did not actively evaluate whether the instructions made sense as they were listening.

In a second study, Markman (1979) found the same pattern of results with older children attempting to follow more complex texts. Children in third, fifth, and sixth grades listened to short essays containing inconsistent information and then answered questions designed to assess awareness of the inconsistencies. The following is an exerpt from a passage about fish:

Fish must have light in order to see. There is absolutely no light at the bottom of the ocean. It is pitch black down there. When it is that dark fish cannot see anything. They cannot even see colors. Some fish that live at the bottom of the ocean can see the color of their food; that is how they know what to eat.

The obvious inconsistency here is that fish cannot see colors at the bottom of the ocean, yet some can see the color of their food. The students generally failed to report any problem with the passage; however, when specifically warned about the inconsistencies, a greater proportion of children (primarily sixth graders) did report them. If children experience such notable comprehension monitoring difficulties while listening, it is probably safe to predict that the problem will be exacerbated while reading.

These apparent problems of self-monitoring can be seen again when watching children read aloud. Several studies of oral reading have revealed differences between good and poor readers, both in types of errors made and in likelihood of spontaneous corrections. Clay (1973) found that beginning readers in the upper half of their class spontaneously corrected 33 percent of their errors, while beginners in the lower half corrected only 5 percent of their errors. Weber (1970) reported that, although good and poor readers in the first grade did not differ in the extent to which they corrected errors that were grammatically acceptable to the sentence context, good readers were twice as likely to correct errors that were grammatically inappropriate.

Difficulties with self-correction persist in the later grades. In a comparison of average and above average sixth grade readers, Kavale and Schreiner (1979) found that average readers (compared with good readers) were more likely to make meaning-distorting errors and were less likely to correct those errors that did occur. Even when good and poor readers are matched on the ability to decode words in isolation, poor readers still make more errors when reading in context (Isakson & Miller, 1976). In addition, poor readers are less likely to detect semantic and syntactic anomalies than are good readers. When good readers encounter an anomalous word, they frequently try to "fix up" the resulting comprehension difficulty by substituting a more sensible word. Poor readers, on the other hand, read the anomalous words without apparent awareness of the problem (Isakson & Miller, 1976). Thus, in addition to keeping track of the success or failure with which their comprehension is proceeding, good readers also take measures to deal with any difficulties that arise.

The same pattern of poor self-monitoring occurs if one considers children's study behavior. If one asks children to read for different purposes (for pleasure, to find some information quickly, or to prepare themselves for a test), third graders do not adjust their reading strategy accordingly (Forrest & Waller, 1979). Similarly, Smith (1967) found that even high school students who were poor readers failed to adjust their reading behavior depending on whether they were reading for details or for general impressions.

Given this inconsistent pattern of monitoring failures it probably is no surprise that young students are less successful at using strategies effectively when attempting to learn from texts. For example, grade school students have difficulty concentrating on main ideas while studying (Brown & Smiley, 1978). Fifth graders rarely appear to do more than reread the passage while some high school students underline, take notes, or outline as they study. Students who spontaneously engage in underlining or notetaking strategies tend to use these devices to highlight the main ideas and, as a result of this selective attention, increase their recall of these central ideas on subsequent tests. The more passive students failing to use such strategies do not improve dramatically as a result of extra study time (Brown & Smiley, 1978).

Another well documented study strategy that skilled readers employ is self-interrogation, although there is considerable evidence that even college students need help in perfecting this skill. Andre and Anderson (1978–1979) recently developed a self-questioning study technique in which high school students were taught to locate sections of text containing important points and to generate questions about them. They found that the process of generating such questions facilitated learning as compared to a read-reread control group and a group that was simply told to make up questions. In addition, the training was more effective for students of lower ability, suggesting that better students had developed effective self-questioning skills, and that this may be more effective than such passive strategies as rereading because it incorporates many metacognitive components. That is, it encourages the reader to set purposes for studying, identify and underline important segments of the material, generate questions which require comprehension of the text to be correctly answered, and think of possible answers to questions. The questioning strategy leads students to an active monitoring of their own learning activities and to the engagement of strategic action.

Student-generated questions are a valuable aid to studying and comprehension. Singer's conception (1978) of "active comprehension" involves reacting to a text with questions and seeking answers with subsequent reading. Such student-generated questions are more effective in promoting comprehension than teacher-generated questions, even for children in elementary school. The ability to ask relevant questions of oneself during reading is, of course, crucial to comprehension monitoring and studying. Collins, Brown, and Larkin (1980) suggest that many failures of comprehension are due to failures in asking the right questions. Similarly, a study by Nash and Torrance (1974) has shown that participation in a creative reading program designed to sensitize readers to gaps in their knowledge (such as in-consistencies and ambiguities) led to a significant improvement in the kinds of questions first graders asked about their reading material. Training in effective question-asking may be an important first step in the development of monitoring skills.

The whole process of learning to learn about reading is the process of becoming aware of what one is doing. As Holt pointed out in *How Children Fail* (1964), such awareness is a prerequisite for all active learning.

> Part of being a good student is learning to be aware of one's own mind and the degree of one's own understanding. The good student may be one who often says that he does not understand, simply because he keeps a constant check on his understanding. The poor student who does not, so to speak, watch himself trying to under-stand, does not know most of the time whether he understands or not. Thus the problem is not to get students to ask us what they don't know; the problem is to make them aware of the difference between what they know and what they don't (pp. 28-29).

This self-awareness is an essential step along the path to expertise. For the proficient reader, many of the monitoring activities have been overlearned to the extent they are no longer totally conscious. Expert readers automatically monitor their comprehension and only pause to take deliberate remedial action when something goes wrong; i.e., they detect a comprehension failure (Baker & Brown, in press; Brown in press). Novice readers, who tend not to engage in spontaneous monitoring, can be helped to do so by being made aware of some of the simple strategies for doing so. In time, and with practice, they may come to monitor their own reading comprehension effortlessly and automatically.

The Development of Self-Regulation

In the normal course of events a large number of children develop the autocritical skills needed for effective learning, even without explicit "cognitive skills training" in the schools. This is not to say that schools are totally successful at this enterprise, and that all students would not possibly benefit from the inclusion in the curricula of direct instruction in metacognitive skills; witness the number of studies that have indicated that college students are less than well informed concerning a potential repertoire of strategic study skills (Brown, Campione, & Day, 1981; Dansereau, Long, McDonald, & Atkinson, 1975). But it certainly is the case that a sizable minority of students, often those from less advantaged backgrounds, have even greater difficulty in adjusting to the largely implicit demands of schools. The battery of learning strategies incidentally acquired by many junior college students is sparse (Brown, Campione, & Day, 1981). How is it that some students spontaneously develop the essential learning skills while others, exposed to the same formal schooling, do not? What are the primary differences between preparation for school of successful and unsuccessful students? Several recent theorists have suggested that deficient mediated learning is the crux of the problem (Brown, 1980; Brown, Bransford, & Ferrara, in press; Brown & French, 1979; Campione, Brown, & Ferrara, in press; Feuerstein, 1979, 1980). All of these theories are based on Vygotsky's concept of internalization (1978), which I will describe briefly to set the stage for the following discussion.

Vygotsky argues that the development of cognitive control is very much a social process. Children first experience active problem solving activities in the presence of others, then gradually come to perform these functions for themselves. This process of "internalization" is gradual; first an adult (parent, teacher) controls and guides the child's activity but gradually the adult and the child come to share the problem solving functions, with the child taking the initiative and the adult correcting and guiding when the child falters. Finally, the adult cedes control to the child and functions primarily as a supportive and sympathetic audience.

This developmental progression from other-regulation to self-regulation is nicely illustrated in successful mother-child learning situations. Consider the following example from Wertsch (1979). The basic situation is that mothers and their young children were given the task of copying a wooden puzzle (a truck). One completed puzzle was used as the model and the mother and child were to complete an identical puzzle. The mother was told to encourage the child if necessary. The following is a sample of a videotaped interaction between a mother and her 2-1/2 year old daughter.

1. C: Oh (glances at model, then looks at pieces pile). Oh now where's this one go? (picks up black cargo square, looks at copy, then at pieces pile)

2. M: Where does it go in this other one (the model)? (child puts black cargo square back down in pieces pile, looks at pieces pile)

3. M: Look at the other truck (model) and then you can tell. (child looks at model, then glances at pieces pile)

4. C: Well? (looks at copy then at model)

5. C: I look at it.

6. C: Um, this other puzzle has a black one over there. (child points to black cargo square in model)

7. M: Um-hm.

8. C: A black one. (looks at pieces pile)

9. M: So where do you want to put the black one on this (your) puzzle? (child picks up black cargo square from pieces pile and looks at copy)

10. C: Well, where do you put it in there? Over there? (inserts black cargo square correctly in copy)

11. M: That looks good.

In this example we can see the mother serving a vital regulatory function, guiding the problem-solving activity of her child. Good examples of the mother assuming the regulatory role are statements 2, 3, and 9 where she functions to keep the child on task and to foster goal relevant search and comparison activities. This protocol represents a mid-point between early stages of development where the mother and child speak to one another but the mother's utterances do not seem to be interpreted by the child as task relevant, and later stages where the child assumes the regulatory functions herself, with the mother functioning as a sympathetic audience.

We would like to argue that supportive "experts," such as mothers in Wertsch's example, master craftsmen in apprenticeship systems (Brown & French, 1979), and more experienced peers in tutoring studies (Allen, 1976), serve a major function of initially adopting the monitoring and overseeing role; these crucial regulatory activities are thereby made overt and explicit.

Ideally, teachers function as just such mediators in the learning to learn process, acting as promoters of self-regulation by nurturing the emergence of personal planning as they gradually cede their own direction. In schools, effective teachers often engage in continual prompts to get children to plan and monitor their own activities. As Dewey pointed out:

> Students need direction in their studying. . . .[They need] times of supervised study, when the teacher learns the difficulties that students are meeting, ascertains what methods of learning they use, gives hints and suggestions, helps students recognize some bad habits that are holding them back. . . .The art of [teaching] then is largely the art of questioning pupils so as to direct their own inquiries and so as to form in them the *independent habit of inquiry* [italics mine] (Dewey, 1910, 1933 edition, p. 265–266).

Schallert and Kleiman (1979) identified four basic strategies used by successful teachers to promote critical thinking. First, they attempted to tailor the information to the children's existing level of understanding. They attempted to activate relevant background knowledge by having students consider new information in the light of what they already knew. Continual attempts were made to focus the students' attention on important facts and, finally, students were helped to monitor their own comprehension because of the teachers' use of clever questioning and such Socratic ploys as invidious generalizations, counterexamples, and reality testing. Thus, expert teachers model many forms of critical thinking for the students, processes that the students must internalize as part of their own problem solving activities if they are to develop effective skills of self-regulation.

Feuerstein's theory is essentially similar, for he holds that cognitive growth is heavily dependent on the quality of mediated learning the child experiences. "Mediated learning is the training given to the human organism by an experienced adult who frames, selects, focuses, and feeds back an environmental experience in such a way as to create appropriate learning sets" (Feuerstein, 1969, p. 6). Mediated learning refers to a learning experience where a supportive other (parent, teacher, peer) is interposed between the learner and the environment and intentionally influences the nature of that interaction. These mediated learning experiences are an essential aspect of development, beginning when the parent selects significant objects for the infant to focus on and proceeding throughout development with the adult systematically shaping the child's learning experiences. This is the principal means by which children develop the cognitive operations necessary for learning independently. By interacting with an adult, who guides problem solving activities and structures the learning environment, children gradually come to adopt structuring and regulatory activities of their own.

Feuerstein believes that the principal reason for the poor academic performance of many disadvantaged students is the lack of consistent mediated learning in their earlier developmental histories because of parental apathy, ignorance, or overcommitment. Quite simply, parents in disadvantaged homes were themselves disadvantaged children and cannot be expected to teach what they do not know; large family size and the need for a working mother does not leave a great deal of time for Socratic dialogue games. In addition, these interactive styles of continually questioning and extending the limits of knowledge are typical of middle-class social interaction patterns and may be alien to some cultures (Au, 1980; Bernstein, 1971).

But mediated learning activities do occur in schools, and middle-class children come prepared to take part in these rituals. Not only do disadvantaged children lack prior exposure but there is some evidence that teachers give less experience in this learning mode to those who, because of their lack of prior experience, need it most. For example, recent observations of reading groups (Au, 1980; McDermott, 1978) have shown that good and poor readers are not treated equally. Good readers are questioned about the meaning behind what they are reading and asked to evaluate and criticize material. A considerable amount of time in the good reading group is "on task;" i.e., reading related activities are occurring, and a sizable amount of group activities are of the optimal "mediated-learning" type. By contrast, in the poor reading groups, little time is spent reading (a lot of time is devoted to discipline) and the poorest readers are rarely asked to read at all. When they are required to read, poor readers receive primarily drill in pronunciation and decoding. Rarely are they given practice in qualifying and evaluating their comprehension (Au, 1980). A case could even be made that the poorest readers receive almost no formal reading instruction in these groups. In the good reading group, the teacher adopts the procedure of asking every child to read. In the poorer reading group, turn-taking is at the teacher's request and, to save everyone from embarrassment, the poorer readers are not called on.

Special education classes are more likely to provide step-by-step instruction for students in basic skills (decoding, etc.) and rarely allow students to figure out answers or to question their assumptions. Heavily programed and guided learning of this type may be a practical and efficient means of getting less successful students to perform better on a particular task. But the teachers not the children are making all the learning decisions. Such experience is less likely to be the appropriate procedure for promoting insightful learning. Students may learn something about a particular task but they are not likely to learn much about how to learn in general.

The development of cognitive skills proceeds normally via the gradual internalization of regulatory skills first experienced by children in social settings (Vygotsky, 1978). Following repeated experience with experts (mothers, teachers, etc.) who criticize, evaluate, and extend the limits of their experience, students develop skills of self-regulation. The development of a battery of such autocritical skills (Binet, 1909) is essential if students are to learn how to learn independently. If for some reason children are deprived of such interaction, the development of such a battery of self-regulatory skills is not likely to occur.

Perhaps there is a more basic problem. Early failure experiences can seriously erode children's self-concepts. Children may have no reason to believe in themselves as active agents in knowing what there is to know in school. If they have no expectations concerning their own ability to control and manage their own school performance, this would surely vitiate any attempts to achieve such self-control. Learned helplessness (Dweck, 1976) can be acquired early. Children's objective knowledge of their own cognitive processes is obviously contaminated by their feelings of personal worth. Competence within a school setting may not be expected by many disadvantaged children and particularly not by those singled out for "special" education in response to their supposed incompetence.

This is a depressing picture but, on an optimistic note, having diagnosed the nature of the problem we should be in a better position to set about rectifying the situation. Remedial training has been devised to provide some of the mediated learning that the less successful student may have lacked (Feuerstein, 1980). Simple training routines for eliciting self-awareness and control of one's own learning achievements have been quite successful at improving the performance of slow learning students (Brown, Campione, & Day, 1981), and we now have a reasonable technology for improving students' cognitive and metacognitive skills with the attendent side benefits of increasing their feeling of personal competence in academic settings (Brown & Campione, 1978; Brown, Bransford, & Ferrara, in press).

Helping Students Learn How to Learn

If we are to help students become independent learners we must attempt to make them more aware of available options to improve their own performance, and of significant factors that must be taken into account when designing a plan for learning. I have argued elsewhere (Brown, 1980; Brown, Bransford, & Ferrara, in press; Brown, Campione, & Day, 1981), that there are four major variables which enter into the learning situation.

These are: 1) the nature of the material to be learned (maps, stories, expository texts, poems, tables); 2) the criterial task, i.e. the end point for which the learner is preparing (multiple-choice, essay exam, understanding instruction, solving problems, learning vocabulary); 3) activities engaged in by learners, their strategies and tactics for making learning an effective process; and 4) general characteristics of learners, such as prior experience, background knowledge, ability, and interests.

This tetrahedral model of the learning situation, which I borrowed from Jenkins (1979), is generally applicable to most individual learning situations (Brown, 1980). Here I will describe how it can be applied to the task of learning from texts. The tetrahedral model is illustrated in Figure 1.

Imagine expert learners designing a plan for learning from texts. First they might consider the *nature of the material* to be learned. They would examine the text itself and make decisions about what kind of material it is—is it a story, an expository text, an instruction book? Major forms of texts have standard structures that can be identified by astute learners to help them set up expectations to guide the reading process. For example, stories in general have a reliable structure (Mandler & Johnson, 1977); a simple form would be that a main char-

CHARACTERISTICS OF THE LEARNER

Bypass Capacity Limitations,
Activate Available Knowledge,
Reason By Analogy

LEARNING ACTIVITIES

Strategies, Rules, Procedures,
Monitor Comprehension,
Macrorules

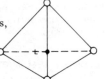

CRITERIAL TASKS

Gist vs. Verbatim Recall,
Generalized Rule Use,
Resolving Ambiguities,
Following Instructions

NATURE OF THE MATERIALS

Text Structure, Cohesion,
Logical Content,
Author's Explicit Cues

Figure 1. An Organizational Framework for Exploring Questions about Learning from Texts

acter reaches some desired goal after overcoming an obstacle. More complex forms include competition, conflict, or sharing among major characters (Bruce & Newman, 1978). Authors strive to provide graphic cues to guide (or misguide) the reader's expectations, as in the typical mystery story. The character of the main protagonist can be hinted at by physical description or early behavior; and general themes of surprise, danger, or villainy are created intentionally by the author and can be used by readers to help them understand the plot. The more the reader knows about such standard story characters, the easier it will be to read and understand stories.

Although not as uniform in structure as stories, expository texts also take predictable forms, such as the compare and contrast mode described by Armbruster and Anderson (1980). Authors flag important statements by such devices as headings, subsections, topic sentences, summaries, redundancies, and just plain "and now for something really important" statements. Expert learners know about such devices and use them as clues to help them concentrate on essential information.

Next the expert might consider the critical task. An important factor in studying is knowing what you are studying for, i.e., knowing what will be required of you as a test of the knowledge you are acquiring. As Bransford and colleagues point out:

> No self-respecting memory expert would put up with the way psychologists run most memory experiments. Experts would ask questions like "What must I remember?" "How many items?" "How much time will there be?" "What's the nature of the tests?" etc. They would know what they needed to know in order to perform optimally—and would settle for nothing less (Bransford, Nitsch & Franks, 1977, p. 38).

If learners know the type of test they will be given, they can appropriately structure their learning activities. The underlying assumption about the relationship between knowledge of the criterion task and studying outcomes is simple: When the criterion task is made explicit to the students before they read the text, students will learn more from studying than when the criterion task remains vague. But, as Anderson and Armbruster (1980) point out, this general rule holds true only if students do modify their study plans accordingly.

Expert learners would also take into consideration their own particular strengths and weaknesses. Some people are "good at numbers," "have a good rote memory," or "tend to forget details." Whatever the psychological reality behind such claims, it is certainly true that everyone has a limited capacity for remembering large amounts of arbitrary material. A reader can keep only a certain amount of information alive at any one time. Effective readers would not overburden their memories by attempting to retain large segments of texts, too many pending questions (Collins & Brewer, 1977), too many unresolved ambiguities, or too many unknown words and abstract phrases. They would take remedial action to rectify the problem, such as looking back, rereading, consulting a dictionary or a knowledgeable other. Similarly, as arbitrary material is difficult to comprehend and retain, experts would try to make the text more meaningful by trying to understand the significance of what they are reading, or by trying to fit the new material into their own personal experience (Bransford, Stein, Shelton, & Owings, 1980; Brown, Smiley, Day, Townsend, & Lawton, 1977). The trick is to make the unfamiliar more familiar and, hence, more memorable.

Based on the evaluation of their own learning capacity and the task at hand, experts would employ appropriate strategies to help them learn better. There is considerable literature on the common study strategies used by experts. Some of the traditional ones are notetaking, summary writing, underlining, and self-questioning, to which can be added more elaborate systems such as mapping and networking (Armbruster & Anderson, 1980). Deliberate attempts to monitor comprehension or studying are also part of the strategic repertoire of the expert.

> Studying actually requires a double or split mental focus. On the one hand, you need to be focused on the material itself (that is, on learning it). At the same time, however, you need to be constantly checking to see that you are actually performing those mental operations that produce learning. In short, you need to monitor your mental processes while studying (Locke, 1975, p. 126).

The predominant characteristics of expert learners are that they are playful, active, and deliberate. They design their own effective routines for learning, routines that are influenced by a consideration of the four points of the tetrahedron shown in

Figure 1. As instructors or psychologists interested in helping less expert students learn how to learn, our main task is to make novices similarly in control of their own activities and similarly aware of the strategy, task, and outcome demands of various learning situations.

I emphasize the need for "cognitive training with awareness" because the whole history of attempts to instill study strategies in ineffectual learners attests to the futility of having students execute some strategy in the absence of a concomitant understanding of why or how that activity works. To give just a few examples, consider notetaking, underlining, and outlining. Successful students commonly report they employ one or more of these activities when appropriate, but attempts to teach the strategies to less successful students have produced equivocal results.

Until recently, by far the majority of studies on underlining or notetaking show these activities to be no more effective than passive studying techniques such as rereading (Arnold, 1942; Hoon, 1974; Idstein & Jenkins, 1972; Kulhavy, Dyer, & Silver, 1975; Stordahl & Christensen, 1956; Todd & Kessler, 1971; Wilmore, 1966). A general summary of the education literature is that such activities are less helpful than one might predict on intuitive grounds; few studies find a clear advantage in the use of underlining or notetaking, and these may be methodologically flawed (Anderson, in press). An important factor in these studies, however, has been that learners have been randomly assigned to treatment groups, that is, forced to adopt one or another strategy. Brown and Smiley (1978) compared high school students who were spontaneous users of these strategies with those who were told to use them. Students who were spontaneous users underlined or took notes that favored the important information. Students induced to use the strategies did not show a similar sensitivity to importance; they took notes or underlined more randomly, and thereby failed to improve as a result of their activities. Taking notes or underlining is not in itself a desirable end. Understanding that one should use these activities as aids to focusing attention appropriately is the desired end point of training.

In support of these findings, the three studies showing positive results of underlining all report an advantage to active studiers. Richards and August (1975) found that college students who actively underlined passages recalled more than students who had appropriate sections underlined for them. Similarly, Schnell and Ricchio (1975) found that high school students who underlined their own text outperformed those who read a version underlined for them, who in turn recalled more than students reading an uncued text. Finally, Fowler and Barker (1974) found that college students who highlighted their texts recalled more of the material they marked (but not of the unmarked text) than did students who received a premarked text.

Similar findings come from the notetaking and outlining literatures (Brown & Smiley, 1978). Again there are more studies showing that these activities are inefficient (Arnold, 1942; Stordahl & Christensen, 1956; Todd & Kessler, 1971; Wilmore, 1966) than there are that report increased perfor- mance as a function of such esoteric pursuits (Barton, 1930; Brown & Smiley, 1978; Salisbury, 1935). But as Anderson and Armbruster (1980) point out, when one considers the outlining literature, in none of the "failure" studies were students *taught* how to outline. But in the major successes, fairly extensive training was given in outlining. For example, Salisbury's training (1935) involved thirty lessons of instruction.

There is considerable evidence then that high school and even college students need to be explicitly taught how to use a complex outlining strategy. Again we see that outlining itself is not a desired end product, and merely telling students it would be a good idea to outline, underline, and take notes is not going to help them become more effective studiers (Brown & Smiley, 1978). Detailed, *informed* instruction of the purposes of outlining and methods of using the strategy intelligently are needed before sizable benefits accrue.

Inducing students to be more active studiers is an old pastime. Dewey (1910) had detailed prescriptions for how to inculcate more effective learning, as did Binet (1909), and how-to-study guides have traditionally been popular (Anderson, in press). In addition, there has been a resurgence of interest in study skills as a topic for scientific investigation, primarily because of the merging of the two disciplines of educational psychology and cognitive science (Glaser, 1978). Hopes for a new discipline of cognitive engineering (Norman, 1980) are becoming realistic. I would like, however, to contrast the current emphasis on awareness training with more traditional study skills training routines, such as the SQ3R (survey, question-read-recall-review) approaches, outlined by Robinson (1941). Although in principle there is nothing wrong with such methods, in practice, training in such cookbook methods often results in "blind rule following" (Brown, 1978; Brown, Campione, & Day, 1981; Holt, 1964) rather than self-awareness and learning to learn. Instructing a student to read a text, ask questions about the topic sentences (undefined), and reread it twice (why not three times?) may be a reasonable recipe for learning certain texts for certain purposes if the learner understands why these activities are appropriate. But if the learner does not understand the significance of these activities, does not know how to check that the strategies are resulting in the desired end result, does now know what the desired end result is, does not know how to adapt the recipe to slightly new situations or invent a new recipe for various types of texts and tasks, then it is not surprising that instruction in the study recipe is less successful at producing expert studiers than one would like. Thus, I agree with Anderson and Armbruster (1980) that almost any study technique can be effective "if its use is accompanied by focused attention and encoding in a form and manner appropriate to the criterion task" and I would add a concomitant understanding on the part of the learner of why the activity should be undertaken and what it is expected to achieve.

The main aim of cognitive training with awareness is to help students become cognizant of the need to adapt their study activities to the demands of the criterial task, the nature of the material, and their own personal preferences and abilities. The goal is to provide novice learners with the information, practice, and success necessary to help them to design effective learning plans of their own. The essential aim of such training would be to make students more aware of the active nature of critical reading and studying and of the importance of employing problem-solving routines to enhance understanding. If less successful students can be made aware of 1) basic strategies for reading and remembering, 2) simple rules of text construction, 3) differing demands of a variety of tests to which their knowledge may be put, and 4) the importance of attempting to use any background knowledge they may have, they cannot help but become more effective learners. Such self-awareness is a prerequisite for self-regulation—the ability to monitor and check one's own cognitive activities while reading and studying (Baker & Brown, in press; Brown, Campione, & Day, 1981).

Summary

As a result of repeated experience in and out of schools, successful students come to learn how to learn from reading. Indeed, reading becomes the primary medium through which they receive instruction. Reading for them is an active process of information gathering, evaluating, and hypothesis testing; they know how to extract information from texts, to critically evaluate its importance, its reliability, and the evidence that supports the data. They monitor their comprehension and retention and evaluate their own progress in the light of the purposes for which they are reading. With repeated experience on these leading school activities, many of these cognitive monitoring processes become automatic. That is, although mature readers typically engage in comprehension monitoring, it is not usually a conscious experience (Brown, in press). When comprehension is proceeding smoothly, good readers proceed as if on automatic pilot until a problem is detected. Some triggering event (Brown, in press; Collins et al., 1977) alerts them to a comprehension failure. Then the understanding process slows down and becomes planned, demanding conscious effort. Study monitoring for the expert involves many automatic, overlearned components; although here the need is greater for deliberate forethought, planning, and checking. In general though, successful students know how to learn from texts.

Less successful students are not as aware of the need to be strategic, plan ahead, monitor, and check their own understanding. They have not yet learned how to learn from texts. Reading is not a primary or preferred mode of obtaining information and the task of studying is often interpreted as

.nvolving nothing more than passive, sometimes desperate, rereading of texts. Such students can be helped to become more active learners via training programs based on awareness and self-control (Brown, Campione, & Day, 1981). In order to become expert learners, students must develop some of the same insights into the demands of the learning situation possessed by the psychologist, the educator, and the expert learner. They must learn about their own cognitive characteristics, their available learning strategies, the demands of various learning tasks, and the inherent structure of the material. They must tailor their activities to the demands of all these forces in order to become flexible and effective learners. In other words, they must *learn how to learn from reading*.

References

ADAMS, M.J. Failures to comprehend and levels of processing in reading. In R.J. Spiro, B.C. Bruce, and W.F. Brewer (Eds.), *Theoretical issues in reading comprehension*. Hillsdale, New Jersey: Erlbaum, 1980.

ALLEN, V. *Children as teachers: Theory and research on tutoring*. New York: Academic Press, 1976.

ANDERSON, T.H. Study strategies and adjunct aids. In R.J. Spiro, B.C. Bruce, & W. F. Brewer (Eds.), *Theoretical issues in reading comprehension*. Hillsdale, New Jersey: Erlbaum, 1980.

ANDERSON, T.H., & ARMBRUSTER, B.B. Studying. In P.D. Pearson (Ed.), *Handbook of reading research*. New York: Longman's, in press.

ANDRE, M.D.A., & ANDERSON, T.H. The development and evaluation of a self-questioning study technique. *Reading Research Quarterly*, 1978-1979, *14*, 605-623.

ARMBRUSTER, B.B., & ANDERSON, T.H. *The effect of mapping on the free recall of expository text* (Technical Report No. 160). Urbana: University of Illinois, Center for the Study of Reading, February 1980. (ED 182 735)

ARNOLD, H.F. The comparative effectiveness of certain study techniques in the field of history. *Journal of Educational Psychology*, 1942, *33*, 449-457.

AU, K. A test of the social organizational hypothesis: Relationships between participation structures and learning to read. Unpublished doctoral dissertation, University of Illinois, 1980.

BAKER, L., & BROWN, A.L. Metacognitive skills of reading. In P.D. Pearson (Ed.), *Handbook of reading research*. New York: Longman's, in press.

BARTON, W.A. *Outlining as a study procedure*. New York: Teachers College, Columbia University, 1930.

BERNSTEIN, B. *Class codes and control* (Volume 1). London: Routledge & Kegan Paul, 1971.

BINET, A. *Les idees modernes sur les enfants.* Paris: Ernest Flamarion, 1909.

BRANSFORD, J.D., NITSCH, K.W., & FRANKS, J.J. Schooling and the facilitation of knowing. In R.C. Anderson, R.J. Spiro, & W.E. Montague (Eds.), *Schooling and the acquisition of knowledge.* Hillsdale, New Jersey: Erlbaum, 1977.

BRANSFORD, J.D., STEIN, B.S., SHELTON, T.S., & OWINGS, R.A. Cognition and adaptation: The importance of learning to learn. In J. Harvey (Ed.), *Cognition, social behavior, and the environment.* Hillsdale, New Jersey: Erlbaum, 1980.

BROWN, A.L. The development of memory: Knowing about knowing, and knowing how to know. In H.W. Reese (Ed.), *Advances in child development and behavior* (Volume 10). New York: Academic Press, 1975.

BROWN, A.L. Knowing when, where, and how to remember: A problem of metacognition. In R. Glaser (Ed.), *Advances in instructional psychology.* Hillsdale, New Jersey: Erlbaum, 1978.

BROWN, A.L. Learning and development: The problems of compatibility, access, and induction. *Human Development,* in press.

BROWN, A.L. Metacognitive development and reading. In R.J. Spiro, B.C. Bruce, & W.F. Brewer (Eds.), *Theoretical issues in reading comprehension.* Hillsdale, New Jersey: Erlbaum, 1980.

BROWN, A.L., BRANSFORD, J.D., & FERRARA, R.A. Learning, remembering, and understanding. In J.H. Flavell & E.M. Markman (Eds.), *Mussen handbook of child development.* New York: John Wiley & Sons, in press.

BROWN, A.L., & CAMPIONE, J.C. Permissible inferences from the outcome of training studies in cognitive development research. *Quarterly Newsletter of the Institute for Comparative Human Development,* 1978, *2,* 46-53.

BROWN, A.L., & CAMPIONE, J.C. Inducing flexible thinking: A problem of access. In M. Friedman, J.P. Das, & N. O'Connor (Eds.), *Intelligence and learning.* New York: Plenum, in press.

BROWN, A.L., CAMPIONE, J.C., & DAY, J. Learning to learn: On training students to learn from texts. *Educational Researcher,* 1981, *10*(2), 14-21.

BROWN, A.L., & FRENCH, L.A. The cognitive consequences of education: School experts or general problem solvers. Commentary on Education and cognitive development: The evidence from experimental research by Sharp, Cole, & Lave. *SRCD Monographs,* 1979.

BROWN, A.L., & SMILEY, S.S. The development of strategies for studying texts. *Child Development,* 1978, *49,* 1076-1088.

BROWN, A., SMILEY, S., DAY, J., TOWNSEND, M., & LAWTON, S. Intrusion of a thematic idea in children's recall of prose. *Child Development,* 1977, *48,* 1454-1466.

BRUCE, B.C., & NEWMAN, D. Interacting plans. *Cognitive Science,* 1978, *2,* 195-233.

BRUNER, J.S. Nature and uses of immaturity. *American Psychologist,* 1972, *27,* 687-708.

CAMPIONE, J.C., BROWN, A.L., & FERRARA, R.A. Research on exceptional children: Implication for theories of intelligence. In R. Sternberg (Ed.), *Handbook of human intelligence.* Boston: Cambridge University Press, in press.

CLAY, M. *Reading: The patterning of complex behavior.* Auckland, New Zealand: Heinemann Educational Books, 1973.

Learning How to Learn from Reading 51

COLLINS, A., BROWN, A.L., MORGAN, J.L., & BREWER, W.F. *The analysis of reading tasks and texts* (Technical Report No. 43). Urbana: University of Illinois, Center for the Study of Reading, April 1977. (ED 145 404)

COLLINS, A., BROWN, J.S., & LARKIN, K.M. Inference in text understanding. In R.J. Spiro, B.C. Bruce, & W.F. Brewer (Eds.), *Theoretical issues in reading comprehension*. Hillsdale, New Jersey: Erlbaum, 1980.

DANSEREAU, D.F., LONG, G.L., McDONALD, B.A., & ATKINSON, T.R. Learning strategy inventory development and assessment (AFHRL-TR-75-40). Lowry Air Force Base, Colorado: Air Force Human Resources Laboratory, 1975.

DENNEY, T., & WEINTRAUB, S. Exploring first graders' concepts of reading. *Reading Teacher*, 1963, *16*, 363-365.

DENNEY, T., & WEINTRAUB, S. First graders' responses to three questions about reading. *Elementary School Journal*, 1966, *66*, 441-448.

DEWEY, J. *How we think*. Boston: Heath, 1910 (2nd ed., Heath, 1933).

DWECK, C.S. Children's interpretation of evaluative feedback: The effects of social cues on learned helplessness. *Merrill-Palmer Quarterly*, 1976, *22*, 105-109.

FEUERSTEIN, R. The instrumental enrichment method: An outline of theory and technique. Unpublished paper, Hadassah-Wizo-Canada Research Institute, 1969.

FEUERSTEIN, R. *The dynamic assessment of retarded performers: The learning potential assessment device, theory, instruments, and techniques*. Baltimore: University Park Press, 1979.

FEUERSTEIN, R. *Instrumental enrichment: An intervention program for cognitive modifiability*. Baltimore: University Park Press, 1980.

FLAVELL, J.H., & WELLMAN, H.M. Metamemory. In R.V. Kail, Jr., & J.W. Hagen (Eds.), *Perspectives on the development of memory and cognition*. Hillsdale, New Jersey: Erlbaum, 1977.

FORREST, D.L., & WALLER, T.G. *Cognitive and metacognitive aspects of reading*. Paper presented at the meeting of the society for Research in Child Development, San Francisco, March 1979.

FOWLER, R.L., & BARKER, A.S. Effectiveness of highlighting for retention of text material. *Journal of Applied Psychology*, 1974, *59*, 358-364.

GLASER, R. (Ed.). *Advances in instructional psychology*. Hillsdale, New Jersey: Erlbaum, 1978.

HOLT, J.H. *How children fail*. New York: Dell, 1964.

HOON, P.W. Efficacy of three common study methods. *Psychology Reports*, 1974, *35*, 1057-1058.

HUEY, E.B. *The psychology and pedagogy of reading*. Cambridge, Massachusetts: The MIT Press, 1968.

IDSTEIN, P., & JENKINS, J.R. Underlining versus repetitive reading. *Journal of Educational Research*, 1972, *65*, 321-323.

ISAKSON, R.L., & MILLER, J.W. Sensitivity to syntactic and semantic cues in good and poor comprehenders. *Journal of Educational Psychology*, 1976, *68* (6), 787-792.

JENKINS, J.J. Four points to remember: A tetrahedral model and memory experiments. In L.S. Cermak & F.I.M. Craik (Eds.), *Levels and processing in human memory*. Hillsdale, New Jersey: Erlbaum, 1979.

JOHNS, J., & ELLIS, D. Reading: Children tell it like it is. *Reading World*, 1976, *16* (2), 115-128.

KAVALE, K., & SCHREINER, R. The reading processes of above average and average readers: A comparison of the use of reasoning strategies in responding to standardized comprehension measures. *Reading Research Quarterly*, 1979, *15*, 102-128.

KULHAVY, R.W., DYER, J.W., & SILVER, L. The effects of note taking and test expectancy on the learning of text material. *Journal of Educational Research*, 1975, *68*, 363-365.

LOCKE, E.Q. *A guide to effective study.* New York: Springer, 1975.

MANDLER, J.M., & JOHNSON, N.S. Remembrance of things parsed: Story structure and recall. *Cognitive Psychology*, 1977, *9*, 111-151.

MARKMAN, E.M. Realizing that you don't understand: A preliminary investigation. *Child Development*, 1977, *46*, 986-992.

MARKMAN, E.M. Realizing that you don't understand: Elementary school children's awareness of inconsistencies. *Child Development*, 1979, *50*, 643-655.

McDERMOTT, R.D. Some reasons for focusing on classrooms in reading research. In P.D. Pearson & J. Hansen (Eds.), *Reading: Disciplined inquiry in process and practice*, Twenty-seventh yearbook of the National Reading Conference. Clemson, South Carolina: National Reading Conference, 1978.

MYERS, M., & PARIS, S.G. Children's metacognitive knowledge about reading. *Journal of Educational Psychology*, 1978, *70*, 680-690.

NASH, W.A., & TORRANCE, E.P. Creative reading and the questioning abilities of young children. *Journal of Creative Behavior*, 1974, *8*, 15-19.

NORMAN, D.A. Cognitive engineering and education. In D.T. Tuma & F. Reif (Eds.), *Problem solving and education: Issues in teaching and research.* Hillsdale, New Jersey: Erlbaum, 1980.

OLSHAVSKY, J. Reading as problem solving: An investigation of strategies. *Reading Research Quarterly*, 1976-1977, *12*, 654-674.

OLSHAVSKY, J. Comprehension profiles of good and poor readers across materials of increasing difficulty. In P.D. Pearson & J. Hansen (Eds.), *Reading: Disciplined inquiry in process and practice*, twenty-seventh yearbook of the National Reading Conference. Clemson, South Carolina: National Reading Conference, 1978.

REID, J.F. Learning to think about reading. *Educational Research*, 1966, *9*, 56-62.

RICHARDS, J.P., & AUGUST, G.J. Generative underlining strategies in prose recall. *Journal of Educational Psychology*, 1975, *67*, 860-865.

ROBINSON, R.P. *Effective study.* New York: Harper & Row, 1941.

SALISBURY, R. Some effects of training in outlining. *English Journal*, 1935, *24*, 111-116.

SCHNELL, T.R., & ROCCHIO, D. A comparison of underlining strategies for improving reading comprehension and retention. In G.H. McNich & W.D. Miller (Eds.), *Reading: Convention and inquiry*, twenty-fourth yearbook of the National Reading Conference. Clemson, South Carolina: National Reading Conference, 1975.

SHALLERT, D.L., & KLEIMAN, G.M. *Some reasons why the teacher is easier to understand than the textbook* (Reading Education Report No. 9). Urbana: University of Illinois, Center for the Study of Reading, June 1979. (ED 172-189)

SINGER, H. Active comprehension from answering to asking questions. *Reading Teacher*, 1978, *31*, 901-908.

SMITH, H.K. The responses of good and poor readers when asked to read for different purposes. *Reading Research Quarterly*, 1977, *3*, 53–84.

SPEARMAN, C. *The nature of intelligence and principles of cognition.* London: Macmillan, 1923.

STORDAHL, K.E., & CHRISTENSEN, C.M. The effect of study techniques on comprehension and retention. *Journal of Educational Research*, 1956, *49*, 561–570.

STRANG, R., & ROGERS, C. How do students read a short story? *English Journal*, 1965, *54*, 819–823.

THORNDIKE, E.L. Reading as reasoning: A study of mistakes in paragraph reading. *Journal of Educational Psychology*, 1917, *8*, 323–332.

TODD, W., & KESSLER, C.C. Influence of response mode, sex, reading ability, and level of difficulty on four measures of recall of meaningful written material. *Journal of Educational Psychology*, 1971, *62*, 229–234.

VYGOTSKY, L.S. *Mind in society: The development of higher psychological processes.* In M. Cole, V. John-Steiner, S. Scribner, & E. Souberman (Eds.). Cambridge, Massachusetts: Harvard University Press, 1978.

WEBER, R.M. A linguistic analysis of first grade reading errors. *Reading Research Quarterly*, 1970, *5*, 427–451.

WERTSCH, J.V. From social interaction to higher psychological processes: A clarification and application of Vygotsky's theory. *Human Development*, 1979, *22*, 1–22.

WHIMBEY, A. *Intelligence can be taught.* New York: Dutton, 1975.

WILMORE, D.J. A comparison of four methods of studying a textbook. Unpublished doctoral dissertation, University of Minnesota, 1966.

Discourse Comprehension and Production: Analyzing Text Structure and Cohesion

Robert J. Tierney
University of Illinois
James Mosenthal
University of Chicago

This paper is intended to serve as an introduction to text analysis as a research tool and vehicle for improving instruction. To this end, seven text analysis models are reviewed together with their pedagogical possibilities. The reviews do not exhaust the text analysis models proposed in the literature or their pedagogical possibilities. In terms of perspective, two major theses are maintained throughout the paper. First, we urge that text analysis be used within the context of understanding that a multiplicity of variables can influence reader-text interactions. Second, we suggest that the various text analysis models can be used as complements, one to another. Distinctions drawn between the various text analysis models should not be used to set the models in competition with one another.

Toward a Text Analysis Perspective

Consistent with contemporary psycholinguistic and cognitive viewpoints is the notion that both the production and comprehension of discourse involve an interaction among reader, text, author, and context. This notion suggests that during discourse production authors do not merely transfer words from within their brains to a text. Likewise, during discourse comprehension, readers do not merely transfer words from a text to their brains. Rather, as depicted in Figure 1, discourse comprehension and discourse production involve a complex interaction among the cognitive structures of the author, the text, the cognitive structures of the reader, and the communicative situation.

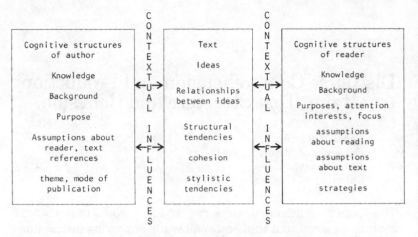

DISCOURSE PRODUCTION   DISCOURSE COMPREHENSION

Cognitive structures of author	CONTEXTUAL INFLUENCES	Text	CONTEXTUAL INFLUENCES	Cognitive structures of reader
Knowledge		Ideas		Knowledge
Background	←U→	Relationships between ideas	←U→	Background
Purpose				Purposes, attention interests, focus
Assumptions about reader, text references	←F→	Structural tendencies	←F→	assumptions about reading
		cohesion		assumptions about text
theme, mode of publication		stylistic tendencies		strategies

Figure 1.   The nature of author, text, and reader relationships during discourse production and comprehension.

Typically, an author goes beyond finding just any set of words to express ideas; an author searches for the words which will create appropriate connotations for the readers of the text. This implies that an author needs to know something about a reader's thoughts including background of experience and interests. It implies that the author has prescribed and can predict the reader's context. It suggests that all these aspects interact back and forth, influencing and being influenced by the production of text. In all, it suggests that what have been labeled text tendencies (i.e., the explicit and implicit ideas, relationships between ideas, structural features, cohesion and stylistic qualities) are constrained by an author's perceptions of an audience, an author's perceived goal for a text, an author's ability to appreciate the effect of a text upon an audience, and the mode and conditions of publication.

During discourse comprehension, the cognitive structures of the reader, the text, and the communicative situation have a similar interactive influence upon a reader's understanding. That is, a reader's knowledge, purpose, interest, attention, and focus influence and are influenced by discourse comprehension. Likewise, the communicative situation, including the physical and sociocultural conditions of the reading situation, constrain comprehension strategies and outcomes. Thus, discourse comprehension can be viewed as involving the construction of meaning wherein the following conditions apply: a) a reader initiates, directs, and terminates any interaction with a text; b) a text is never fully explicit nor is comprehension of a text exclusively textual; c) a reader inserts, substitutes, deletes, and focuses ideas toward refining an interpretation which seems plausible, connected, and complete; d) a number of factors contribute to the extent to which a reader's understanding will vary from the author's intended message. To reiterate a major thesis, discourse comprehension evolves from a myriad of complex interacting influences.

Procedural Models for Text Analysis

In recent years, the fields of linguistics, cognitive psychology, and computer science have afforded a number of systems for examining the contribution of text features to discourse comprehension. In this regard, the work of Dawes (1966), Frederiksen (1975), Grimes (1972), Halliday and Hasan (1976), Kintsch (1974), Meyer (1975a, 1975b), and Rumelhart (1975) have been seminal. These systems, which might be labelled procedural models for text analysis, can be broadly defined as systems for examining the characteristics of text and knowledge of text from a semantic perspective. An implicit tenet of most of these systems is the notion that a text is the reflection of the writer who produced the text and that some specificity relative to discourse production and discourse comprehension can be derived by analyzing and comparing a subject's knowledge to the characteristics of the text itself.

The uses of text analysis for the researcher and theorist seem obvious. Text analysis provides the means for a systematic examination of the effects of selected text characteristics upon reading comprehension. Indeed, over the past decade, numerous valuable insights relative to discourse comprehension have been derived from research based upon text analysis models. For example, text analysis research has suggested that certain aspects of text structure do influence the amount and type of information recalled and that tenable predictions can be made as to where distortions, omissions, additions, substitutions and restructuring will occur. Chodos and Mosenthal (Note 1), Kintsch (1974), Mandler and Johnson (1977),

Rumelhart (1975), Stein and Glenn (1978), and Thorndyke (1977) have shown the influence upon reading comprehension of a generalized story structure which most readers possess. McKoon (1977), Meyer and McConkie (1973), and Meyer (1975a, 1977) have shown the influence of the hierarchical structure of expository prose and the importance of the position of ideas within text structure. Clements (1975) demonstrated the influence of the staging of ideas. Marshall (1976) and Tierney, Bridge, and Cera (1979) have demonstrated the influence of propositional content and interpropositional relationships.

From a practical perspective, educators interested in applying text analysis findings and technology need to be aware of what text analysis can and cannot do. In general, it is our argument that text analysis has the potential to be used and misused. Within the context of an appreciation of reader-text interactions, analyses of text features seem both warranted and appealing. Outside this context, such analyses and their derivatives may be misguided.

The next section is intended to familiarize the reader with what text analysis can and cannot do. In this section, six different means of examining text are presented: story grammars, event chain formulations, expository prose predicate structures, mapped patterns, propositional analysis, and cohesion. Our discussion includes a brief overview of each text analysis system and some commentary relative to its utility in research and educational practice. This section is then followed by a general discussion of what seems to be the potential application of text analysis.

Propositional Analyses

Based upon Fillmore's case grammar (1968), the primary concern of many recent discourse models has been on semantics with an emphasis on propositions and propositional structures. For example, models by Kintsch (1974) and Frederiksen (1975) are among the popular models concerned with propositional analysis. Basic assumptions of these models have been that a sentence is comprised of one or more propositions reflecting the knowledge of the speaker or writer, and that the pivot of each proposition is the verb.

Kintsch's propositional text base. As Turner and Green (1977) state, the use of prose texts in research requires a system for formally representing the meaning of texts. Kintsch's propositional system (Kintsch, 1974) addresses that requirement. Basic terms of Kintsch's sytem are the proposition, or idea unit, and the text base, or the list of connected propositions constituting a text.

Kintsch (1974) refers to the set of propositions for a text as its microstructure or text base. Three types of text base are distinguished: the text base structure, the template text base, and the protocol text base. The text base structure is equivalent to the knowledge base of the author who generated the text and can only be inferred. The template text base represents a model of the text, and it comprises a list of connected propositions which can be arranged into a hierarchical network. The protocol text base represents the stated recall of a reader for a text and is scored by comparing it to the template text base.

The construction of a template text base and a protocol text base requires reducing the text to an ordered list of propositions or idea units, each unit composed of relations and arguments. Arguments are the concepts represented by one or more words in the text. Relations are the pivotal concept in the proposition and connect the arguments so that together, arguments and relations represent single ideas.

As an example, consider a template text base for the opening sentences of "An Occurrence at Owl Creek Bridge," by Ambrose Bierce (1978).

Text: A man stood upon a railroad bridge in Northern Alabama, looking down into the swift water 20 feet below. The man's hands were behind his back, the wrists bound with a cord. A rope loosely encircled his neck.

Template Text Base:
1. (QUALITY OF, BRIDGE, RAILROAD)
2. (STAND, MAN, 1)
3. (LOCATION: IN, 2, NORTHERN ALABAMA)
4. (QUALIFY, BELOW, 20 FEET)
5. (QUALITY OF, WATER, SWIFT)
6. (LOCATION: 4, 5, $)
7. (LOOK DOWN, 3, 6)
8. (PART OF, 2, HANDS)
9. (PART OF, 2, BACK)
10. (LOCATION: BEHIND, 8, 9)
11. (BIND, $, WRISTS, CORD)
12. (PART OF, 2, NECK)
13. (ENCIRCLE, $, 12, ROPE)
14. (QUALIFY, 13, LOOSELY)

Each line represents a proposition. The relation is written first in the proposition, followed by its arguments. Consider the three propositions which make up the clause, "A man stood upon a railroad bridge in Northern Alabama." In Proposition 1, the relation dominating the proposition is QUALITY OF. The arguments are BRIDGE and RAILROAD. The relation QUALITY OF signifies a modifying proposition. In the second proposition, STAND is the relation, and MAN and RAILROAD BRIDGE are the arguments. Notice that instead of writing RAILROAD BRIDGE, the number of the proposition denoting "railroad bridge" is substituted. STAND signifies a predicate proposition. Predicate propositions represent actions or states. In Proposition 3, the relation is LOCATION and is specified by IN. Proposition 2 and NORTHERN ALABAMA are the arguments. LOCATION signifies a connective proposition. Connective propositions relate whole propositions or facts with other propositions or facts.

The relations QUALITY OF, STAND, LOCATION are representative of the three classes of propositions which define all propositions. The three classes are predication, modification, and connection. The classification of propositions is based on the way a relation binds its arguments. While the relation and its arguments may be depicted by words in the text, they represent abstract word concepts which are not to be confused with the words explicitly stated in the text. For purposes of preparing a text base, the relation and its arguments are represented by capitalized words to indicate they are word concepts. Note also, in the example of STAND, that tense is not represented in proposition. Turner and Green explain that tense is a product of syntax and is therefore not included in a semantic representation of text. A discussion of the classes of propositions follows.

As stated, predicate propositions represent actions or states. Usually, these relations are verbs. Their arguments fill certain slots defined in relation to the verb dominating the proposition. For example, in Proposition 11, the verb BIND has a slot for the "one who binds," called the AGENT. In the text under consideration, the AGENT is not specified and the symbol $ is substituted. BIND also has a slot for the person or thing "bound" called the OBJECT. This slot is filled by WRISTS. Finally, BIND has a slot for the instrument used for "binding" called the INSTRUMENT. This slot is filled by CORD. With this additional notation, Proposition 11 could be written (BIND, A\$, O:WRISTS, 1:CORD). It is a matter of preference whether the slots are designated in the proposition. In the template text base, STAND (Proposition 2), LOOK DOWN (Proposition 7), BIND (Proposition 11), and ENCIRCLE (Proposition 13) are predicate propositions.

Modifier propositions qualify arguments of a proposition or a whole proposition. Propositions 1, 4, 5, 8, 9, 12 and 14 are examples of modifying propositions. There are four types of modifying propositions: Qualifiers, Partitives, Quantifiers, and Negations. QUALITY OF and QUALIFY are qualifiers with adjectival and adverbial functions, respectively. PART OF is a partitive type of modifier proposition whose function is to define the relationship of a part to a whole (see Propositions 8, 9, 12). Besides qualifiers and partitives there are quantifier and negating types of modifier propositions. Quantifiers are usually signalled by the relation NUMBER OF. Negations are signalled by the relation NEGATE.

Connective propositions serve a special function in that they are the only means of coordinating propositions representing separate sentences. There are eight major classes of connectives with each class having many examples. In a connective proposition the class of the connective is given followed by the word concept which is the example of the class, as in (CONJUNCTION: AND . . .). The arguments of the proposition follow AND. The remaining classes follow with an example of the class (DISJUNCTION: OR . . .), (CAUSALITY: CAUSE . . .), (PURPOSE: IN ORDER TO . . .), (CONCESSION: ALTHOUGH . . .), (CONTRAST: BUT . . .), and (CONDITION: IF . . .). The final class is CIRCUMSTANCE and has three subclasses TIME, LOCATION, and MANNER. In the template text base, the only connective propositions are CIRCUMSTANCE propositions denoting LOCATION. They are characterized by the word concepts IN (Proposition 3), 20 FEET BELOW (Proposition 6), and BEHIND (Proposition 10).

It must be remembered that Kintsch's reason for creating a text base is to provide a legitimate breakdown of ideas in text against which recalls, broken down into protocol text bases, may be compared. It is as if Kintsch has provided a means for comparing "deep structures" of text and recall. As a research tool, Kintsch's system is quite powerful.

But the propositional text base is not only understood as a tool. Kintsch means his propositional analysis to provide a means of describing, experimentally, the mental processes involved in comprehension of text (see Kintsch & van Dijk, 1978). The first part of the comprehension process organizes the "meaning elements of a text" into a coherent micro-structure. The ideal microstructure is approximated by the template text base, while the actual microstructure generated by the reader is approximated by the protocol text base. The second aspect of the comprehension process is the generation of a macrostructure from the microstructure. This aspect repre-sents a condensing of information into a manageable unit for memory—Kintsch calls it the "gist" of the text. It is important to understand the relationship of the two aspects of the com-prehension process to the structural representation of text. On the one hand, the structural theory underlying the construction of a template text base and protocol text base is, as Kintsch describes it, "a semiformal statement of certain linguistic intuitions" (Kintsch & van Dijk, 1978, p. 365). The compre-hension model is applied to the template text base and generates an expected protocol text base. The experimental success of such an endeavor is dependent on a system that will generate macropropositions as legitimately as the micropropositions of a text base are generated. However, the generation of macro-propositions and an overall macrostructure of text is a process that is not as mechanically sound as the rules for generating the microstructure and will not be discussed at this time.

The strength of Kintsch's system lies in its simplicity and in its ability to represent well "linguistic intuitions" about the surface structure of text. Also, the system is not confined to a text type as are story grammars and Meyer's system for describing expository text structure. Rather, Kintsch's system is flexible enough to deal with any text type. With that flexibility, Kintsch's system represents a powerful tool for research in reading comprehension. It must be pointed out that Kintsch's system is not a tool for testing or teaching but is rather a tool for research that complements a theory of discourse comprehension.

Frederiksen's semantic and logical networks. Based on the premise that an examination of comprehension must account for the interplay between text-based and knowledge-based processes, Frederiksen's model offers a text analysis framework which purports to address the text, reader, and communicative context, and which is based upon the semantic content and logical structure of the text. In brief, the semantic content consists of propositions that are represented as networks of concepts connected by labelled binary relations. The concepts and connectors parallel the arguments and relations represented in a Kintsch analysis. The logical structure represents the logical, causal, and algebraic relations between propositions (Frederiksen, 1975, 1977, Note 2; Frederiksen, Frederiksen, Humphrey, & Otteson, Note 3). In a Kintsch analysis these would be represented by connectives relating distinct propositions.

For an illustration of the use of Frederiksen's framework, consider a reader's recall of selected sentences (see Table 1). The sentences were taken from a story; the reader's recall was taken from a recall for the entire story. At the lowest level, Frederiksen's framework would define the semantic content and logical structure of the text. At subsequent levels of analysis, Frederiksen's framework affords a concurrent text-based analysis of inferences and a functional examination of their role. For example, in Table 1, the semantic content and logical structure of a text is represented by numbered propositions. The abbreviated symbols denote some of the concepts and relationships defined by Frederiksen's semantic and logical network system. Tables 2 and 3 provide a modified version of Frederiksen's Taxonomy of Text-Based Inferences and his list of Functional Contexts.

In undertaking a Frederiksen analysis, the following guidelines for analyzing a text and scoring recalls are used.

Analyzing a text. The first step is to define the text in terms of its semantic content and logical structure. This requires breaking the text down into propositions or idea units and defining the concepts and relationships represented within and between propositions.

Within propositions, the semantic network specifies relations and two types of concepts—objects and actions. Objects are defined as things occupying space. Actions are

Table 1

Frederiksen Semantic and Logical Networks

Text:

His shirt was jumping back and forth.
His mother came running.

Recall:

The shirt was jumping back and forth on the
bed. Then Johnny's mother came running.

Message Base (Knowledge Structure) of Text

01 ('Johnny) - PAT @ TEM (PRES) - (has) - OBJ - (:shirt)
      (shirt) - DEF - NUM - (one)
02 ("01) - AGT @ TEM (PAST) ASPECT (CONT) - (jump) - MAN -
      (back and forth)
03 ('Johnny) - PAT @ TEM (PAST) - (has) - DAT - (:mother)
04 ("C3) - AGT @ TEM (PAST) - (came) - MAN - (running)

Key to Symbols in Network

(   )   concept
(:)   concept to be determined and quantified
(')   concept not to be determined and quantified
(")   reference to proposition usually cited by number
@   marks an operation on the relation

Relations

Case relations, resultive propositions

AGT	Agent	participant in the act
DAT	Dative	recipient of the act (animate)
OBJ	Object	recipient of the act (inanimate)

Case relations, processive propositions

PAT	Patient	participant in the act
DAT	Dative	recipient of the act (animate)
OBJ	Object	recipient of the act (inanimate)

Other

MAN	Manner	adverbial
DEF	Determination	(definite)
TOK	Determination	(indefinite)
NUM	Quantification	
PAST	one of a variety of tenses	
CONT	one of a variety of aspects	

         Tierney and Mosenthal

Table 2

Modified Frederiksen Taxonomy of Text-Based Inferences

Identification Operation*

1. Attribute inference
2. Category inference
3. Time inference
4. Locative inference
5. Part-whole inference
6. Degree inference
7. Manner inference
8. Identity inference

Frame Operations*

9. Act inference
10. Case inference
11. Instrument inference
12. Result inference
13. Source inference
14. Goal inference
15. Theme inference
16. Frame transformation

17. Qualifier inference
18. Disembedding

Event Generation**

19. Event generation (synonymous)

Algebraic Operations**

20. Algebraic inference

Dependency Operations**

21. Causal inference
22. Conditional inference
23. Contrastive inference
24. Concessional inference
25. Conjuncture inference
26. Disjunctive inference

---

*Refers to:

a. synonymous slot substitute
b. superordinate slot substitute
c. subordinate slot substitute
d. semantically different slot substitute
e. generation of relation and concept

**Refers to:

a. plausible and relevant
b. implausible and irrelevant
c. irrelevant, plausible

---

defined as things which occupy an interval of time and which involve change. There are two major subclasses of actions—resultive and processive. Resultive actions involve a physical or cognitive change; processive actions involve no change in state.

Represented within the semantic network are three types of relations—stative, manner, and case. Stative relations are relations which distinguish an object from other objects. They include determination, quantification, identification, classification, attribution, locative, temporal, and part-whole. The

Table 3

Frederiksen's Functional Contexts of Inferences in Reading Comprehension

Types	Function
First Stage inference -resolution of ambiguity -resolution of cataphora -Dietic Inference: person, place, time	Interpretation of a current sentence by replacing anaphoric elements in proposition, with referrents and resolving ambiguities by selecting a preferred reading
Connective inferences	Connecting disconnected propositions
Extensive inference	Generating new propositions which extend meaning given by original set
Structural inference -segmentation -topical inference -reduction	Segmenting and organizing a text, building a coherent model of a text as a whole

Note: Based on Frederiksen (Note 2) and Frederiksen et al. (Note 3).

major relationships represented within any text are the case relationships. Case relationships specify the relationship of an action and fit into different frameworks depending upon whether they represent processive or resultive actions. Processive actions have the following case framework:

$$(object) \quad - \quad (processive\ action) \quad - \quad (object)$$
$$(theme)$$
$$(goal)$$

Resultive actions have the following case framework:

$$(object) \quad - \quad (resultive\ action) \quad - \quad (object)$$
$$(source)$$
$$(result)$$
$$(instrument)$$
$$(goal)$$

All case relationships are further specified by tense, qualifier, and aspect relations. To illustrate, consider the following representation of the sentence *John can swim well.* This sentence represents a processive action involving the present tense and a qualifier. Also embedded within the proposition is a relationship involving manner. Using Frederiksen's system, the sentence would be represented as follows:

(John) — Pat @ Ten (Pres) @ Qual (can) — (swim) — Man — (well)

Alternatively, consider the representation of a sentence involving a resultive action: *John ran down the road.* This sentence would be represented as follows:

1.0 (John) — Agt @ Ten (Past) — (ran) — Result — (1.1)
1.1 (John) — Loc — (road, down)

It should be noted that case relations represent the major relations evident in a text and that not all slots are filled within the case framework. Some slots are mandatory; other slots are optional. Also, it should be noted that selected slots require a proposition which is embedded. As illustrated in the last example, the embedded stative proposition detailing location was given the same number as the major proposition, but a decimal was added to tag it as embedded.

In addition to the semantic network, Frederiksen proposes a logical network in order to specify relationships across propositions. That is, the logical network represents the causal, logical, and algebraic relations which connect propositions temporally, causally, comparatively, conjunctively, and concessionally. For example, suppose a sentence within a text defined an explicit relationship between two propositions. Consider the sentence, *The dinosaurs died because they could not find food.* In all, three propositions would be needed to represent this sentence. Two would represent case relationships; one would specify the causal relationship between the other two propositions.

1. (dinosaurs) — Pat @ Ten (Past) @ Qual (can) @ (neg) — (find) — obj (food)

2. (dinosaurs) — Pat @ Ten (Past) — (die)

3. (1) — cau (2)

As the example illustrates, Proposition 3 specifies the causal relationship and, therefore, represents the logical network.

Thus, the semantic and logical networks together define the content and structure of a text. In so doing, these networks purport to provide a representation of the writer's knowledge structure which is referred to as the message base of a passage. This message base serves to define the characteristics of a particular text and can serve as a template for studying discourse processing including inferential operations. In all, it represents the first level of analysis using Frederiksen's system.

Scoring recalls. Scoring recalls represents the second and third levels of analysis. Specifically, scoring recalls entails preparing a semantic and logical network of each subject's recall and comparing each to the message base of the original passage. This involves marking every item in the subject's recall that corresponds to the message base as defined for the original text. When all of the explicitly stated items have been marked, each proposition in the recall is analyzed to determine the types of inferences represented by the information generated by the reader. In accordance with Frederiksen's taxonomy of inferences, this entails a concurrent examination of inference type, inferential operations and inferential functions. For example, suppose a reader generated a causal relationship between two previously disconnected propositions. According to Frederiksen's second and third levels of analysis, this inference would be classified as a dependency operation involving a causal inference toward connecting disconnected propositions.

Of the various text-analysis frameworks presented, Frederiksen's system of analysis appears to be the most comprehensive. Indeed, some might argue that Frederiksen's methodology is too detailed and, therefore, too time-consuming and difficult to manage. In terms of propositional analysis, Frederiksen's system has some advantages over other microanalyses such as that proposed by Kintsch. Unlike Kintsch, Frederiksen leaves unfilled any slot which is not explicitly cued by the text. Rather than fill slots likely to be inferred, Frederiksen offers a taxonomy of inferences. Thus, if Frederiksen's model of text analysis and taxonomy of inferences are used concurrently, Frederiksen's system would offer a more systematic and objective procedure for examining a reader's text-based recall.

From a theoretical perspective and as a research tool, Frederiksen's analysis represents a valiant attempt to address the issue of text-based inferences and to synthesize the work being done both in linguistics and in psychology. Unfortunately, in attempting to determine the underlying representation of a text, Frederiksen's system, along with Kintsch's system, is often limited by the inability of the researcher and even the writer to recognize underlying message bases represented within the text. Also, it offers no guidelines for addressing either implied meanings or indirect speech acts involved in conversations.

With the evolution of Frederiksen's system, however, versions of his text analysis procedures have been used successfully to glean important information concerning the influence of the semantic content and logical structure upon reading comprehension (Marshall, 1976; Bridge, 1977; Tierney, Bridge, & Cera, 1979; Pearson, Note 4). The major advantage of Frederiksen's system, however, is the flexibility it affords. Analysis can be done at various levels and the system can be applied to almost any text. The major limitations are that Frederiksen's system does not consider implied meanings or structural qualities beyond the interpropositional level, and his categories for inferences seem to overlap. Obviously, unless it were used in a very general way, Frederiksen's text analysis model would be well-nigh impossible for teachers to use.

Cohesion

Unlike structural explanations of content, cohesive analyses describe the patterns in the fabric or texture of a text. In accordance with this conceptualization, text is viewed as "language in use" and as "language . . . relevant to its environment" (Halliday, 1977). This contrasts with "language in the abstract" and "decontextualized language like words in a dictionary or sentences in a grammar book" (Halliday, 1977). As viewed by Halliday and Hasan (1976), a text is a semantic unit of any length and function—so long as it does function (as a sign, a recipe, a book). The text is the basic unit of the semantic system. It is a unit defined by its functional relevance.

According to Halliday and Hasan (1976), cohesion is displayed in the ties that exist within text between a presupposed item and a presupposing item. For example, in the sentences "John makes good meals. Last night, he made spaghetti." *he* is the presupposing item and *John* is the presupposed item. Text derives texture from the fact that it functions as a unity with respect to its environment and the fact that this unity can be described by the ties that exist between presupposing and presupposed items. It is these cohesive ties within a text that establish a text's continuity. That is, cohesive ties represent a kind of linguistic mortar which connects the text together. As Halliday and Hasan suggest:

> The concept of ties makes it possible to analyze a text in terms of its cohesive properties and give a systematic account of its patterns of texture (p. 4).

Halliday and Hasan detail various types of cohesive ties evident in texts: reference, substitution/ellipsis, lexical cohesion, and conjunction. Each type reveals presupposed and presupposing items. The connection of such items across sentences defines the semantic continuity, texture or cohesiveness of a text.

Reference. Reference in extended text typically includes what Halliday and Hasan label personals, demonstratives, and comparatives. The personals include the personal pronouns and their possessive forms: *he, him, his, they, them, theirs, their, it, its.* The demonstratives include: *this, these, that, those, here, there, then* and *the.* The comparatives typically are adjectives or adverbs presupposing an item already mentioned: *same, equal, better, more, identically, so.* Generally, an instance of referential cohesion occurs when an item in a text can only be interpreted by reference to a preceding item in the text. Consider the following examples of personal, demonstrative, and comparative reference.

a. Personal:
   The three young businessmen had lunch together.
   They ended up drinking much too much.
   (*they* refers to *the three young businessmen*)

b. Demonstrative:
   Dr. Forbes drove eight miles in a blinding snowstorm
      to get to Plainfield to see the Gardner boy. Two days
      later he had to drive there again.
   (*there* refers to *Plainfield*)

c. Comparative:

John sold him three tires for the price of one.

Jack asked, "Why didn't you give me the same deal?"

(*same* refers to *three tires for the price of one*)

When dealing with reference in written text, the assumption is made that the referential ties are endophoric or text-determined (within the text) as opposed to exophoric or situationally-determined (outside the text). For example, if an adolescent was overheard to say "that's bad," we would not know what he was referring to unless we saw the custom-made van he was looking at. This is an example of exophoric reference—it is reference dependent upon the actual situation. If a similar situation were part of a novel, *that* would refer endophorically to the words *custom-made van*, or the description of the van given in the text.

It is also assumed that endophoric reference is either anaphoric (presupposing an item that appears in preceding text) or cataphoric (presupposing an item that appears in subsequent text). However, cataphoric reference occurs primarily within a sentence and so can be explained by the structure of the sentence. Consider the following example of cataphoric reference:

The player who slacks off in practice won't play in the game.

The player refers forward to *who slacks off in practice.* Rarely are there instances of cataphoric reference in text which extend across sentences. However, cataphoric reference can occur across sentences and is to be considered genuinely cohesive in those cases:

He actually did it. He asked her out.

(the second sentence is cohesive with *it*)

Thus, we are left with a description of referential cohesion within the written text that assumes the cohesive tie to be predominantly endophoric and anaphoric.

Substitution and ellipsis. Substitution and ellipsis are distinguished in the following way: Substitution replaces one item with another, and ellipsis omits an item that is assumed. An example of substitution is:

My razor is dull. I need a new one.

(*one* substitutes for *razor*)

An example of ellipsis is:

> I can only remember the names of 48 states. I need to name two more.

(two more *states* is understood)

Three categories of substitution and ellipsis are described by Halliday and Hasan. They are nominal substitution/ellipsis, verbal substitution/ellipsis, and clausal substitution/ellipsis. In substitution, the word(s) appearing in text can refer back to a noun phrase, a verb phrase or a clause. In ellipsis, the word(s) omitted can be a noun phrase, a verb phrase or a clause.

In substitution, the three categories are defined by the use of explicit word substitutions.

Nominal: *one, ones, same*

> Look at these pictures from the scrapbook. That one is the oldest.
> (*one* substitutes for *picture*)

> These books are no good. Get me some better ones.
> (*ones* substitutes for *books*)

> John is an excellent cook. The same can't be said of his wife.
> (*the same* substitutes for *is an excellent cook*)

Verbal: *do*

> Why are you fidgeting? I didn't know I was doing so.
> (*doing so* substitutes for *fidgeting*)

Clausal: *so, not*

> Are gas prices going up? The paper says so.
> (*so* substitutes for *gas prices are going up*)

> Are gas prices going up? I hope not.
> (*not* substitutes for *gas prices are not going up*)

At one point, ellipsis is described as substitution by zero. But the mechanics of substitution and elliptical cohesion are complex enough that Halliday and Hasan preserve the two separate identities. Generally, ellipsis can be defined as the omission of an item that is understood or assumed. For example:

Nominal ellipsis

Which game do you want to go to?
The first.
(*game* is understood in the response)

Verbal ellipsis

Has he tasted John's cooking?
He may have.
(*tasted John's cooking* is understood in the response)

Clausal ellipsis

Jack was going to get some beehives.
Who was?
(*going to get some beehives* is understood in the response)

Up to this point, substitution and ellipsis have been understood as the replacement of a word(s) by another word(s) and the omission of a word(s) whose presence is understood. There is more to it. The nature of the relationship between presupposed and presupposing items in reference and substitution/ellipsis is essentially different. A reference tie describes identity; substitution/ellipsis describes contrast. Consider the sentence:

These books are no good. Get me some better ones.

Ones substitutes for *books*. Yet, the substitution is not an identity of reference. Rather, the message of the response is contrastive. Halliday and Hasan say that the substitute repudiates the preceding message. *Ones* actually refers to the nonidentified books which are better. *Ones* does refer to the word-concept *book*, but only as a means of contrasting *better* with *these*.

Conjunction. Conjunction is described as an instance of semantic connection. Typical connectives such as *and, but, so,* and *next* can identify conjunctive cohesion. For example:

He is cheap sometimes. But he can be generous when he wants to.
They'll be back at 10. So come over early.

Conjunctive items within a sentence, as with other cohesive items within the sentence, can be described structurally. But in connecting separate sentences, the conjunctive item receives a cohesive emphasis that characterizes the relationship between the two sentences. As Halliday and Hasan state,

> conjunctive elements are cohesive not in themselves but indirectly, by virtue of their specific meanings. They are not primarily devices for reaching out into the preceding ... text, but they express certain meanings which presuppose the presence of other components in the discourse (1976, p. 226).

Halliday and Hasan describe four types of conjunctive relations. They are additive, adversative, causal, and temporal. There is a great wealth of possible conjunctive words and phrases which communicate many shades of meaning. These shades of meaning are indicated by the following examples: conjunctive relations of the additive type are characterized by such connectives as *and, nor, furthermore, by the way, thus, in the same way.* Examples of adversative connectives are *yet, but, however, in fact, on the other hand, rather, in any case.* Some causal connectives are *so, because, it follows.* Finally, examples of temporal connectives are *finally, then, meanwhile, to sum up.*

Lexical cohesion. Lexical cohesion is broken into two parts, reiteration and collocation. Reiteration, as with reference, establishes a relationship of identity:

Dick and I did the climb to Window Rock. The climb was easy.

(*climb* in the second sentence reiterates *climb* in the original statement)

However, in lexical reiteration the presupposing item is presupposing because it is reiterative.

There is another difference between lexical reiteration and reference. In being reiterative, a word need not be identical to the presupposed item. Consider the following example:

a. We parked the car and started the climb to Window Rock.
b. The climb
c. The ascent
d. The task
e. The thing

> was easy.

The presupposed item is *climb* in (a). In (b) the same item is repeated, in (c) a synonym is substituted, in (d) a superordinate word-concept is substituted, and in (e) a general noun is substituted. These four categories represent variations in the system of reiteration.

Reiteration has qualities similar to substitution. Though not precisely contrastive, the meaning of a presupposing item in an example of reiteration need not make explicit reference back to a presupposed item. Consider the following example:

  a. That Siamese cat is beautiful.
  b. That cat has won many awards.
  c. There's another Siamese cat entered in this competition.
  d. Both cats are beautiful.
  e. Most Siamese cats are beautiful.

In (b) the reference is identical between *cat* and *cat* in (a). In (c) *another Siamese cat* excludes the *cat* in (a). In (d) *both cats* includes *cat* in (a). In (e) *cats* is unrelated referentially to *cat* in (a). These four different relationships to the presupposed item are labelled identical, exclusive, inclusive, and unrelated. These relationships are determined by text usage whereas the same word, synonym, superordinate, general word types mentioned above are descriptive of the system of reiteration, independent of usage in text.

Lexical collocation can be simply described as "the association of lexical items that regularly co-occur" across expanses of sentences if need be (Halliday & Hasan, 1976, p. 285). Consider the similar lexical environment shared by such words as *wool, ewe, sheep,* and *lamb.* In a text, this sequence of words is referred to as a cohesive chain. Meaning is generated by the associations the reader makes between the ideas represented by the words. Such meaning is a kind of synthesis of the elements in a shared lexical environment. Consider the following cohesive chain: *newsstand, Sunday newspaper, funnies, read, papers, Sunday crossword puzzle.* If a writer were describing a Sunday morning sequence of a day in the life of a city dweller, the above chain and the shared lexical environment it defines might be expanded to include such words as *deli* and *bagel* and, perhaps, even *happy.* The writer might join the Sunday morning sequence with a Saturday night sequence tying *movie, bar,* and *friends* to the Sunday morning vocabulary. The obvious expanding associative potential of collocational items emphasizes the semantic power of a shared lexical environment independent of text structure.

The study of the concept of cohesion represents a necessary counterpoint to the study of structure and content in prose. Early in this section, cohesion was referred to as the mortar of an interpretable text. Cohesive language, the bulk of any text, not only makes the text interpretable in its function as mortar, it plays a major role in determining the text's characteristic "feel," its affective power.

Two examples follow which point out the mortar-like quality of cohesion and its affective power. The first example takes an excerpt from John Osborne's *Look Back in Anger* (1977, Act II, Scene 1). A fairly complete table of the cohesive items in the passage is given. The table is a simplified version of the tabular form Halliday and Hasan use to chart the cohesive items in the passages they analyze. Sentences or phrases that are equivalent in meaning or that are specific statements of a previous general statement are included as examples of lexical collocation. Arrows within the PRESUPPOSED ITEM column indicate a series of items cohesive one with another. The first item is the item immediately presupposed; the second item in the series is more distant in the text from the presupposing item, etc. The arrows are supplied as a means of showing the mortar-like quality of cohesive ties. A sample text follows. Its cohesive analysis is presented in Table 4.

Alison: 1 Did you manage all right?

Helena: 2 Of course. 3 I've prepared most of the meals in the last week, you know.

Alison: 4 Yes, you have. 5 It's been wonderful having someone to help. 6 Another woman I mean.

Helena: 7 I'm enjoying it. 8 Although I don't think I shall ever get used to having to go down to the bathroom every time I want some water for something.

Alison: 9 It is rather primitive, isn't it?

Helena: 10 Yes. 11 It is rather.

Table 4

A Cohesive Analysis of the Sample Text
Using Halliday and Hasan Model

Sentence Number	Cohesive Item	Type	Presupposed Item
1	you	Reference	Helena (sentence 1 refers exophorically to situation)
2	of course	Ellipsis	of course I managed all right.
3	(have) prepared (most of the meals in the last week)	Lexical Collocation	managed (all right)
4	you have	Ellipsis	you have prepared most of the meals in the last week → managed all right
5	someone help	Lexical Reiteration Lexical Collocation	Helena sentence 4 → sentence 3
6	another woman	Reference Lexical Reiteration	someone someone → Helena
7	it	Reference	help(ing) → sentence 4 → sentence 3
8	although sentence 8	Conjunction Lexical Collocation	sentence 7 and sentence 8 it → help(ing) sentence 4 → sentence 3
9	it	Reference	having to go down to the bathroom every time I want some water for something
10	it rather	Reference Lexical reiteration, Ellipsis	it → having to go . . . rather ( ) rather primitive (E)

The second example is given to show the affective, associative power of collocational items. The shared lexical environment, used or created by the writer in his choice of words, helps determine the perspective and the character of the text as a whole. The opening paragraph of Wolfe's *Electric Kool-Aid Acid Test* (1977) demonstrates this point. Only the collocational items of the paragraph are discussed.

That's good thinking there, Cool Breeze. Cool Breeze is a kid with 3 or 4 days' beard sitting next to me on the cramped metal bottom of the open back part of the pickup truck. Bouncing along. Dipping and rising and rolling on these rotten springs like a boat. Out the back of the truck the city of San Francisco is bouncing down the hill, all those endless staggers of bay windows, slums with a view, bouncing and streaming down the hill. One after another, electric signs with neon martini glasses lit up on them, the San Francisco symbol of "bar"—thousands of neon-magenta martini glasses bouncing and streaming down the hill, and beneath them thousands of people wheeling around to look at this freaking crazed truck we're in, their white faces erupting from their lapels like marshmallows—streaming and bouncing down the hill—and God knows they've got plenty to look at (p. 1).

In the discussion below, phrases, not just individual words, are identified as collocational. Also, as noticed in the long middle sentence, collocational items need not be restricted by sentence structure and sentence boundaries. There are several cohesive chains (chains of words sharing the same lexical environment) found in this paragraph. Consider the following chains:

a. cramped metal bottom . . . open back part . . . pick up truck . . . rotten springs . . . boat . . . back of the truck . . . freaking crazed truck
b. sitting . . . bouncing along . . . dipping . . . rising . . . rolling . . . bouncing down the hill . . . bouncing . . . streaming down the hill . . . streaming and bouncing down the hill
c. endless . . . one after another . . . thousands . . . hundreds . . . thousands
d. city of San Francisco . . . staggers of bay windows . . . slums with a view . . . San Francisco
e. electric sign . . . neon martini glasses . . . symbol . . . bar . . . neon-magenta martini glasses . . .

The (a) and (b) chains, within the context of the entire passage, create a "feel" for the "freaking crazed truck." Together with the (c) chain, the (a) and (b) chains also help determine the feel for San Francisco and the environment of the martini glass symbol for bar. None of this feel is factual and therefore easily articulated in a retelling. Rather, this feel represents an affective factor in the reader's comprehension of a text.

Structural analyses of text dispense with any consideration of cohesion and its effect on recall. Comprehension scores based on recall of the story outline do not incorporate the felt quality of a reader's comprehension of a story. Analyzing the cohesive element in an evaluation of a text could lead to new insights into the text's or author's influence upon the reader's comprehension and appreciation of text. However, from the researcher's point of view, it is questionable to what extent the influence of cohesive relations can be systematically studied. Halliday and Hasan's examples of cohesion in text are only descriptive. That is, while they assess the character of cohesion's presence, they do not offer standards for interpreting and analyzing cohesive patterns.

If the researcher cannot be sure of the nature of cohesion patterns across text or the influence of cohesive patterns upon comprehension, the teacher can only use cohesion indirectly. For example, prior to the use of a text, teachers might examine its cohesive patterns. This might include an examination of possible anaphoric ambiguities, macrorelations across sentences and cohesive chains. Beyond these rudimentary suggestions, the ramifications of cohesive analyses for the classroom teacher have yet to be explored.

Story Grammars

A story grammar exists as an approximation of a reader's internalized grammar for a single protagonist narrative (Mandler & Johnson, 1977; Rumelhart, 1975; Stein & Glenn, 1978; Thorndyke, 1977). This internalized story structure involves invariant categories which foster reader instantiations. Generally, these categories are hierarchical and include the equivalents of setting, event structure, episodes, initiating event for the episode, a reaction to the initiating event, internal and external response components to the reaction, attempt and consequent components and a final resolution. Consider the following story:

1. Dick lived on a farm in Vermont.
2. One night he heard a fox in the chicken coop.
3. He knew he had to kill it.
4. Dick got his rifle
5. and went to the chicken coop.
6. He surprised the fox with a chicken in its mouth.
7. Dick shot the fox where it stood.
8. Dick buried the fox.

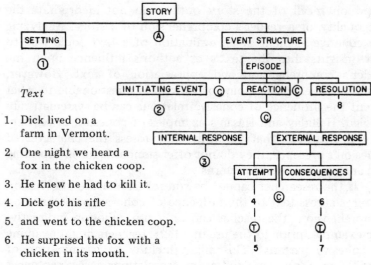

Text

1. Dick lived on a
   farm in Vermont.

2. One night we heard a
   fox in the chicken coop.

3. He knew he had to kill it.

4. Dick got his rifle

5. and went to the chicken coop.

6. He surprised the fox with a
   chicken in its mouth.

7. Dick shot the fox where it stood.

8. Dick buried the fox.

Figure 2a. Story grammar analyses of sample text.

This story could map onto a tree diagram as depicted in Figure 2a. In some stories, subcategories of Character, Time and Location may be subordinate to the Setting. Multiple episodes could occur under the Event Structure if the story demanded it. Episodes could also be embedded within other categories of the story structure (an Initiating Event might be an episode in its own right). In order to allow a story grammar to generate stories of varying complexity, structural nodes in the grammar must allow for such embedding to take place. For example, in the grammar constructed by Mandler and Johnson (1977), the Ending category, corresponding to the Resolution category in Figure 2a, has three subordinate nodes. They are [Event*(AND Emphasis)/Emphasis/Episode]. The brackets indicate that one and only one of the three enclosed subcategories is possible. The asterisk indicates that there can be no more than one event. The parentheses indicate an optional complement to Event*. The slash lines separate the three choices. In turn, each of the three subcategories has its own subordinate nodes. The evident hierarchical complexity allows for the generation of stories with complex event structures.

Of all the story grammarians, Mandler and Johnson (1977) provide a grammar that can accommodate more complex stories. They make their grammar manageable by isolating the relational terms that connect individual nodes. These terms are AND, THEN, and CAUSE. The AND term indicates simultaneity. THEN indicates a temporal or sequential relationship. And CAUSE connects two nodes, the first of which provides the reason for the second to happen. The relational terms are abbreviated A, T, C and are inserted between nodes in the tree diagram. The tree diagram in Figure 2b has incorporated these labels.

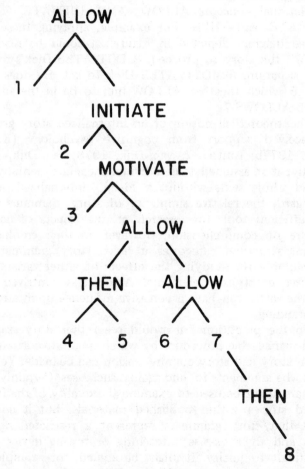

Figure 2b. Story grammar analyses (continued).

The use of such relational terms in the grammar is an improvement over other grammars which omit them. It is not that the A, T, C terms introduce new information; rather, the terms make the grammar and its representation more readable and specify the relationship between inferred and stated propositions. In the above story, Proposition 3 might have been omitted, in which case the internal response is inferred and is assumed to be the cause of Dick's getting the rifle.

Rumelhart (1975) further discriminates between uses of relational terms. He suggests semantic interpretation rules intended to allow the reader to decode the syntactic rules of the grammar. His semantic interpretation rules include the relational concepts ALLOW, AND, INITIATE, CAUSE, MOTIVATE, and THEN. For example, applying these rules, the tree diagram depicted in Figure 2a could be read as 1 ALLOWS the story to proceed. 2 INITIATES Dick's reaction to the situation. 3 MOTIVATES Dick to act. He does 4 and THEN 5 which together ALLOW him to be in the situation 6 which ALLOWS 7.

The theoretical notion of an internalized story grammar has received support from cognitive psychology (Kintsch, 1977a, 1977b; Kintsch & van Dijk, 1978; van Dijk, 1977). Basically, it is assumed that individuals cannot mentally comprehend whole texts without a "deep," internalized plan. In this regard, the relative simplicity of story grammars makes them efficient tools for research on the effects of narrative structure on comprehension. However, in their emphasis on invariant structural categories in text, story grammars may be unsuitable for studying the effects of either variant story structures or stylistic elements. Across less contrived narratives, the latter can have a pervasive influence upon a reader's understanding.

To the practitioner it would seem that story grammars offer a manageable procedure by which qualitative assessments of both story and story comprehension can be made. Yet there seem to be arguments for and against such uses. Certainly, story grammars might be used to examine the quality of the form of selected stories within published materials. But it could be argued that story grammars represent a restricted range of stories and their use as a teaching or testing device would be difficult to justify. It might be argued, for example, that existing story grammars fail to address alternate purposes for reading and writing, confine their consideration of story features to a single protagonist narrative and represent an internalized structure that need not be taught. For example, used as a grid against which a subject's recall is matched, story grammars would appear to give an equal weight to all parts of a story. Maybe to the reader what might be considered a structurally unimportant proposition reflects the major theme of a story. The point is that rigid assessments based upon story grammars do not seem legitimate or consistent with their intended use. They afford no affective component, no pragmatics which would make the reader equally as important as the text.

Event Chain Formulation for Narratives

An event chain formulation for narratives is not patterned after an internalized story structure or a single-protagonist episodic structure (Trabasso & Nicholas, in press; Warren, Nicholas & Trabasso, 1979). In its representation, an event chain depicts, for each protagonist, several broad classes of events (states, events, actions, cognitions, displays, impulses, and goals) and logical connectives (motivation, physical cause, psychological cause, enablement, temporal succession, and temporal coexistence). Certain a priori rules constrain the possible combination of event types and connectives. For example, only certain classes of events (action, display and event) can have a causal relationship which is physical. In stories involving multiple protagonists, the events related to each protagonist shift horizontally in accordance with a shift in characters.

As an illustration of the structure of an event chain, consider the following brief story and its depiction in Figure 3.

1. It was the weekend.
2. Martyn was playing in the sand tray.
3. Karyn felt mischievous.
4. She decided to tease Martyn.
5. When Martyn was not looking,
6. she turned the hose on.
7. Martyn was covered with water.
8. He grabbed the hose.
9. He was very angry.
10. So to get even with Karyn,
11. he sprayed her.

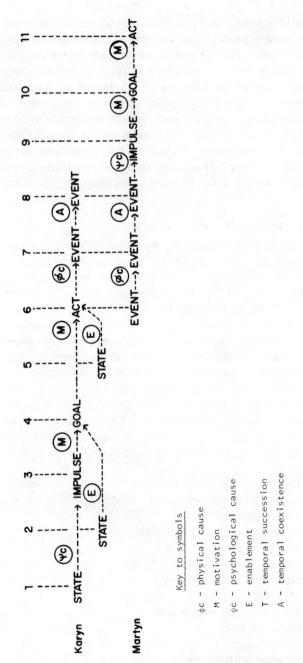

Figure 3. Event chain for the narrative involving Karyn and Martyn.

Tierney and Mosenthal

The figure depicts the event chain of the story with each event numbered and labelled. Their interconnections are represented by a labelled arrow; the shift in protagonist is depicted by a shift in horizontal lines from Karyn and Martyn.

In conjunction with their formulation of event chains, Warren, Nicholas, and Trabasso (1979) and Trabasso and Nicholas (in press) propose a taxonomy of inferences. Their taxonomy provides categories for the types of inferences a reader might make within and across event chains. The categories of inference within the taxonomy include three broad types: logical, informational, and value inferences. The informational inferences involve the determination of the "who," "what," "when," and "where" within stories. The logical inference category addresses the "how" and "why" of stories. Value inferences address the "so what" of the story. Table 5 provides additional detail regarding the subclasses and functions of each category.

Table 5

Taxonomy of Inferences Based on Event-Chain Formulation

Class	Function
1. Logical Inference	
a. motivation	Inferring causes for a character's given voluntary thoughts, actions, or goals (or vice versa), e.g., John was angry. He left.
b. psychological cause	Inferring causes for a character's given voluntary thoughts, actions, or feelings (or vice versa), e.g., John tripped on the stone. He shouted.
c. physical cause	Inferring mechanical causes for given objective events or states (or vice versa) e.g., Lightening hit. The tree fell. David smashed the car. His passenger was injured.
d. enablement	Determining the conditions necessary but not sufficient for a given event to occur. Determine the event a certain condition allows, e.g., It was windy. They could fly the kite.

Table 5 (continued)

Class	Function
2. Information Inference	
a. pronominal	Specify the antecedents or pronouns, e.g., Chuck was late. He was mad.
b. referential	Specify the related antecedents of given actions or events when the reference is not pronominally marked, whether or not they are explicitly stated in other propositions, e.g., Carol found her father's car in front of the school. She ran and hopped in.
c. spatio-temporal	Determine the place or time of a single or series of propositions, e.g., It was Friday afternoon. They ran to the football park. The children were all ready.
d. world-frame	Determining a world context to account for inferences, e.g., They saw the lions, tigers, seals, and monkeys.
e. elaborate	Flushing out additions which do not contribute to the logical process of the story.
3. Value Inferences	Judging the morality, convention, and anomaly in character's thoughts and actions or in story style or construction, e.g., John wanted to tease Peter. He asked him if he could leave the party. Peter was shocked and angrily shouted obscenities. Was shouting obscenities a good way to deal with John?

Note: Based upon Warren, Nicholas, and Trabasso, 1979.

In an attempt to define practical limits to inferencing, the authors address what they term a "relevancy hypothesis." The relevancy hypothesis states that the reader, understanding a narrative, should make only those inferences determined by and integral to the progress of the narrative. In other words, the reader should make only those inferences necessary to determine what happened and why. While certain inferences

Tierney and Mosenthal

may be consistent with the text and add color to the story, they are irrelevant to the flow of the narratives.

As with story grammars, an event chain formulation is a manageable procedure which can afford valuable qualitative data on text, readers, and discourse processes. But there are several advantages which an event chain formulation has when compared with a story grammar: a) an event chain analysis is not restricted to a single protagonist situation; b) an event chain formulation does not ascribe a singular framework or model to all narratives; c) a portion, rather than the whole, of a text can be subjected to this type of analysis; and d) assuming the adequacy of the taxonomy of inferences and the legitimacy of the relevancy hypothesis, discourse processes can be categorized and evaluated. On the negative side, an event chain formulation fails to address the influence of variant reader purposes and afford a structural analysis of only the events within a story. With regard to reader purposes, the relevancy hypothesis erroneously assumes common purposes across different texts, readers, and reading situations. In terms of the scope of an event chain formulation, unfortunately, larger structural units such as setting and resolution are not addressed.

From the viewpoint of a practitioner, an event chain formulation might be useful for purposes of examining the flow of a narrative and deriving testing and teaching paradigms. For example, given the difficulty some readers often have in understanding narrative involving multiple protagonists, it may prove beneficial to have readers map the chain of events within the episodic structure of complex narratives.

Expository Prose Predicate Structures

In *The Organization of Prose and Its Effects on Memory*, Meyer (1975a) provides an expository analog to story grammars. Specifically, Meyer provides a structural analysis of prose based upon the relationships in the content of a passage. As Meyer states, her analysis

> ... depicts the relationships among the content of the passage. It shows how an author of a passage has organized his ideas to convey his message, the primary purpose of his writing endeavor (p. 3).

Whereas the story grammarians assume a culturally internalized story grammar for narrative text, Meyer suggests that in expository text there is not an expository grammar that individuals in a culture share. Rather, there is only the superstructure created by the author.

Meyer's structural analysis of prose is based on relationships which she defines as predicates. There are two types of predicates, lexical and rhetorical. Generally, a lexical predicate dominates the arguments of a sentence. The arguments of the sentence are connected by role relations which are always subordinate to the dominant lexical predicate. Consider the first example in Figure 4(a). In the tree diagram, the lexical predicate BLEW dominates the structure of the sentence. Each of the three brackets defines the role of an argument and the argument. WIND is the force that acts on the patient, WEATHERVANE, in a specific range or area of action, the ROOF. The lexical predicate and its arguments define a lexical proposition. Based on the work of Fillmore (1968) and Grimes (1972), Meyer details nine types of role relationships.

Rhetorical predicates relate ideas that typically extend across sentence boundaries. More importantly, they are the means by which an author organizes the whole text. The rhetorical predicates of a text define its general organization. Based upon Grimes (1972), Meyer describes three types of rhetorical predicates: paratactic, hypotactic, and neutral. A rhetorical predicate is paratactic if the main arguments of a text all receive equal time. Hypotactic rhetorical predicates describe texts whose arguments are organized hierarchically. Neutral rhetorical predicates are ones that can be paratactic or hypotactic depending on the author's purpose.

As stated above, rhetorical predicates represent the principle by which any piece of expository prose is organized. Rhetorical predicates can also dominate a paragraph and, in turn, be dominated by the rhetorical predicate of a chapter which is, in turn, dominated by another rhetorical predicate which dominates the whole text. In other words, there is in a text of any length a hierarchical organization of ideas defined by the organizational principles carried in the rhetorical predicates.

Figure 4(b) is an example of a response rhetorical predicate, a type of paratactic rhetorical predicate. It represents the

a. Lexical Predicate

The wind (force) blew (lexical predicate) the
weathervane (patient) off the roof (range).

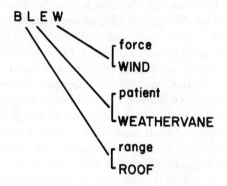

b. Response Rhetorical Predicate

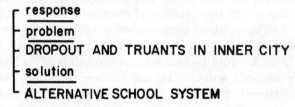

Figure 4.   Meyer structural analysis of prose (the predicates).

organizational structure of an article on alternative schools.
The vertical line indicates the paratactic or equivalent status
of the arguments. Underlined words with lowercase letters
indicate rhetorical predicates or components of a rhetorical
predicate. Thus, response is the label of the rhetorical predicate
which dominates the entire article. The first component of a
response predicate is the problem . The item which defines
the problem of the response predicate is given next and is
written with capital letters. The solution predicate is the complement component to the problem . Its argument follows,
also in capital letters.

From her work on rhetorical predicates, Meyer concludes that top-level structural nodes such as problem and solution are stored in memory preferentially and are most easily accessed in recall tasks. Thus, in the above example, the relationship of truancy and alternative schools has priority in memory storage—not necessarily as individual facts but as principles to which the rest of the information in the article is made subordinate. Meyer concludes that information organized at hierarchically inferior levels is less easily remembered, if not deleted from the individual's organization of the information in memory.

What follows is a text and a structural representation of a portion of the content of the text. The representation is done according to Meyer's guidelines for depicting content structure. Left-most entries are hierarchically dominant to right-most entries. Small case, underlined words identify rhetorical propositions. Capitalized words with dotted underlining are lexical predicates from the text. Words in small case but not underlined identify the role of an argument in a lexical proposition. Non-underlined capitalized words are words taken from the text. Rhetorical predicates and role relations in the diagram are somewhat self-explanatory. Also self-explanatory is the left to right display of dominant-subordinate information.

The content structure of a text may be broken down to whatever level desired. For example, an entry such as 14 in Figure 5 could be broken down in terms of its lexical predicate. In Meyer's work, texts are broken down to the point where significant items for recall are identified in isolation in the content structure. Retellings are scored according to the extent to which they reflect the dominant rhetorical structure of the text and articulate subordinate propositions and relationships:

Cracking the Cycles of Depression and Mania[1] by Joel Greenberg

SOME PERSONS WITH AFFECTIVE DISORDERS APPEAR TO BE OUT OF PHASE WITH THE NORMAL 24-HOUR DAY. CHANGING THEIR SLEEP-WAKE CYCLES CAN TRIGGER DRAMATIC IMPROVEMENTS.

Despite significant advances in understanding and treating depression and manic-depression, these "affective" disorders still carry with them some of the more curious mysteries in behavioral science. The puzzle involves an apparent cyclic or "up and down" characteristic in certain patients. Many depressives, for example, suffer most in the morning (sleep disturbance is thought to be central to depression); others show some bizarre hormonal activity that appears to be out of synch with normal metabolism; and still others—particularly manic-depressives—seem to function on a daily and annual calendar of their own.

Perhaps shedding some light on affective illness are newly reported research results from the National Institute of Mental Health's Clinical Psychobiology Branch in Bethesda, Maryland. The findings indicate that slightly abnormal biological rhythms—both long and short term—may be key factors in the development of depression and manic depression.

It was found that melatonin—an indicator of brain norepinephrine activity—seems to run through a cycle in which it peaks in January and July and hits valleys in May and October, while platelet serotonin appears to be on a reverse cycle, with its activity reaching peaks in May and October. Both norepinephrine and serotonin have been implicated in depression.

"We've known for a long time that there are annual rhythms and seasonal variations in a lot of illness," says NIMH Clinical Psychobiology Chief Frederick K. Goodwin, who conducted much of the research. "Affective illness is [frequently] a recurrent phenomenon." and the research results suggest "the possibility of some long-term cyclic process."

In the other portion of the work, Goodwin and his colleagues observed that the daily biological rhythms of some persons with affective disorders are slightly out of phase with the standard 24-hour day. In bipolar, or manic-depressive patients, the researchers had noticed that several days before the periodic manic phase set in, the patients would go to bed and wake up somewhat earlier than usual. If such a sleep-wake change was associated with the shift away from depression, the investigators reasoned, perhaps intentionally manipulating the pattern would help depressives—which it did.

```
1    Response
2    problem
3    APPEAR TO BE

4       patient
5    PERSONS WITH AFFECTIVE DISORDERS

6       latter
7    OUT OF PHASE WITH NORMAL 24-HOUR DAY
8       evidence
9    ARE SHEDDING SOME LIGHT ON AFFECTIVE DISORDERS  covariance, antecedent

10      patient
11      RESEARCH RESULTS

12         evidence
13         collection
14      NOREPINEPHRINE AND SEROTONIN HAVE BEEN IMPLICATED IN DEPRESSION

15            specific
16            collection
17         MEASURING THE HORMONE MELATONIN

18               specific
19            SEEMS TO RUN

20                  patient
21               MELATONIN

22                     attribution
23                  AN INDICATOR OF NOREPINEPHRINE ACTIVITY

24                  range
25               THROUGH A CYCLE

26                     explanation
27                  PEAKS IN JANUARY AND JULY AND HITS VALLEYS IN MAY AND OCTOBER

28               (MEASURING) PLATELET SEROTONIN

29                  specific
30               APPEARS TO BE ON A REVERSE CYCLE

31         ARE

32            patient
33         DAILY BIOLOGICAL RHYTHMS

34               attribution
35            OF SOME PERSONS WITH AFFECTIVE DISORDERS

36            latter
37         SLIGHTLY OUT OF PHASE WITH THE STANDARD 24-HOUR DAY

38            explanation
39         WOULD GO TO BED AND WAKE UP SOMEWHAT EARLIER THAN USUAL

40               setting time
41            SEVERAL DAYS BEFORE THE PERIODIC MANIC PHASE SETS IN

42      covariance, consequent
43      MAY BE

44         force
45      SLIGHTLY ABNORMAL BIOLOGICAL RHYTHM

46         patient
47      KEY FACTORS IN THE DEVELOPMENT OF DEPRESSION AND MANIC DEPRESSION

48      solution
49   CHANGING SLEEP-WAKE FACTORS CAN TRIGGER DRAMATIC IMPROVEMENTS

50      explanation
51   REASONED

52         agent
53      INVESTIGATORS
```

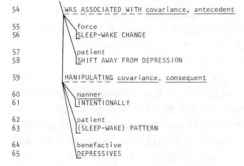

```
54       WAS ASSOCIATED WITH covariance, antecedent
55          force
56         SLEEP-WAKE CHANGE
57          patient
58         SHIFT AWAY FROM DEPRESSION
59       MANIPULATING covariance, consequent
60          manner
61         INTENTIONALLY
62          patient
63         (SLEEP-WAKE) PATTERN
64          benefactive
65         DEPRESSIVES
```

Figure 5.   The content structure of "Cracking the Cycles of Depression and Mania" (not all information in the text is diagramed).

Meyer claims that her structural analysis procedures provide the researcher with the basis for describing prose passages, examining reading comprehension and studying the effects of structural manipulation of prose upon comprehension. Meyer states that, given a system for describing the organizational structure of prose passages, research now has a means of describing and comparing prose structures. Also, given the structural dimension, recall tasks can be effectively scored and compared. Meyer claims that content structure can now be used to study such topics as individual differences in reading comprehension, the influence of prior knowledge on reading tasks, and the effect of variant positioning of top-level structural variables within the text.

Likewise, Meyer claims that these structural analysis procedures have afforded results and a technology which might have relevance to educators, writers, and publishers. She suggests that writers should place information they want readers to remember high in the content structure of their prose. She suggests that a tightly structured text is more readily comprehended than a loosely structured text. She urges teachers and students to diagram text structures in an effort to discern the importance of ideas. In all, she sees structural analysis of text in terms of

> . . . providing data for a theory of learning from prose, information about individual differences in learning, a potential diagnostic tool for educators to identify areas of learning problems, and a model for writers of text questions, texts, and other prose materials (Meyer, 1977, p. 199).

Critics of Meyer would argue that she makes the tool the subject matter. That is, Meyer fails to consider the differential and interactive contributions reader and context will and should play in discourse comprehension.

For the theorist, Meyer's work raises some interesting questions. The story grammarians acknowledge the presence and power of generic structure for stories in the mind of the reader. Meyer does not necessarily believe there are no generic structures for which the rhetorical predicates she describes are approximations. Obviously, familiarity with a particular paratactic organizational structure in a text will help a reader encode information organized according to the principle of that structure. Obviously, the reader comes to the reading task with some prior knowledge that can help comprehend the information at hand. However, in accordance with her intent—to scientifically study the effect of prose structure on memory—Meyer makes no claims to be representing approximations to what might be called a generic system of structural principles for organizing prose texts.

Mapped Patterns

An alternative to Meyer's structural analysis procedures is a technique called mapping. Mapping involves defining the organizational pattern of ideas within text. To this end, a map of a text is developed which reflects the pattern of relations within a text.

Based upon the work of Hanf (1971) and Merritt, Prior, and Grugeon (1977), a team of researchers at the Center for the Study of Reading has developed a mapping technique to serve as a procedure for diagramming idealized representations of texts (Anderson, 1978). The mapping technique incorporates the visual-spatial conventions for diagramming ideas and the nature of relationships between ideas. The scheme includes seven fundamental relationships between ideas: concept and example, concept and properties, concept and definition, temporal succession, cause and effect, conditional, and comparison. (These relationships and their mapping scheme are depicted in Figure 6.) The relationship between concept and its characteristics is depicted as a segmented box similar to a lined outline. The notation for a relationship between a concept and examples is similar to a Venn diagram. The compare and contrast notation is similar to a double entry table; the causal and temporal notation is similar to flowcharting.

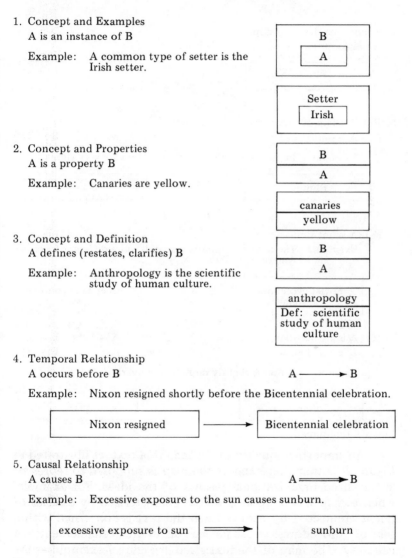

1. Concept and Examples
   A is an instance of B

   Example: A common type of setter is the Irish setter.

2. Concept and Properties
   A is a property B

   Example: Canaries are yellow.

3. Concept and Definition
   A defines (restates, clarifies) B

   Example: Anthropology is the scientific study of human culture.

4. Temporal Relationship
   A occurs before B

   Example: Nixon resigned shortly before the Bicentennial celebration.

5. Causal Relationship
   A causes B

   Example: Excessive exposure to the sun causes sunburn.

Figure 6.   Summary of mapping relationships and symbols.

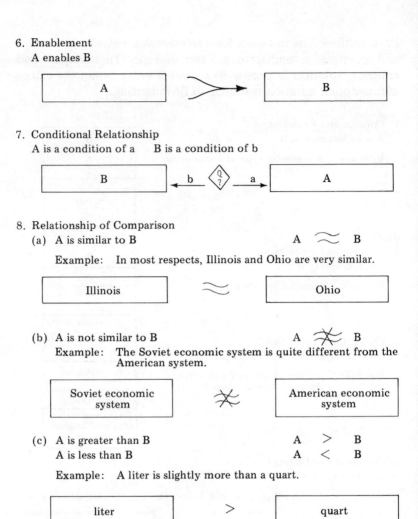

6. Enablement
   A enables B

7. Conditional Relationship
   A is a condition of a   B is a condition of b

8. Relationship of Comparison
   (a) A is similar to B   A ≈ B

   Example: In most respects, Illinois and Ohio are very similar.

   (b) A is not similar to B   A ≠ B
        Example: The Soviet economic system is quite different from the
                   American system.

   (c) A is greater than B   A > B
        A is less than B   A < B

   Example: A liter is slightly more than a quart.

Figure 6 (continued)

An important quality of the map of a text, as illustrated in Figure 7, is that the shape of the map is supposed to represent an idealized organizational pattern of the ideas. For example, when a map based upon a text is characterized by a series of boxes connected by arrows, then the text is concerned with a set of procedures, a sequence of events, enablement, or causality. The map of the text given in Figure 7 exemplifies the last three types.

As a text analysis tool, mapping offers some unique possibilities over other techniques. In its simplicity it affords

Tierney and Mosenthal

For more than two hundred years most people got their milk from their own cattle or from a nearby dairy herd. But in time, new inventions made the dairy industry a big business. In 1851, Gail Borden, founder of a milk company, found a way to take some of the water out of milk. This made it keep much longer. Four years later, Louis Pasteur introduced the pasteurization process. This process killed the bacteria in milk that caused it to spoil. Next, a special milk bottle was designed. This was followed by the invention of machines that could fill bottles and cap them automatically.

These discoveries had a great effect on the dairy industry. They meant that milk could be stored longer. It could be safely shipped over long distances. Preparing and distributing milk soon became a large-scale business. Recently, in a single year, more than sixty billion quarts of milk were sold in the United States.

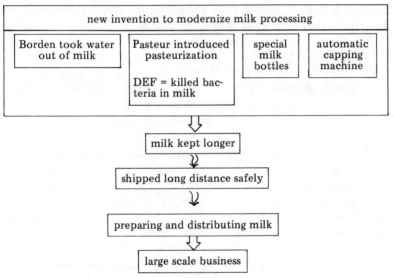

Figure 7. Example of a map of a text.

researchers, writers, teachers and students an accessible proce-dure by which the characteristics of discourse can be examined and against which a reader's comprehension can be compared. The overall shape of a map affords an appreciation of the "totality" of a text. The notational details and the task of formulating the map afford an appreciation of both the com-plexity and explicitness with which ideas and relationships exist within a text.

As an instructional procedure, it has certain advantages over outlining in that it offers an examination of the relationships between ideas. As with other procedures, however, one must wonder whether or not mapping may encourage text-bound interpretations. As Tierney and Spiro (1979) argue:

> Instructional techniques that sponsor rigid procedures on students
> ... may interfere with approaches a reader might more naturally
> and effectively bring to bear given the exigencies of text, task and
> reader knowledge (p. 136).

Indeed, Anderson (Note 5) has suggested that the worth of mapping seems to vary across the reader's intended purposes, the nature of the mapping activity and the demands of the text itself. As Anderson explained, students may profit from mapping the important ideas and those sections of text that are confusing; however, they should in no way be expected to map extended chunks of text (e.g., chapters).

Applications of Text Analysis

Although the results of text analysis seem encouraging, it would be amiss to suggest that text analysis is not without limitations. Certainly, text analysis provides a means for systematic examinations of characteristics of text and their differential influence upon comprehension. Already, numerous studies have provided invaluable insights through the use of a text analysis procedural model. But the findings apply to a restricted range of text types, text features, and reading situations. Text analysis does not afford an analysis of every text characteristic, across every text, across every reading situation.

Researchers intent on text analysis must remain cognizant of what is being measured, the context within which things are being measured, the realiability with which features can be discerned, and those aspects of text eluding analyses. Consistent with our first major thesis, researchers should examine text features within an interactive framework. That is, researchers should remain alert to the influence of those variables which interact with text features. Furthermore, researchers intent on text analysis should closely examine the purpose of their research pursuit. A researcher may wish to subject a passage or passages to a variety of analyses which have the potential to afford valuable insights. For certain purposes, a researcher may find that text analysis is not an appropriate tool; alternatively, a researcher may find a variety of text analyses to be appropriate.

While text analysis procedural models have and will have research applications, less obvious is whether text analysis will serve the classroom teacher and associated reading personnel. Already, we have argued that it would be amiss to use text analysis models, at least in their present forms, to derive reading comprehension performance scores. Also, we have suggested that instructional paradigms based upon text analysis models could stifle reader-text interactions. Although certain text features appear to have a differential influence upon reading comprehension, we are unaware of any research to confirm that teachers or curriculum materials should either highlight, emphasize or teach thoese features. Indeed, it should be noted that text analysis procedures were never intended to serve as curriculum guides, and very few of the authors sampled in the previous section have ever advocated such uses.

Despite these limitations, some pedagogical applications of text analysis seem intuitively appealing. For example, it does seem reasonable to suggest that text analysis procedures might be used for the following purposes:

1. *To examine and appreciate the differential responses of readers to text features.* A text analysis procedural model may offer a teacher a framework for examining and systematically unravelling the relationship between the information gleaned by readers and the presentation of information in the text. For example, by comparing readers' recall with an appropriate analysis of the original text, questions similar to the following can be pursued: What influence did the readers' background knowledge have upon their interpretation? How was their knowledge altered and what new information did they learn? How many and what types of inferences did the readers make? What information did readers restructure, clarify, abstract? Indeed, a simplified form of text analysis can be used to match the reader's recall against an analysis of the text. Readers can match their ideas against the explicit ideas in the text, or against a map of the text or a structural representation of these ideas. In so doing, readers could discuss the nature,

basis, and legitimacy of their deletions, insertions and substitutions; teachers could probe the extent to which a reader's interpretation was plausible and consistent with desired learning outcomes.

2. *To examine and appreciate the text demands placed upon readers.* Knowledge of the characteristics of text can afford teachers an appreciation of the demands a text places upon a reader. For example, an examination of text characteristics, via text analysis, may afford answers to the following: What information does the text contain explicitly? What information will readers likely infer? How is the text organized? What text characteristics are likely to detract from or contribute to idiosyncratic reader interpretations? By undertaking even simplified adaptations of text analysis, teachers can be acquainted with the explicit information within a text, the organization of ideas across a text and information authors assume their readers will bring to the text. If a teacher were planning to use a text selection for the purpose of addressing causes of certain events, a simplified text analysis might be used to examine incidences of causal, temporal or conditional chains within the text. If a teacher were planning to use a text to introduce a new concept, analysis might be used to examine the extent to which new learnings are tied to explicit text-based information or familiar reader-based concepts. If a teacher were planning to question readers on a text, a simplified structural representation of a text might afford an appreciation of the ideas keyed within the text.

3. *To examine and appreciate the relevance and plausibility of a reader's text-based inferences.* By focussing on certain questions (e.g., What information do readers incorporate into their knowledge structures? What sorts of derived information do readers acquire?), text analysis can afford a systematic examination of the plausibility and relevance of reader-generated knowledge. That is, the extent to which a reader's idiosyncratic response is reasonable can be discerned more readily. To this end, our discussion of text analysis systems offers a variety of procedures which could be adopted and adapted for these purposes. Specifically, event chain formulations and Frederiksen's semantic and logical networks could provide curriculum developers and teachers a detailed listing of inference types. Toward qualitative and subjective evaluations of inferencing, the relevancy hypothesis proposed by Trabasso and Nichols and

the selected subcategories proposed for Frederiksen's taxonomy of inferences could be applied to assess the reasonableness of idiosyncratic responses by readers.

4. *To afford teachers and readers a metacognitive awareness of text demands.* Brown (in press) has stated that some readers seem uninformed about the task of reading and might profit from knowing more regarding the nature of discourse demands. That is, readers might profit from metacognitive explanations of the relationships which exist between text characteristics and their interpretations. For example, teachers and their students could explore through discussion the extent to which their various idiosyncratic interpretations match the explicit/implicit text features. Through the use of mapping, event-chain formulation, story grammars, or even cohesive analysis, teachers and students might study the impact of how ideas are patterned differently across texts.

5. *To suggest instructional and testing procedures consistent with text demands.* Given that texts are used as a primary means for instruction in most school settings and given that text-based tests are used as a primary means of assessment, the demands imposed on a reader by text-based teaching and text-based testing should be examined. By comparing the characteristics of texts against teacher expectations, a simplified form of text analysis can afford at least minimal appreciation of the nature of the demands imposed upon readers. Toward the improvement of tests, texts, and instructional support, then, some form of text analysis might guide the teacher in the selection, perusal, and development of tasks. This might entail examining the extent to which answers to questions are supported by text-based information. It might require some reflection on the extent to which the apparent purposes of an author for his text coincide with its instructional uses. The point is that the ideas represented in a text should be examined prior to assuming their saliency. Without these types of examinations, texts are apt to be used by publishers, test-developers, and teachers for purposes other than those for which they are either capable of serving or intended to serve.

Concluding Remarks

To reiterate, the purpose of this paper was to introduce readers to text analyses as a research tool and as a vehicle for examining instruction. The uses of text analysis have been sampled—not exhausted. In terms of perspective, it has been our thesis that text analysis has the potential to be used and misused. Within the context of an appreciation of reader-text interactions, analysis of text features seem both warranted and appealing. Outside this context, an overemphasis upon such analysis or their derivatives may be misguided. Hopefully, this paper will prompt appropriate uses of these models. Finally, the reader should be reminded that this paper is not intended as the primary source for any single text analysis model proposed herein.

Reference Notes

1. Chodos, L., & Mosenthal, P. *Fourth graders' comprehension of story structures under three recall conditions.* Paper presented at the meeting of the National Reading Conference, New Orleans, December 1977.
2. Frederiksen, C.H. *Inference and the structure of children's discourse.* Paper presented at the meeting of the Society for Research in Child Symposium on the Development of Discourse Processing Skills, New Orleans, 1977.
3. Frederiksen, C.H., Frederiksen, J.C., Humphrey, F.M., & Otteson, J. *Discourse inference: Adapting to the inferential demands of school texts.* Paper presented at the annual meeting of the American Educational Research Association, Toronto, 1978.
4. Pearson, G. *Representing meaning in text.* Paper presented at the American Educational Research Association, April 1977.
5. Anderson, T.H. Personal communication, January 1, 1979.

References

ANDERSON, T.H. *Study skills and learning strategies* (Technical Report No. 104). Urbana: University of Illinois, Center for the Study of Reading, September 1978. (ED 161 000)

BIERCE, A. An occurrence at Owl Creek Bridge. In R.V. Cassill (Ed.), *The Norton anthology of short fiction.* New York: W.W. Norton, 1978.

BRIDGE, C.A. The text-based inferences generated by children in processing written discourse. Unpublished doctoral dissertation, University of Arizona, 1977.

BROWN, A.L. Metacognitive development and reading. In R.J. Spiro, B. Bruce, & W.F. Brewer (Eds.), *Theoretical issues in reading comprehension.* Hillsdale, New Jersey: Erlbaum, 1980.

CLEMENTS, P. The effects of staging on recall from prose. Unpublished doctoral dissertation, Cornell University, 1975.

DAWES, R.M. Memory and distortion of meaningful written material. *British Journal of Psychology,* 1966, *57,* 77–86.

FILLMORE, C.J. The case for case. In E. Bach & R.T. Harms (Eds.), *Universals in linguistic theory*. New York: Holt, Rinehart & Winston, 1968.

FREDERIKSEN, C.H. Representing logical and semantic structures of knowledge acquired from discourse. *Cognitive Psychology*, 1975, 7, 371-458.

FREDERIKSEN, C.H. Discourse comprehension and early reading. In L. Resnick & P. Weaver (Eds.), *Theory and practice in early reading*. Hillsdale, New Jersey: Erlbaum, 1977.

GRIMES, J.E. *The thread of discourse*. Ithaca, New York: Cornell University, 1972.

HALLIDAY, M.A.K. Text as semantic choice in social contexts. In T.A. van Dijk & J.S. Petofi (Eds.), *Grammars and descriptions*. New York: de Gruyter, 1977.

HALLIDAY, M.A.K., & HASAN, R. *Cohesion in English*. London: Longman, 1976.

HANF, M.B. Mapping: A technique for translating reading into thinking. *Journal of Reading*, 1971, 14, 225-230.

KINTSCH, W. *The representation of meaning in memory*. Hillsdale, New Jersey: Erlbaum, 1974.

KINTSCH, W. *Memory & cognition*. New York: Wiley, 1977(a).

KINTSCH, W. On comprehending stories. In M. Just & P. Carpenter (Eds.), *Cognitive processes in comprehension*. Hillsdale, New Jersey: Erlbaum, 1977(b).

KINTSCH, W., & van DIJK, T.A. Toward a model of text comprehension and production. *Psychological Review*, 1978, 85, 363-394.

MANDLER, J.M., & JOHNSON, N.S. Remembrance of things parsed: Story structure and recall. *Cognitive Psychology*, 1977, 9, 111-151.

MARSHALL, N. The structure of semantic memory for text. Unpublished doctoral dissertation, Cornell University, 1976.

McKOON, G. Organization of information in text memory. *Journal of Verbal Learning and Verbal Behavior*, 1977, 16, 247-260.

MERRITT, J., PRIOR, D., & GRUGEON, D. *Developing independence in reading*. Milton Keynes, England: The Open University Press, 1977.

MEYER, B.J.F. *The organization of prose and its effects on memory*. Amsterdam: North Holland, 1975(a).

MEYER, B.J.F. Identification of the structure of prose and its implications for the study of reading and memory. *Journal of Reading Behavior*, 1975, 7, 7-47(b).

MEYER, B.J.F. The structure of prose: Effects on learning and memory and implications for educational practice. In R.C. Anderson, R. Spiro, & W.E. Montague (Eds.), *Schooling and the acquisition of knowledge*. Hillsdale, New Jersey: Erlbaum, 1977.

MEYER, B.J.F., & McCONKIE, G. What is recalled after hearing a passage? *Journal of Educational Psychology*, 1973, 65, 109-117.

OSBORNE, J. *Look back in anger*. New York: Bantam, 1977.

RUMELHART, D.E. Notes on a schema for stories. In D.G. Bobrow & A.M. Collins (Eds.), *Representation and understanding: Studies in cognitive science*. New York: Academic Press, 1975.

STEIN, N.L., & GLENN, C.G. An analysis of story comprehension in elementary school children. In R.O. Freedle (Ed.), *New directions in discourse processing*. Norwood, New Jersey: Ablex, 1979.

THORNDYKE, P.W. Cognitive structures in comprehension and memory of narrative discourse. *Cognitive Psychology*, 1977, 9, 77-110.

TIERNEY, R.J., BRIDGE, C.A., & CERA, M.J. The discourse processing operations of children. *Reading Research Quarterly*, 1979, *14*, 539–573.

TIERNEY, R.J., & SPIRO, R.J. Some basic notions about reading comprehension: Implications for teachers. In J. Houste and R. Covey (Eds.), *New perspectives in comprehension*. Bloomington: Indiana University Monographs on Language and Thinking, 1979.

TRABASSO, T., & NICHOLAS, D.W. Memory and inferences in the comprehension of narratives. In F. Wilkening & J. Becker (Eds.), *Information integration by children*. Hillsdale, New Jersey: Erlbaum, in press.

TURNER, A., & GREENE, E. *The construction and use of a propositional text base* (Technical Report No. 63). Boulder: The University of Colorado, April, 1977.

van DIJK, T.A. Semantic macrostructures and knowledge frames in discourse comprehension. In M.A. Just & P.A. Carpenter (Eds.), *Cognitive processes in comprehension*. Hillsdale, New Jersey: Erlbaum, 1977.

WARREN, W.H., NICHOLAS, D.W., & TRABASSO, T. Event chains and inferences in understanding narratives. In R. Freedle (Ed.), *New directions in discourse processing*. Norwood, New Jersey: Ablex, 1979.

WOLFE, T. *Electric Kool-Aid Acid Test*. New York: Bantam, 1977.

Footnotes

1. Adapted from an article of the same title in *Science News*, *114*, 22, November 25, 1978, 367.
2. The research reported herein was supported in part by the National Institute of Education under Contract No. US-NIE-C-400-76-0116. It was completed while Dr. Tierney was on leave from the University of Arizona. The authors would like to thank Tom Anderson, James Cunningham, Peter Johnston, Judith A. Langer, Jean Osborn, M. Trika Smith-Burke, and Peter Winograd for their comments on this paper.

Children's Language and World: Initial Encounters with Print

Jerome C. Harste
Carolyn L. Burke
Virginia A. Woodward
Indiana University

Significant insights, important for reading teachers and educators, have been gained from research in the area of written language development among preschool children. Clay (1975) demonstrated that very young children are busy discovering written language for themselves long before formal instruction. Read (1975) explained the rule-governed relationships which children generate in their invented spellings. Ylisto (1967) showed that the young child approaches print with an expectation that it be meaningful. Durkin (1963) found that early readers tend to be early scribblers, and Ferrierro's research (1978) with preschool children from Mexico suggested that the findings of Clay, Read, and Ylisto about the development of written language are not only true for preschool children of highly literate parents, but also true for preschool children whose parents are illiterate.

Research studies such as these are extremely important because, in a very real sense, one cannot hope to adequately address the issue of optimum instruction at any level without knowledge and understanding of the natural process of written language growth and development.

The research reported in this paper is best viewed as an attempt to further explain the process of growing print awareness. The major aim is to identify early and universal language learning strategies for the purpose of furthering our understanding of written language growth and development.

One major assumption which governed our initial plan of research was that written language growth and development parallels oral language growth and development. We hypothesized that what was known about oral language growth and development would prove useful for understanding written language growth and development.

While much research in the area of written and oral language development has been conducted (see Dale, 1976 for a review of oral language development; Loban, 1976; Olson, 1977), the work of Halliday (1975) was especially seminal for us. Not only had Halliday demonstrated that written language is related to oral language, but also that language is inherently social. Using this perspective, Halliday concluded from a longitudinal study of his son, Nigel, that oral language development might best be described as a "saga in learning to mean." Like Ylisto, Halliday found that meaning, or semantics, was the driving force in language growth. It is from discovering what language does (both semantically and pragmatically) that children discover its form (both syntactically and graphophonemically).

Another major premise of our research was that written language growth and development is a sociopsycholinguistic process (Harste & Burke, 1979). In order to understand the cognitive and linguistic processes involved in reading and writing, we must look at the linguistic, situational, and cultural context in which that processing occurs.

The data (see Figure 1) we collected from three four-year-olds attending a preschool program in which many foreign college students enroll their children cogently illustrates the sociopsycholinguistic nature of the written literacy process. These uninterrupted writing samples were collected when the children were told, "Write everything you can write."

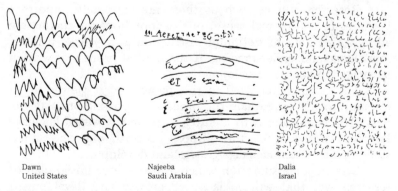

Dawn
United States

Najeeba
Saudi Arabia

Dalia
Israel

Figure 1. Uninterrupted writing samples from three children, age four.

Harste, Burke, and Woodward

In contrast to the other samples, Dawn's scribbles look undeniably English. When Najeeba finished her writing she said, "Here, but you can't read it, because it is in Arabic." Najeeba then went on to point out that in Arabic one uses "a lot more dots" than in English. Dalia is an Israeli child whose whole writing bears the predictable look of Hebrew. From ongoing encounters with print in each of their respective early written language environments, it appears that these children have developed identifiable expectations for print. To analyze their developing print awareness, the cognitive and linguistic decisions which each child made must be considered in relation to the sociolinguistic context of their early written language environment.

Figure 2 poses a transactional view of the process involving a language setting and a mental setting with each providing an environment for the other (Rosenblatt, 1938, 1978; Harste & Carey, 1979; Carey & Harste, 1979).

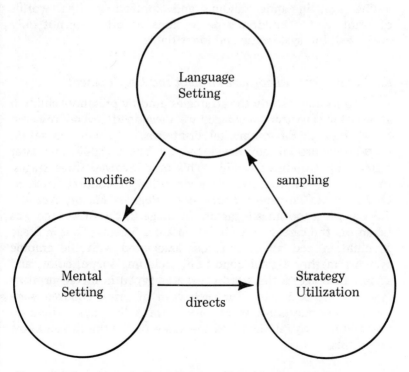

Figure 2. A sociopsycholinguistic view of the language process.

"Language Setting" as a concept is meant to suggest that any instance of language (either oral or written) contains multimodal cues (linguistic, situational, and cultural) available for processing (Neisser, 1976). In considering a given text, the *language setting* which includes where the language is found (home, school store), in what culture (United States, Israel, Saudia Arabia), and for and by whom it was produced (peer, superior, subordinate) modifies the *mental setting* in terms of what schema the reader accesses. The accessed schemata direct *strategy utilization* and, hence, sampling of the language setting. Strategy utilization in both reading and writing differ due to cultural and language settings.

What makes the multicultural data in Figure 1 so exciting is that it provides vivid evidence that a) written language, like oral language, is learned naturally from ongoing natural encounters with print prior to formal language instruction; b) children in literate societies are actively involved, at a very young age, in understanding and controlling their worlds of print; and c) children's perceptions of print are not only organized, but systematic and identifiable.

Exploring Written Language Growth and Development

To formally study the strategies used by preschool children approaching written language, we developed several research tasks. Task 1—Environmental Print—was a further adaptation of a procedure initially developed by Ylisto (1967) and later refined by Goodman (1976). This task involved three stages. In Stage 1, children were shown print in context, such as *Crest; with Fluoristan; Toothpaste; Regular Flavor; Net wt. 1.5 oz.* on a toothpaste carton. In Stage 2, the Crest logo was taken off the carton and placed on a 3 x 5 card. (Thus in Stage 2, children had all of the cues associated with the graphic systems in the original condition, including shape, color, and style.) In Stage 3, the word *Crest* was typed in mixed primary type on a 3 x 5 card. For each item of print, children were asked three questions: What do you think this says? Where do you think it says it? and Tell me some of the things you know about this.

Task 2—Language Experience Story Dictation and Reading —involved giving children a shoe box of toys (ranging from a toy truck to a spool of thread) and asking them to select three items with which to tell us a story. Stories dictated by the children were transcribed by the researchers with care taken to maintain the children's language patterns. Upon completion of the story, children were given the transcription and asked to read the story to the researcher. One day later children were asked to reread the story from the same transcription.

Task 3—Uninterrupted Writing—involved giving children a blank sheet of typing paper and asking them to write their name and anything else that they could write. At each point that a child stopped writing we repeated the direction, "Write everything you can write." This procedure was continued until the child self-terminated the task by saying such things as "That's all" or "I can't write anymore." Once the task was terminated, children were asked to read back to the researcher what they had written.

We administered these tasks to twenty children ages three to six. Selected observations will be presented and discussed in the form of language stories and the four major strategies we identify will be described.

Expecting Print to be Meaningful: The Strategy of Semantic Intent

All children in our sample demonstrated an expectation that written language would make personal sense. This leads us to believe that children seem to discover early that written language is functional. If this were not the case, there would be no reason for its development and presence in societies (see Goodman & Goodman, 1976, for an excellent discussion of this issue). It is this dimension of functionality which also makes written language predictable. We do not encounter "Baskin Robbins" on a shoe store, nor the sign "Shoe Store" on an ice cream parlor. The print we encounter makes sense in terms of its context.

From our data it appears that semantic intent is simply a natural extension of a more generic strategy used by children in discovering the world. We found that children as young as three demonstrate application of this strategy when approaching written language. Just as form follows function in oral language development (Halliday, 1975), these data suggest the same principle operates in written language development.

Access to the semantic system of language constitutes real access to literacy in that it permits further orchestration of the written language event to occur. To suggest the practical implications of this strategy, four language stories are presented.

Nathan and Crest. Nathan's story takes place in Stage 1 of the Environmental Print Task when we showed him the Crest toothpaste carton and asked, "What do you think this says?"

With almost no hesitation Nathan, age three, responded, "Brush teeth."

In order to fully appreciate Nathan's response, one must think of what alternatives he had available but failed to use: "Once upon a time . . . ," "336-6925," or "one cup sugar." Nathan, however, doesn't respond with any of these but, rather, with "Brush teeth." In doing so, Nathan demonstrates that he knows how print works in relation to context.

Many other manufacturers have elected to name products using this functional description option, i.e., "Mop & Glo," and "Spray & Wash." So Nathan's option isn't totally unexpected. It falls within the semantic parameters which we as adults use to label print in the environment. Not only is it predictable, it's fairly sophisticated. "Brush teeth" is about the right kind of written language phrase length for use when naming environmental print. What we see, then, in Nathan's response is an expression of the whole notion of context.

The reason each of us can supply an appropriate context, not only for "Brush teeth" but for each of the other responses listed as ones Nathan might have given, is that within each text, whether oral or written, is an assumption about context—likely location, by whom, and for whom it was produced.

Conceptually, Nathan's response "Brush teeth" conjures up the whole world image of someone standing in front of a sink in the act of brushing teeth. It is important to note that the response Nathan gave is dynamic, capturing relationships between whole world objects and events, even though what was shown him was a static decal on the side of a box. From this static print information, Nathan appeared to construct a very real sense of situation.

Harste, Burke, and Woodward

Nathan's response was personal, suggesting that he assumed the print shown him would be meaningful in terms of his world and what he knows. The expectation for written language is what we term "semantic intent," and this is an important and early developing reading and writing strategy.

What the child has discovered about written language can be thought of as a personal model, the sum total of those strategies which the child has acquired and which allow anticipation and cognition. It is important to understand that the term "model" is used in its denotative sense, as a set of assumptions through which experience is perceived and acted upon. We see the notion of semantic intent as an important component of the young child's model of reading and writing. Having once acquired this strategy, the child is able to discover other regularities which written language possesses. This is illustrated in the three remaining language stories.

Boyd and Dynamints. The second language story involves a three year old named Boyd.

We asked Boyd, showing him a package of Dynamints, "What does that say?"

He responded, "Fresh-A-Mints."

One can almost feel the Dynamints bursting forth with flavor in Boyd's mouth! From visual cues available in the optic array Boyd, too, was able to create a sense of situation.

Boyd's story, like Nathan's, serves as an example of print processing as a meaning transaction involving the strategy of semantic intent.

Unlike the first example, however, Boyd's response (Fresh-A-*Mints* for Dyna*mints*) seems at least in part controlled by the graphic display with which he was presented. While this may have been accidental, we had too many of these kinds of "accidents" happen for us to accept this explanation. We suspect that when children are allowed to discover the regularities of print, they reach generalizations and begin to orchestrate information about a variety of language systems. How this process works is illustrated in the next language story.

Alison and the McDonald's Cup.

We showed Alison, age four, a McDonald's cup and asked her, "What does that say?"

Alison had decided that we liked pointing so she took her finger to the line of print that read "Please put litter in its place" and began to say, "McDonald's." Before she got the "Mc" out, however, she moved her finger down to McDonald's and said, "McDonald's," emphasizing the *Mc* and the *Donald's*. She looked at the cup a moment and then turned to the examiner and said, putting emphasis on the *Mc*, "Do you know why they call it *Mc*Donald's?" "No," the examiner said, "Why?"

"Because they wanted it to read McDonald's," came the response.

The examiner followed by asking, "Where does it say *Mc*?" Alison took her finger and pointed to *Mc* and once again followed by saying, "McDonald's," with perfect morphemic synchronization between hand and voice.

A great deal transpired during this brief sequence. Clearly, one gets the feeling that Alison knows a good deal about letter and sound relationships at her young age, or why would she have rejected "Please put litter in its place" as saying McDonald's? Alison anticipated the response "McDonald's," but when she went to point it out, the information in the optic array ("Please put litter in its place") did not agree with her print expectations. She explored other print on the cup and upon finding McDonald's she elected it as a better match in terms of anticipated message and form.

The monologue involving the *Mc* in *McDonald's* is interesting and illustrates both the power of observation and the type of language hypothesis testing in which young children engage (Smith, 1978). No one has to tell Alison whether she's right or wrong; the visual information allows her to check her own hypothesis and thus gain control of written language form.

It is important to note that it was Alison's functional expectation for print that permitted her exploration and growing control of the language form. The predictability of the print setting in terms of what Alison knew about her world allowed this language growth. Just as it is not accidental that print in a literate society is functional so, too, it should not surprise us that it is this element of functionality which makes print settings predictable. A more explicit instance of how this process leads to linguistic awareness is illustrated in the next language story.

Alison and Wendy's Cup. Showing Alison a cup from a Wendy's restaurant, we asked "What does that say?"

She responded by running her finger under *Wendy's* and saying "Wendy's" and under *Hamburgers* by hesitating and then saying, "Cup."

Alison then looked at the experimenter and reflected, "That's a short sound for a long word."

This language story again demonstrates the notions of semantic transaction and hypothesis testing. One can see in Alison's response an expectation about sound length and graphic display. She seems puzzled by the incongruence and mentions it, thereby indicating that despite its irregularity, semantically the word "cup" makes sense and hence is acceptable to her. While this strategy may lead to a moment of doubt, it serves her well. Alison seems to be testing the semantic priority principle of language. It is Alison's confidence that this print setting has to make sense—indeed does make sense—that seems to allow her the opportunity to implicitly draw a generalization about written language form.

Accessing One's Communication Potential: The Strategy of Negotiability

Young children do not seem to isolate their print knowledge from information they have acquired via other communication systems. Children freely utilize what they know about alternative and available communication systems to make sense of their print world. The three language stories which follow demonstrate the cognitive flexibility young children display in an attempt to make meaning from information available in the optic array. Alison, Megan, and Mara use all they have learned about print in their search for meaning. Cook-Gumperz (1977) terms such cognitive flexibility "negotiability" to capture the child's willingness to use any available communication means in the interest of maintaining the message. Its intuitive use by children argues strongly for the existence of a generalized communication potential out of which more specialized communication systems are generated.

Alison and Jell-O. We showed Alison the word Jell-O in mixed primary type (Stage 3) and asked, "What does that say?"

Alison hesitated a moment, shrugged her shoulders, and then said, "I don't know, it should be a telephone number."

In order to make this response, Alison obviously had transformed the two *l*'s into ones and the *O* into a zero. Whether it was the hyphen which triggered this transformation is hard to determine, just as it may have been the *J* and *e* which made her hesitate before suggesting "it *should* be a telephone number."

Alison utilizes all she has learned, not only about print but also about the numerical communication system to make sense of this print. Negotiation, in this sense, is a marshalling strategy which makes available all of the knowledge resources she possesses.

One might think of the language user as having an information base acquired from encountering the mathematical, linguistic, artistic, dramatic, and other communication systems which abound in our world. This base of knowledge represents one's communication potential. Negotiability is the strategy which allows us to use this potential in an attempt to express what we wish to mean.

We see negotiability as an important strategy in written language growth and development. It represents the child's discovery that what is known about one communication system can support understanding of other communication systems. How this process works is more clearly illustrated in the language story which follows.

Megan's Present. In Task 3—Uninterrupted Writing, Megan, age four wrote her name on the top left-hand corner of her paper, spelling it O-K-U-N-V-L-O. Then turning her paper on its side, she added A-O-A-M-K working right-to-left so the final product was reversed by adult standards. Still writing with the paper sideways, Megan drew a castle-like outline across her paper, like so: ⌐ᴗᴗ⌐ . Megan then proceeded to draw a present, replete with ribbon.

After pausing a moment she announced, "That's all."

The researcher asked Megan to read what she had written.

Megan said, pointing to where she had written her name, "This is how I write my last name. And this," pointing to A-O-A-M-K, "is my nickname, Angel. And this is a sort of castle. And this says present."

She then proceeded to color her present with black ink—first the package, then the ribbon, making the thing one black blob.

After observing her handiwork, Megan reflected a moment and said quite emphatically, as much to herself as to the researcher, "No, it doesn't."

Snatching up the pen again she wrote P-K-P-L and announced, "Now, *that* says present."

Megan, like most children in our sample, was not intent upon impressing us with a demonstration of what she knew. This, like any other setting, was simply an opportunity to engage in the process, to experiment, to test hypotheses.

She twice demonstrated her ability to freely move to alternate communication systems to express herself. Her representation for "castle" seems to rest on the borders between art and language, utilizing qualities of both. Her initial rendering of "present" as a drawing insured that her thoughts would be preserved and thus available to be resolved into P-K-P-L.

In doing so, Megan's performance not only demonstrates the notions of negotiability across communication systems and how it is that growth and development in one communication system supports growth and development in another system, but further suggests that Megan's knowledge of grapheme-phoneme relationships is extensive, organized, and systematic (note, for example, Megan's decision to begin her nickname *Angel* with an "A" and *present* with a "P"). (For an extensive discussion on grapho-phonemic rules known by school-aged children, see Read, 1975.) In Megan's response, one gets the clear notion that what she has discovered about language is not isolated bits and pieces of language data, but a compilation of interrelated strategies which allow her first and foremost to mean. Negotiability is a meaning based problem solving strategy as Mara's language story so cogently demonstrates.

Mara's Writing. We asked Mara, age five, to write everything she could write.

Mara began by writing her name, then paused and said, "Can I write names I know?"

The examiner responded by repeating the direction, "Write everything you can write."

Mara wrote L-A-U-R-A directly under Mara.

Moving down the page in column-like fashion Mara wrote L-A-U . . . , paused, and asked, "What comes after the 'u' in Laurie?"

The examiner said, "Just do the best you can. Write everything you can write."

Mara finished Laurie spelling it L-A-U-I-E, and then added M-A-R-Y and B-E-T-H, announcing the latter to be her mother's name.

Mara then took a long pause, drew a line under the word *Beth* and announced, "Next I'll write some words I know."

Mara proceeded again making a column, writing Y-E-S (with a reversed "s"), N-O (with a reversed "n"), O-N (with a reversed "n"), L-O-V-E, Y-O-U, and I-N (reversing both the order of the letters and the "n").

Mara studied her *in* and said, "I think that's backwards. Is that backwards?"

The examiner responded, "Just do the best you can. I want you to write everything you can write."

At this point, Mara accepted her *in* as written, drew a solid black line under it, and stopped.

After thinking a bit she announced, "I can write numbers," and proceeded to write numbers 1 to 30 in a column under her word list. Reaching the bottom of the page with a number 9, Mara started a second column and wrote numbers 10 to 30.

Mara made all of her 3s, 7s, and 9s backwards. Some of Mara's 2s were written conventionally, but others were reversed. Never batting an eye, Mara wrote the number 22 such that it contained a conventionally written 2 and a backwards 2. Fours also presented problems, as did 6s. All numerals were recognizable, despite the instability as to direction.

When Mara finished writing numeral 30, she announced, "That's all I can write."

Mara read what she had written with no difficulty.

Mara's language story provides a nice contrast to those of *Alison and Jell-O* and *Megan's Present.* Mara is, of course, older than Alison or Megan. Also, in many ways, she is wiser and less of a risk-taker. She now knows there is a correct and an incorrect form. To be safe she sticks with what she feels she knows. The result makes Mara's performance more hesitant and less free than that of Megan or Alison.

Mara's performance also demonstrates what the older child's base of knowledge may look like. Mara has clearly separated data appropriate to alternative communication systems. The information she possesses in her knowledge base is, in this sense, tidier. However, she freely uses an alternate communication system (math) to give her the needed support to complete her task. Alternate communication systems are for her a resource, a communication potential, much as they are for adults when they accompany written text with diagrams and pictures, or oral text with gestures.

Orchestrating the Written Language Event:
The Strategy of Hypothesis-Testing

If one views each instance of written language as the orchestration of a complex social event, then the initiate written language user is faced with a problem of some magnitude. As varied elements in this event are perceived, new hypotheses must be generated and tested. These hypotheses are concerned with pragmatics (what language for what context), semantics (how I can say what I mean), syntax (how I get the flow of my message captured on paper), graphics (how I place-hold what I wish to say), and the orchestration of these systems (how I synchronize these systems). Within each of these areas there are a range of hypotheses which need formulation and fit.

From this perspective what should surprise us is the impressive amount of mastery young children display across alternate written language settings. Truly the most salient feature of any language user's response to written language is the ongoing hypothesis testing it displays. For the written language user, hypothesis testing is not only a strategy, but a risk taking attitude of "I can find out."

To fully appreciate the power of this strategy and its net effectiveness one has to be impressed with the multifaceted aspects of mastery displayed in the responses we have already examined.

While the written language event may seem complex enough on its own, intervention by helpful adults may make the event more complex, convincing children to trade in their personal strategies for those of instruction. Having recognized the complexity of the process, educators often take this to mean that the task must be simplified for the initiate user. But his assumption is misguided. As the following language stories show, the complexity of language presents no problem but, rather, language in its natural complexity helps youngsters to gain control.

Leslie and the Crest Carton. We showed Leslie, age six, a carton of Crest toothpaste (Task 1) and asked, "What does that say?"

Leslie, hesitating a total of 5 seconds (during which time she seemed fidgety and uncomfortable) finally produced, "Cr-Cr-Crost."

When urged to tell us where she'd seen this before, Leslie responded, "In the stores."

When further urged to tell us anything else she could about this thing, Leslie responded, "It's toothpaste. It comes in big and small and you can brush your teeth with it."

Later, during a home interview, we asked Leslie's mother what brand of toothpaste the family used. She responded, "Crest. We always have."

Leslie's behavior, like Mara's, seems cautious and as such stands in stark contrast to the behavior of Nathan, Boyd, Megan, and Alison. We found that children three and four years of age responded rapidly to the Crest carton with responses such as "Brush teeth," "Toothpaste," and "Crest." Children five and six years of age hesitated longer than the three or four year olds and often seemed reluctant to produce responses such as "Toothpaste" or "Colgate." Despite differences in response time, we seriously doubt that five and six year olds in our sample knew less about language than did three and four year olds; rather, we believe this phenomenon to be an artifact of increasingly refined language formation. With more information to consider, responses become measured.

Four of the five six year olds in our study were in the first grade where they were receiving phonics instruction in letter names and sounds. Even though data were collected only 22 days after the opening of school, each of these children responded to the environmental print in Stages 1, 2, and 3 by sounding out the word. Most of these children, when shown *Crest*, hesitated and responded, "Cr-Cr-Cr-Toothpaste," or made a similar response.

It is interesting to note that in the final analysis most six year olds selected a semantically acceptable response after initially focusing on the graphic information available. One cannot help wondering, however, how long it would take these children to abandon what they knew about language to favor instead the phonetic strategy being emphasized in their instructional program (like Leslie's "Crost").

This experience raises the possibility that the high incidence of nonsense word production found among beginning first and second grade readers (Biemiller, 1970; Barr, 1974–1975; Cohen, 1974–1975) may simply reflect their instructional history and may not represent natural development at all. Six year olds in our study appear almost too trusting; all too willing to turn in the strategies they have discovered about language for those which their teachers, operating from an alternate theoretical model of the process, emphasize during instruction. In the final analysis, this may be the most serious consequence of any formal language instruction which fails to build upon young children's natural language understanding.

Dawn's language story illustrates how some instructionally encouraged hypotheses can influence orchestration.

Dawn's Writing. We asked Dawn, age four, to write everything she could write (see Figure 1, Dawn/United States).

Dawn began by writing what looked like "N," "O," and "M" and then proceeded to do what some have termed "scribble drawing," left-to-right, line-for-line, down the page. When Dawn had completely filled the page, the examiner asked her to read what she had written.

Dawn read, pointing left-to-right and moving top-to-bottom, "My name is Dawn. I go to University School. I used to go to Children's Corner. My brother Timmy goes to University School too," making sure that when she came to the final "too" in her story she was on the bottom utmost lefthand corner of the page.

Later, when we asked Dawn to write her name and draw a picture of herself so that we could remember her, she did so spelling her name D-A-W-N very clearly and conventionally.

Dawn's performance is impressive, especially in light of the fact that many early formal language programs feel these skills must be taught to children two years later. Dawn's "scribbles" look like English cursive writing, and they demonstrate Dawn's control of left-to-right and top-to-bottom directionality.

Probably the most interesting element of Dawn's performance is her unique attempt to capture the flow of language on paper. From other examples of uninterrupted writing, we have ample evidence that on other occasions Dawn wrote letters and words. In this instance, the process of writing letters and words stood in her way of producing a message, so Dawn freely tested an alternate form of expression using the English forms she acquired from past encounters.

Dawn's performance reflects a developmental strategy which some children develop to handle syntax or the flow of language. Our data clearly challenge both the "scribble" and "drawing" conceptualizations undergirding this term and suggest, instead, that this behavior provides important insights into new language hypotheses being tested by the child. It seems that Dawn clearly understood the function of written language. Given this context she produced, as we can tell from her reading, an appropriate text. It was her focus on pragmatics and semantics which allowed her to test a more economic graphic form. What looks like "scribble drawing" from one theoretical perspective marks development from another.

As a result of the many questions our data raises, Hill (1978) collected uninterrupted writing and reading samples from four three year old children over a year and a half. Her data suggests that "scribble drawing" represents a much later developmental stage—one that appears long after the child has begun experimenting with letters and other recognizable but representational placeholders for meaning.

The Linguistic Data Pool: Strategy of Fine Tuning Language with Language

Functional spellings in children indicate they not only spell the way words *sound*, but the way they *look* and *mean*. Take, for example, F-L-I-Y-I-N-G for flying and A-L-I-N-O for a lion (Jason, age six). In each of these instances there is a close sound/graphic match indicating the rule-governed relationships these children have developed between speaking and writing. But equally interesting is the inclusion of the Y in flying and the addition of the O in lion. Clearly, these do not reflect sound patterns solely or there would be no reason why the child added O to the end of his spelling of lion or failed to add just another I to his spelling of flying. Rather, what is reflected in these instances is visual memory of what the child has seen in reading. This provides evidence of the inter-relationships between reading, speaking, listening and writing.

The single language story included in this session strongly suggests that oral and written language grow and develop in parallel rather than serial fashion. The instructional assumption that the expressions of language are developmentally ordered from listening to speaking to reading to writing needs further examination in light of these findings. Data collected from the children in our sample, as illustrated in the following language story, demonstrates the relationships among the various expressions of language are more complex than a serial development hypothesis would suggest.

Alison's Turnip Story

On the first occasion, Alison (age 4.1) selected an eraser (which she imagined to be a stop sign), a little plastic truck, and a spool of thread. The story which Alison both enacted with these objects and dictated follows:

> Once there was a needle of thread. When he was walking along he found a car driving. He jumped over the car. And when they came to a stop sign they found it wasn't a stop sign.

Reading her story immediately after dictation, Alison produced:

> Once there was a little needle of thread walking along the road. Suddenly she came to a car and she jumped over it. When she came to a stop sign she found it wasn't a stop sign.

Rereading her story one day later, Alison produced:

> Once there was a needle of thread and he was walking along. He found a car driving. He jumped over the car and when they came to a stop sign they found it wasn't a stop sign.
> The end.

On the second occasion, five months later, Alison again selected the spool of thread, but then ventured off to select a paint brush and some play money with which to tell her story. In dictating her story she freely assigned these objects alternate roles (Turnip, Grandma, Granddaughter, Puppy, Beetle) so that she could enact her story as she told it. Her story as dictated follows:

> Once upon a time there
> was a turnip. The
> granddaddy came out and
> tried to pull out the
> turnip. He called the grandma
> and they both tried to
> pull out the turnip. The

grandma called the granddaughter
and they all three tried to
pull out the turnip. The
granddaughter called the puppy.
They all four tried to pull out
the turnip. The dog called
a beetle. The other beetle called
another beetle and another beetle
called another beetle. And all
seven tried to pull out the
turnip. They all pulled out the
turnip.
The end.

When she completed dictating her story, Alison was handed the pages of her story and asked to read them to the researcher. Although her turning of pages failed to correspond to what she was reading, Alison's rendition was surprisingly close to the dictated text in terms of both semantic and syntactic structure.

One day later, Alison was again asked to read the story she had written.

Alison responded, "But I don't remember what it is about."

The examiner paused, waited and finally putting Alison's story in front of her said, "Well you just do the best you can."

Alison, glancing at the text, pointed to the t-u-r-n-i-p in the middle of line two, and announced, "Oh, now I remember . . . turnip."

Alison's second rendition of the story was like the first, very close to what was dictated both semantically and syntactically, although once again her turning of pages failed to correspond with what she was reading. (Alison did, however, turn to the last page once she realized her story was ending.) Alison added another beetle in her second reading, having either forgotten exactly how many she included in her first story or wishing to prolong the retelling experience.

In light of Alison's reading and page turning behaviors, it is unclear what role graphics played in her reading and re-reading of these texts. Clearly, her need to see the word *turnip* to recall her second story suggests that graphic information was significant.

Even though she added a story sequence in her second reading, Alison's renditions of her texts are surprisingly like the originals. While Alison shows that she sees print as controlled, she is not controlled by print. Instead, she is controlled by meaning rules!

Alison's second story is particularly recognizable as that underlying the children's literature selection, *The Great Big Enormous Turnip* (Tolstoy, 1968). Yet, what seems important is not the similarities in story so much as the differences. Alison's story is clearly a new event with new text, just as distinctive as the original. What she has borrowed is a story structure or ideational scaffolding. Past encounters with literature have given her the necessary frameworks for presentation of her texts. Both of Alison's stories introduce a protagonist, initiating event, and an attempt (Stein, 1978). These higher-order cognitive schemata not only help Alison to organize her ideas but also facilitate her reading and rereading.

Alison's reading of her stories was controlled and, unlike her general speech, indicated a cognizance on her part that written language differs from oral language in distinctive ways. Obviously, it was Alison's experience with alternate language encounters (speaking, reading, writing, listening) which allowed her the opportunity for making this discovery and developing this control.

Alison's performance demonstrates the interrelatedness of growth in the language arts. Information received via one expression of language (story structure via listening to stories) became available data for output in another expression of language (writing via story dictation).

What children learn from reading becomes available lingusitic data for oral language development. One can get a feel for this interrelationship in Alison's story dictation, as Tolstoy's structure clearly provides her a workable strategy for her own language story dictation.

On Strategies: Some Concluding Remarks

Two things remain to be said. First, we believe the strategies of semantic intent, negotiability, hypothesis testing, and fine tuning of language are not separately employed but rather are complementary and synergistic. Second, we believe these strategies are universal and undergird all writing activities for every writer.

The validity of this first tenet lies in each of the language stories presented. We do not have time to discuss the second statement in this paper, but its importance is apparent.

Having said this much, however, is not enough. It remains the business of the final section of this paper to tie these findings to the theory from which they spring. It is only in this way that subsequent research and practice may be affected.

Conceptual and Instructional Implications

When shown the official United States Post Office logo and asked, "What does that say?" preschool children responded:

"A birdie flew." (Nathan, age three)

"American picture sign." (Alison, age four)

"Put in mail." (Jonathan, age five)

"U.S. Mail." (Emily, age six)

A behavioral interpretation of these responses may lead some to conclude that Nathan, Alison, and Jonathan are "non readers," while Emily is a "reader."

It is true that Emily's observed response, "U.S. Mail," matched the print on the logo, while Nathan's, Alison's, and Jonathan's did not. To note only such gross differences in their response products is to miss the more important similarities in the process each went through.

Nathan's and Jonathan's responses conjure up specific whole world images of a bird flying and a letter being mailed. Alison's response is equally interesting. Clearly, her "American picture sign" is a label much like "U.S. Mail"; however, Alison's response gives important insights into both perception and cognition. From available visual information, Alison rapidly made a meaningful association with other information which she knew about her world. That one abstraction (eagle) represents another abstraction (America) is seemingly an instance of high level cognitive processing. Yet, this four year old leads us to suspect that even those things which we consider highly abstract—like logos and print—are not controlled abstractly but concretely in terms of information already possessed (in Alison's case, as a "picture sign").

Alison's, Nathan's, and Jonathan's responses clearly are not "errors," but rather reflections of sophisticated cognitive processing strategies which allow these children to make sense of their world.

It is only in the instance of Emily's "correct" response that a traditional internal processing model, such as that shown in Figure 3, seems adequate.

A Traditional Internal Processing Model (Neisser, 1976)

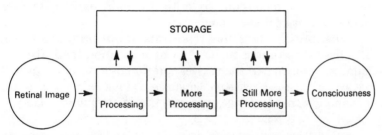

Figure 3.   A traditional internal processing model from Ulric Neisser, *Cognition and Reality*. San Francisco: W.H. Freeman and Company, 1976, p. 17.

This model suggests that Emily saw *U.S. Mail* and began processing this image at increasing levels of sophistication, i.e., as individual graphemes which needed to be related to phonemes stored in memory (Level 1—Processing), as combinations of graphemes which needed to be related to English orthographic spelling patterns stored in memory (Level 2—More Processing), as words which needed to be identified in terms of one's lexical data bank stored in memory (Level 3—Still More Processing), and so on until recognition or consciousness.

Meaning in this model is something to be reached via more fundamental processing; the result, not the intent. Figure 3 is a static model: The input is static; the output *appears* static.

We use the term "appears" deliberately, thereby suggesting that even in instances, like Emily's, where the response appears bound and thereby explainable in terms of the graphic input alone, the "true process" shares much similarity to that used by Nathan, Alison and Jonathan.

Data presented in this paper seriously question the assumptions underlying the internal processing model of language.

Because of this model's pervasiveness within early childhood education and reading programs, it seems important to point out the instructional, conceptual, and practical implications which this model has led to and which the data in this paper challenge.

This conceptualization of print processing has led to early language programs which stress ordered sequencing of skills: from letter and sound relationships to syllabication, to blending, to words, to word patterns, to literal comprehension, to inferential comprehension, to critical comprehension, to ever "higher" forms of literary analysis.

Conceptually, it is this representation of print processing which has led to rubrics such as "print acquisition" and "reading readiness," which in themselves presuppose notions of oral language as learned, written language as taught. Emig (1976), for example, ranks language processes as primary and secondary:

> with talking and listening characterized as first-order processes; reading and writing as second-order. First-order processes are acquired without formal or systematic instruction; second-order processes . . . tend to be learned initially only with the aid of formal and systematic instruction (p. 122).

Practically, it is this conception of the process which has led theorists such as Mattingly (1972) to think of written language literacy as hinging on breaking an abstract linguistic code: oral language is natural; reading and writing unnatural. Given such a conception, no wonder many, including Mattingly, are surprised

> that a substantial number of human beings can also perform linguistic functions by hand and eye. If we had never observed actual reading and writing we would probably not believe these activities possible (Mattingly, 1972, p. vii).

In contrast to this view, our contention is that written language literacy is a natural extension of all learning generally, and language learning specifically. Theoretically, this view suggests that as active cognitive organisms, children encounter their environment by identifying features of meaning which they perceive as salient. Babies who encounter a dog, to use an example from Neisser (1976), perceive the dog not only in terms of visual cues, but auditory, haptic, and olfactory cues. Features of meaning related to these cues become organized in their schema of DOG. Later each of these features of meaning (a doglike smell, or even the sound of the spoken word *dog*) triggers the entire DOG schema.

Oral language, from this perspective, is seen as developmentally quite natural, much like other cognitive distinctions which we assume and expect young children to make. What is not so apparent is that written language control develops similarly. If the word *dog* is written on a card and hung around the animal's neck, it is likely that in sampling the optic array the word *dog* may well come to be a distinctive feature of meaning embedded in the DOG schema which, when encountered later, would call from memory all that is known of the canine family.

While most people do not hang labels on their dogs, it would not be surprising to encounter a *Beware of the Dog* sign in the presence of some dogs. From experiences of this sort, features of print become distinctive features of meaning embedded in whole world schema.

Control of much environmental print can be explained in this manner. Very young children learn to control the word *stop*, for example, not because some obliging adult says, "That sign says stop," each time a stop is made but, rather, because the child's very presence in this language encounter provides all of the perceptual information needed for control. Later, the word alone allows comprehension, not because it was accessed entirely through graphemes, but also through instantiation of relevant whole world schemata.

Reading and writing are sociopsycholinguistic processes and, as such, children develop models of written language from natural, ongoing encounters with print. Conceptually, this premise is illustrated in Figure 4 and suggests that when *The Child*, bringing all that she or he knows about the world, including strategies for finding out, encounters *The Language Process*, information is provided which permits the discovery of how the language process works. Specific language information available includes how the graphophonemic, syntactic, and semantic systems of language operate in relation to one another and in relation to those things known about their world.

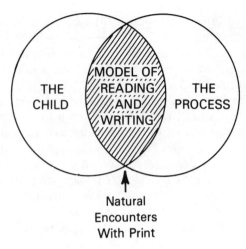

Figure 4. A personalized model of reading and writing prior to formal language instruction.

Data collected and presented in this paper suggest that preschool children have discovered much about print prior to formal language instruction. The child's *Model of Reading and Writing*, as illustrated through the various language stories presented, is a functional expectation for print. It describes how language operates in alternate contexts and suggests a growing control of English orthography, wordness, left-to-right and top-to-bottom directionality, grapheme-phoneme correspondence, and syntax. Taken together, these data suggest that written language, like oral language, is learned naturally from encountering written language in use. Further, these data suggest that formal instructional programs which assume that the young child knows little if anything about print and which focus primarily on the more abstract systems of language such as letters and words may fail to allow children to access what they already know about language and/or convince them that the strategies which they have used to make sense of their world do not apply to written language control.

To avoid this, we might best begin formal language instruction by building upon the variety of rich language acquisition strategies which children have informally developed on their own. Four such key strategies identified in this paper include those of semantic intent, negotiability, hypothesis testing, and fine tuning language through language.

Harste, Burke, and Woodward

In this regard the lesson to be learned is clear. When children in our sample found themselves working in relatively underdeveloped reading and writing systems, they made several decisions in common. First, they related to strongly personal information—the writing of their name or the reading of the logo of their favorite fastfood restaurant. Second, they used whatever generalized features they had factored out of these systems—letters, linear organization, phoneme-grapheme correspondence, the use of a wavy line—to place-hold or intuit the message. Third, when pressed to continue communicating beyond their competence they maintained their focus on the sharing of meaning while intuitively and unselfconsciously lapsing into alternate communication systems.

In similar regard we must come to understand that what the child knows about one expression of language can support growth and development in another. This conceptualization presupposes a parallel growth and development among the expressions of language. What the child learns about language from having read a book, for example, becomes available linguistic data for output in another expression of language, like writing. What the child knows about how oral language operates becomes available data for the discovery and testing of how written language operates. Each encounter with language develops expectations for the forms in which they may be cast. The process is cyclic. What is learned from one encounter becomes the anticipatory data available for subsequent encounters. It is through their experience as writers that young language users in our sample fine-tuned their reading strategies.

Figure 5 suggests that each of us can be considered to possess a personal pool of language data fed by all of the language phenomena perceived out of our world; a pool which constitutes the sum of our current definition of language; a pool from which we draw data for processing each time we use language. The pool of language data is composed of a set of relations concerning how meaning is shared through language. The data for the pool enters as part of listening, speaking, reading, or writing experiences, and exists as any one of the expressions of language. The lines which we as literate individuals draw between the varying expressions of language and the alternate communication systems are arbitrary. Focusing a young learner's attention upon them can only constitute a distraction in learning to mean (Burke, 1978).

Figure 5. Linguistic data pool.

As teachers, we need to be concerned not only with what children do once they encounter print, but with what anticipations they hold for language generally as well as what decisions they make about reading and writing on the way to the process. Our role as teachers is best thought of as assisting children to discover the predictability of written language in a variety of real world, whole language contexts. Written language activities provided for children should be meaningful, open-ended, situationally valid and contextually rich enough to allow access to their natural written language learning strategies of semantic intent, negotiability, hypothesis-testing and fine-tuning language through language.

Written language growth and development is a sociopsycholinguistic process. This relationship, we believe, opens vistas to what is instructionally possible and provides much needed enriched conceptualization for the exploration of written language literacy.

References

BARR, R. The effect of instruction on pupil reading strategies. *Reading Research Quarterly*, 1974–1975, *10*, 555–582.

BIEMILLER, A. The development of the use of graphic and contextual information as children learn to read. *Reading Research Quarterly*, Fall 1970, *6*, 75–96.

BURKE, C.L. *Reading as communication: Reading as language.* Paper presented at the Annual Meeting of the National Council of Teachers of English, Kansas City, November 25, 1978.

CLAY, M. *What did I write?* London: Heinemann Educational Books, 1975.

COHEN, A.S. Oral reading errors of first grade children taught by a code emphasis approach. *Reading Research Quarterly*, 1974–1975, *10*, 616–650.

COOK, GUMPERZ, J. *Social-ecological perspectives for studying children's use of persuasive arguments.* Paper presented at the Department of Sociology Seminar, Indiana University, November 8, 1977.

DALE, P. (Ed.). *Language development: Structure and function* (2nd ed.). New York: Holt, Rinehart & Winston, 1976.

ECO, U. *A theory of semiotics.* Bloomington, Indiana: Indiana University Press, 1976.

EMIG, J. Writing as a mode of learning. *College Composition and Communication,* 1976, 122-128.

GOODMAN, K.S., & GOODMAN, Y.M. *Learning to read is natural.* Paper presented at a Conference on Theory and Practice of Beginning Reading Instruction, Pittsburgh, April 13, 1976.

GOODMAN, Y. *A study of the development of literacy in preschool children.* NIE Research Grant Proposal, 1976.

HALLIDAY, M.A.K. *Learning how to mean.* London: Edward Arnold, Ltd., 1975.

HILL, M. Look I can write: Children's print awareness from a sociopsycholinguistic perspective. Unpublished doctoral research, Reading Department, Indiana University, 1978.

LOBAN, W. *Language development.* Urbana, Illinois: National Council of Teachers of English, 1976.

MATTINGLY, I. Reading, the linguistic process, the linguistic awareness. In Kavanaugh & Mattingly (Eds.), *Language by eye and ear.* Cambridge: MIT Press, 1972.

McINTYRE, M.L. A modified model for the description of language acquisition in the deaf child. Unpublished master's thesis, California State University at Northridge, 1974.

NEISSER, U. *Cognition and reality.* San Francisco: W.H. Freeman, 1976.

OLSON, D. From utterance to text: The bias of language in speech and writing. *Harvard Educational Review,* 1977, *47,* 257-281.

READ, C. *Children's categorization of speech sounds in English* (Technical Report No. 197). Urbana, Illinois: National Council of Teachers of English, Committee on Research, 1975.

ROSENBLATT, L.M. *The reader, the text, the poem.* Carbondale: Southern Illinois Press, 1978.

SMITH, F. *Understanding reading.* New York: Holt, Rinehart & Winston, 1978.

STEIN, N.L. *How children understand stories: A developmental analysis* (Technical Report No. 69). Urbana, Illinois: University of Illinois at Urbana-Champaign, Center for the Study of Reading, March 1978.

TOLSTOY, A. *The great big enormous turnip.* (Illustrated by Helen Oxenbury.) New York: Franklin, Watts, 1968.

Footnote

The research reported here was supported by the Maris M. Proffit Research Grant awarded by the School of Education, Indiana University, Bloomington, Indiana. The children in this study represented a random sample of all preschool aged children attending a local preschool in Monroe County, Indiana. Using parental educational attainment, income, residence, and occupation, this sample was identified as middle to high *SES.* Since the writing of this paper, the three authors have received funds from the National Institute of Education to continue work in this area.

Situational Differences in the Use of Language

William S. Hall
University of Maryland
Larry F. Guthrie
Far West Regional Laboratory
San Francisco, California

A continuing problem in American Education is how to curb the widespread school failure of children from nonmainstream home backgrounds. While many explanations exist for this state of affairs, considerable emphasis has been placed on the idea that there are cultural and situational differences in the functions and uses of language (Labov, 1970; Hall & Freedle, 1975; Hall & Guthrie, 1979). In this article we present the issues underlying the hypothesis that minority groups and the poor use language in ways that systematically put their children at a disadvantage at school (Hall & Guthrie, 1980; Gearhart & Hall, 1979). We will examine the consequences of these issues for children whose home language differs from their school language and then will present an example from our research which will amplify our understanding of school and home language variation. It is our thesis that oral language is directly linked to a child's cognitive and emotional experiences at school and thereby affects the learning to read experience.

Cultural variation in the function and uses of language has important consequences for speakers of dialects, particularly with respect to educational performance. Three types of consequences can be posited: social, cognitive, and educational.

The *social consequences* of a variant way of using language can affect teacher-pupil as well as peer relationships. The consequences of a teacher's attitude toward a given dialect—including vocabulary differences—are profound. For example, attitude toward dialect can affect a teacher's initial judgments about how smart a child is likely to be, how the child will fare as a learner, how the child will be grouped for instruction, and how the child's contributions in class will be treated. These in turn can affect the child's attitude about self as a school learner (i.e. willingness to participate, expectations about results of participation, etc.). There are also consequences of variation in language use with respect to one's standing with peers. It is often suggested that, for high status, peer and school settings require opposing rules for using or not using a variety of speech. Therefore the child desiring peer approval may use language which does not conform to school language.

Also at issue is whether different patterns of language socialization in the home—in this case, vocabulary use—have discernible *cognitive consequences*. Vocabulary differences clearly reflect differences in public access to one's ideas. These differences lead to different opportunities to talk about a given meaning and, as a result, different speech communities have different access to members' and others' ideas. At a deeper level, there is evidence suggesting that unrecognized differences in vocabulary result in mis-estimates of memory capacity and "general intelligence."

Finally, differences in language use can have *educational consequences*. Instructional situations often require students to reflect on their use of language (metalinguistics), their strategies for learning (metacognition) and their emotions and behavior (metabehavior). The possible consequences of variation from the school language in the acquisition of school skills may be illustrated for reading and the ability to deal with metabehavioral information. In reading, semantic mismatches between readers' word meaning and authors' word meaning may affect children's expectations about the gist of the language they are reading. Moreover, it is often suggested that different cultures may promote different levels of metalinguistic awareness, and some cultures may provide vocabulary items which are therefore useful for their development and use in reading. Variation in language socialization may also differentially facilitate or support the child's growing ability to analyze and make analytical statements about certain kinds of behavior which are not always reflected in everyday life. Such "meta" behavioral abilities include perceptual awareness (like the ability to analyze a perceptual array into a set of geometrical or mathematical relationships), as well as behavioral awareness (such as the ability to analyze the emotions of a person or those of a fictional character). Since such analysis is a hallmark of schooling, it is a prime area for analyzing home/school mismatches (Scribner & Cole, 1973).

Problems of misunderstanding increase directly with the dissimilarity of cultural backgrounds. The less knowledge speakers share about their social situation, the less they can depend on their knowledge of the broader context of their interaction to make sense of each other despite lexical misinterpretations, and the more likely a participant will fear social censure for exposing a misunderstanding. Listeners may fear that they will appear ignorant or implicitly critical of the speaker's competence. Similarly, if speakers suspect that listeners misunderstand, they may fear that publicly "repairing" the misunderstanding would display their own initial incompetence or implicitly criticize the listener's competence.

Critical Questions

While no list is exhaustive, the statement of the issues gives rise to several questions we have considered critical in our study of situational (home-school) differences in language use (Hall & Guthrie, 1979, 1980).[1] In a major study (Hall & Guthrie, 1980), we have focused the set of issues around eight specific questions concerning cultural differences. These same questions may also prove fruitful for teachers to consider: 1) Are there differences in the way black and white speakers structure portions of the lexicon? 2) Are there differences between vocabulary used in the home and in the school situation? 3) Admitting that both phonology and grammar are equally important determinants of dialect assessment, does phonology play a greater role in producing misunderstanding between teacher and student? 4) To what extent do children rely on nonverbal as opposed to verbal cues in obtaining information from the environment and communicating information about the environment to others? 5) To what extent are children likely or able to hypothesize or predict with linguistic information? 6) Do children adjust their speech to reflect the contextual needs of a situation? 7) Concerning the metabehavioral activities of the children, are they able to describe their own behavior and inner states, what is the nature of the lexicon children have developed to describe their own behavior and inner states, and what kind of metalinguistic awareness have children developed? 8) What is the proportion of different uses of questions across different cultural groups? We will focus our discussion on the four questions we feel are most cogent for classroom teachers to consider.

Question 1. *Are there differences in the way black and white speakers structure portions of the lexicon?*

There might be certain differences in the way in which speakers of black dialect and standard English structure prepositions. For example, black Harlem adults have been observed to say the following to children: "John, sit *to* the table." In this instance, a standard English speaker would probably say: "John, sit *at* the table." The question is whether the rendering "sit *to* the table" does not give the child a different relationship between himself and the object *table* than that interpretable from "John, sit *at* the table." Essentially, the first instance is more factive (indicating fact) than locative (indicating place). Such potential differences in structuring the lexicon are of special interest because of their implications for cognitive functioning as it is exemplified in standardized test performance.

On a broader scale, the reason for asking this question is due to its centrality in human experience. Space and time, both of which can be readily revealed through prepositions, are basic coordinates of experience. Since only one object can be in a given place at a given time, spatial locatives provide an indispensable device for identifying referents. "Hand me the spoon on the table" identifies the spoon that the speaker is referring to. The place adverbial, "on the table," indicates a search field, and the head noun, "spoon," provides the target description. As Miller and Johnson-Laird (1976) indicate, how a search is to be executed depends on the particular preposition relating the target to the landmark: on, in, at, by, under, etc. How children learn to delimit the search field and the cultural variations in it is of extreme interest.

Question 2. *Are there differences between vocabulary used in the home and in the school situation?*

Evidence on this question is being sought: A search is being conducted of naturally occurring data with respect to lexicon. Hall and Tirre (1979) have searched their corpus for the use of words from four standardized intelligence tests: The Stanford-

Binet, the WISC-R, the WPPSI, and the Peabody. They found that, overall, speakers produced more of the target words at home than at school, and that middle-class children produced more of the words at home than did lower-class. No overall differences were found for race or social class.

Question 3. *Admitting that both phonology and grammar are equally important determinants of dialect assessment, does phonology play a greater role in producing misunderstanding between teacher and student?*

This question can be seen to relate directly to the role of dialect in learning to read. Simons (1973), for example, has noted that one major behavioral consequence of the differences between the black dialect and standard English phonological systems for reading acquisition is that certain written words are pronounced differently by black dialect than by standard English speakers. The results of these differences are words that have a pronunciation unique to black dialect, e.g., *nest/ness, rest/ress, hand/han*. Moreover, there are words whose black dialect pronunciation results in a different word, e.g., *test/tess, mend/men, walked/walk, cold/coal, find/fine*. The latter result is an extra set of homophones for black dialect speakers. These differences in pronunciation could interfere with the black dialect speaker's acquisition of word recognition skills. These differences may also provide opportunities for miscommunication between teacher and student during phonics instruction.

Question 4. *To what extent do children rely on nonverbal as opposed to verbal cues in obtaining information from the environment and communicating information about the environment to others?*

This question, in part, involves the ways children acquire information from others and, further, how their information acquisition differs and/or is similar to that of adults. Cultural and social-class differences may also be significant in this area. There may be greater use of nonverbal cues in one culture than in another, or specific nonverbal rules may be the cause for miscommunication. Byers and Byers (1972) found that white children were more successful in communicating nonverbally with a white teacher than were black children, even though the teacher paid as much attention to both. More recently, in a study of a fifth grade debating club, McDermott and Hall (1977) have shown that performance on a task depends to a large degree on how people define the situation they are in.

An Analysis of Internal State Words

Having presented some of the questions around which our current research revolves, we would like to describe in detail one direction our analysis has taken. This involves the use of internal state words, which can be seen as indicators of cognitive development. Internal state words are those concerned with mental states, e.g. *think, know, like, angry, see,* and *want.* Table 1 lists some examples of the vocabulary types that we are investigating. These have been divided into three categories—cognitive, perceptual, and affective—and into parts of speech as well. The list is not meant to be exhaustive of the words in these categories which can be found in our corpus, but the list should clarify for the reader which words are of concern for us. As pointed out in Gearhart and Hall (1978) and Hall and Nagy (1979), internal state words represent one way in which to investigate the possible

Table 1
Categories of Internal State Vocabulary
with Examples of Possible Types

Verbs	Nouns	Adjectives
Cognitive		
know	knowledge	certain
know how		
think	thought	thoughtful
believe	belief	believable
understand (see, get)	understanding	understanding
wonder		
imagine	imagination	
guess	guess	
make sure		sure
suppose		
doubt	doubt	doubtful
remember	memory	
recall		
forget		forgetful
realize		
(pretend)		
(learn, pick up)		
remind	reminder	
dream	dream	
(appear)	(appearance)	
(seem)		

Table 1 (continued)

Verbs	Nouns	Adjectives
Perceptual		
see	sight	
look	look	
(appear)	(appearance)	
(seem)		
watch		
hear		
listen	sound	
touch		
(feel)		
taste	taste	
smell	smell	smelly
Affective		
frighten	fear	afraid, scared
	anger	angry
like	like	
love	love	loving
hate	hate	
brother		
(feel)	feeling	
hope	hope	hopeful
(stand)		
	comfort	comfortable
	(bad) mood	
	concern	concerned
		sorry
	worry	worried
		upset

A Metalinguistic Category: Lexical Definition

(call)		
(name)	name, word	
(mean)		
(stand for)		

cognitive consequences of early socialization. Internal state words reflect cognitive or metacognitive processes. While the use of such words (think, know, want, hear) is not necessarily associated with metacognition, or vice-versa, the internal state lexicon *is* often used to describe (if not organize) cognitive or metacognitive processes. For this reason, the distribution of internal state words in childrens' vocabulary would seem to indicate their ability to describe and monitor their own internal states. Furthermore, it appears likely that more efficient communication could be a product of the ability to use words.

Our investigations revealed that two of our speakers (Rog and Toh) and the people they interact with used internal state words 1 to 3 percent of the time. We examined the data by categories as illustrated in Table 2. In this table we have depicted for each speaker in each situation, the relative proportion of his/her total internal state tokens in each particular internal state category. Table 2 indicates that, at home, both Toh's mother and Toh used words from all three domains with roughly equal frequency. Rog's mother tended to use primarily cognitive words and Rog, perceptual words. While Toh and Rog both used perceptual words more than either cognitive or affective words, the greater extent to which Toh diverged from a preoperational concern with external appearances and perceptual experiences appears related to the greater diversity across domains by Toh's mother as compared to Rog's mother.

At school, both boys' teachers looked quite alike in this analysis, with about equal concern for cognitive and perceptual words. Toh's teacher did use a couple of affective words, Rog's teacher none, a modest difference at best, but one which corresponds to differences between Toh's and Rog's mothers. The greater use of perceptual words by teachers than by mothers makes sense in view of teachers' interests in encouraging sustained attentional involvement in some fairly focused task.

The data on diversity of tokens among these three categories corresponds to the data on diversity of *types* within as well as across all three internal state domains (see Table 3). There was a substantially greater diversity of affect expressed both at home and at school for Toh than for Rog, and greater diversity across all three domains as well. These data correspond to differences between Toh and Rog. The two teachers differed in this type analysis with regard to the diversity of cognitive words used: Rog's teacher used only one cognitive word (know) yet used it just about as often (from the token data in Tables 1 and 2) as all 5 types used by Toh's teacher.

Table 2
Distribution of Internal State and Lexical Definition
Tokens for ROG and TOH Speakers at Home (Dinner) and at
School (Directed Activity), with Proportion of Total
Internal State Tokens over Total Tokens for Each Speaker

ROG[a]

Situation	Vocabulary Domain	Speaker		
		Child	Mother	Teacher
Dinner	cognitive	3	28	
	perceptual	21	5	
	affective	0	5	
	(lexical)	(0)	(0)	
Total internal state tokens/ Total tokens		$\dfrac{24}{1036} = .02$	$\dfrac{38}{1576} = .02$	
Directed Activity	cognitive	1		8
	perceptual	6		11
	affective	1		0
	(lexical)	(1)		(1)
Total internal state tokens/ Total tokens		$\dfrac{8}{451} = .02$		$\dfrac{19}{92} = .02$

TOH[a]

Situation	Vocabulary Domain	Speaker		
		Child	Mother	Teacher
Dinner	cognitive	5	28	
	perceptual	14	18	
	affective	4	28	
	(lexical)	(2)	(0)	
Total internal state tokens/ Total tokens		$\dfrac{23}{1222} = .02$	$\dfrac{74}{2199} = .03$	
Directed Activity	cognitive	1	10	
	perceptual	5	12	
	affective	4	2	
	(lexical)	(0)	(0)	
Total internal state tokens/ Total tokens		$\dfrac{10}{693} = .01$	$\dfrac{24}{1154} = .02$	

[a]Code names for subjects.

Hall and Guthrie

Table 3
For Each Speaker (x Situation), the Proportion of
Total Internal State Tokens in Each Particular
Internal State Domain (Cognitive, Perceptual, Affective)

ROG

		Speaker		
Situation	Vocabulary Domain	Child	Mother	Teacher
Dinner	cognitive	.13	.74	
	perceptual	.87	.13	
	affective	.00	.13	
		(N=24)	(N=38)	
Directed	cognitive	.12		.42
School	perceptual	.75		.58
Activity	affective	.12		.00
		(N=8)		(N=19)

TOH

Dinner	cognitive	.22	.38	
	perceptual	.61	.24	
	affective	.17	.38	
		(N=23)	(N=74)	
Directed	cognitive	.20		.42
School	perceptual	.50		.50
Activity	affective	.40		.08
		(N=10)		(N=24)

It can be argued that exposure to a number of different types could facilitate the child's construction of differentiated and flexible domains of lexical knowledge. Toh's mother and his teacher appear to provide that kind of environment for Toh. In contrast, Rog's teacher appears to be constricting Rog's experience with words of internal state. While both teachers use fewer types of words than the mothers (as would be expected from the rather focused nature of the directed activities taped), Rog's teacher provides virtually no diversity at all. We might also point out that Rog's mother shows in this analysis a fairly even distribution of type diversity among the three categories, even through her token data (Tables 1 and 2) showed a preponderance of cognitive tokens. This is because several affective and perceptual words were used only once.

Toh's mother was more concerned with feelings, emotions, and attitudes than was Rog's mother. Similarly, Toh's teacher displayed at least some concern with affect; Rog's teacher, none. These data correspond with the children's vocabulary. Toh used words concerning affect both at home and at school; Rog, neither. Would children whose mothers and teachers were concerned with affects and attitudes be at any advantage when they entered school?

At first one might think that these affective concepts are essentially irrelevant to traditional academic tasks and to our concern with metacognitive processes. But there are two ways in which they are quite fundamental to school performance. The first has to do with the child's growing concepts of personal attitudes toward tasks and accomplishments. Children who are learning about internal states and their relation to external states and interactions have opportunities to learn to recognize and evaluate their own motivations for doing things. School, then, could be experienced and "accomplished" in a more personal, independent, and self-defined way for such a child than for a child who is less knowledgeable or aware of feelings and motivations. The second has to do with critical school skills related to reading comprehension. While learning to read might seem a dry, impersonal school task, in fact what is asked of children are complex interpretations of characters' thoughts, feelings, and intentions. Having learned to recognize these in themselves and those close to them would help children learn to do so for characters in stories. Such children would more easily interpret beyond the information given and concern themselves with underlying personal and interpersonal dimensions of characters' actions. Our data for Toh suggest that he will be at an advantage for these kinds of interpretive school tasks as compared to Rog. This would be the case even if it were not for the additional burden on Rog, much of the time, to *transform* the story content from themes predominant in the majority culture to ones that are familiar and interpretable to him. If anything, Rog needs a teacher with particular concern to develop his skills for these kinds of affective and intentional interpretations, and instead he has a teacher who (in these data) shows no concern with such tasks.

Semanticity: The Second Step

Once tokens are located, they are coded for what we have called "semanticity" (i.e., the relation of the word's meaning to the utterance meaning as a whole).[2] If you examine a word in the context of its utterance, how critical is it that the child interpret *any* meaning for the word in order to assign a reasonable interpretation to the utterance? There are what we are calling pragmatic uses for these words, in which the semantic content concerned with internal states is not contributing to the topical focus of the proposition, and so the utterance meaning may be quite interpretable without understanding the internal state words. In contrast, *semantic uses* are codes for those utterances in which internal state words are intended to contribute to topical content. *Reflections* are those uses which appear to call explicitly for metacognitive abilities. For example, "How did you know . . . ?" or "I realized that if I could just remember . . . ." When internal state words are used as reflections, their content (thinking, remembering, knowing) generally contributes to the discourse topic. *Genuine expressions* of internal states also contribute substantial content, yet it is usually the object of the internal state which becomes the topic (*what* one was thinking about).

There are consistent differences between the teachers' pragmatic and semantic usages. The Toh data show these speakers primarily using words to express some literal meaning. The Rog speakers were using words for pragmatic functions almost as often as for semantic functions.

The Toh data, as compared to the Rog data, show the greater frequency with which these words were included in the turns of Toh speakers as compared to Rog. Further, Toh adult speakers used internal state words semantically in approximately 15 to 18 percent of their turns, as compared to 10 percent for Rog's mother and 6 percent for Rog's teacher. Correspondingly, Toh used an internal state word semantically in roughly 7 percent of his turns, as compared to 2 to 3 percent for Rog. These data suggest that explicitly expressed concern with mental states and activities is more frequent in one child's world than in another's. In these data, Toh had more opportunity than did Rog to learn the meanings of words in these domains. These are, then, illustrations of the kinds of cultural differences we will continue to examine.

Mental Activities: Toward Higher Level Units

One area of investigation we consider to be of extreme importance is the role of internal state words in relation to higher level cognitive activities and interpreting mental states. In our future research, it will be of interest to determine the occasions in which mothers and teachers introduce and use specific lexical items. Of critical interest will be those occasions in which: a lexical item is a match (ideal for learning) or a mismatch to some corresponding mental activity; the occasion for a lexical item is the child's spontaneous mental activity; a lexical item is used to misrepresent a mental state or activity (the child's or anyone else's).

In this chapter we have addressed the issues around the home/school mismatch hypothesis. This hypothesis states that differences in rules for language use in the home may account for the lower school achievement levels of nonmainstream children. While this idea is attractive, empirical evidence for it is still lacking. We have yet to identify specific points of mismatch. Basic to our thinking on new directions for research is the idea that some sort of ethnographic approach will be required. Unless we have some idea of how children and adults of various ethnic and social class groups actually use language, we cannot begin to design appropriate programs to deal with language differences of nonmainstream children and their teachers.

Despite the efforts of federal and state agencies, countless educators, researchers, and social workers, nonmainstream children in America continue to fail. Obviously, a different approach is called for, but exactly what that approach should be is unclear. We have suggested that to find a solution to this problem we must step back and carefully examine it at a more fundamental level, beginning with naturally occurring language data. Without a clear notion of how the language of mainstream and minority children differs and how it varies according to cultural or situational constraints, one should not begin to prescribe programs for change. Too many remediation and intervention programs have been based on assumed, incomplete, or invalid evidence.

Once we have answers to questions at the level they are asked here, then perhaps real solutions to the academic problems of nonmainstream children can be found.

References

ASHER, S. *Referential communication* (Technical Report No. 90). Urbana: University of Illinois, Center for the Study of Reading, June 1978. (ED 159 594)

BROWN, R. *A first language.* Cambridge, Massachusetts: Harvard University Press, 1973.

BYERS, R., & BYERS, H. Nonverbal communication and the education of children. In C. B. Cazden, V. P. John, & D. Hymes (Eds.), *Functions of language in the classroom.* New York: Teachers College Press, 1972.

GEARHART, M., & HALL, W. S. *Internal state words: Cultural and situational variation in vocabulary usage* (Technical Report No. 115). Urbana: University of Illinois, Center for the Study of Reading, February 1979. (ED 165 131)

GLUCKSBERG, S., KRAUSS, R. M., & HIGGINS, F. The development of referential communication skills. In F. D. Horowitz (Ed.), *Review of child development research* (Volume 4). Chicago: University of Chicago Press, 1975, 305-345.

HALL, W. S., COLE, M., REDER, S., & DOWLEY, J. Variations in young children's use of language: Some effects of setting and dialect. In R. O. Freedle (Ed.), *Discourse production and comprehension.* Hillsdale, New Jersey: Ablex, 1977.

HALL, W. S. & DORE, J. *Lexical sharing in mother-child interaction: Some cross-cultural variations.* Mimeo, 1978.

HALL, S. & FREEDLE, R. O. *Culture and language.* New York: Halstead, 1975.

HALL, W. S. & GUTHRIE, L. F. *On the dialect question and reading* (Technical Report No. 121). Urbana: University of Illinois, Center for the Study of Reading, 1979a. (ED 169 522)

HALL, W. S. & GUTHRIE, L. F. *Cultural and situational variations in language function and use* (Technical Report No. 145). Urbana: University of Illinois, Center for the Study of Reading, 1979b. (ED 179 944)

HALL, W. S., & NAGY, W. *Theoretical issues in the investigation of words of internal report* (Technical Report No. 146). Urbana: University of Illinois, Center for the Study of Reading, October 1979. (ED 177 526)

HALL, W. S., & TIRRE, W. C. *The communicative environment of young children: social class, ethnic, and situational differences* (Technical Report No. 125). Urbana: University of Illinois, Center for the Study of Reading, May 1979. (ED 170 788)

LABOV, W. The logic of nonstandard English. In F. Williams (Ed.), *Language and poverty.* Chicago: Markham, 1970.

LITOWITZ, B. Learning to make definitions. *Journal of Child Language,* 1977, *4,* 289-304.

McDERMOTT, R.P., & HALL, W.S. The social organization of a successful and unsuccessful school performance. *Quarterly Newsletter of the Institute for Comparative Human Development,* 1977, *3,* 10-11.

MILLER, G.H., & JOHNSON-LAIRD, P.N. *Language and perception.* Cambridge, Massachusetts: Harvard University Press, 1976.

NELSON, K. Structure and strategy in learning to talk. *Monographs of the Society for Research in Child Development,* 1973, *38* (1-2 Serial No. 149).

NELSON, K. *How young children represent knowledge of their world in and out of language: A preliminary report.* Paper presented at the Thirteenth Annual Carnegie Symposium on Cognition, Carnegie-Mellon University, May 1977.

NELSON, K., & BROWN, A. The semantic-episodic distinction in memory development. In P. Ornstein (Ed.), *Memory development.* Hillsdale, New Jersey: Erlbaum, 1978.

SCRIBNER, S., & COLE, M. The cognitive consequence of formal and informal education. *Science,* 1973, *182,* 553-559.

SHATZ, M. The relationship between cognitive processes and the development of communication skills. In B. Keasey (Ed.), *Nebraska symposium on motivation.* Lincoln: University of Nebraska, 1978.

SHATZ, M., & GELMAN, R. The development of communication skills: Modifications in the speech of young children as a function of listener. *Monographs of the Society for Research in Child Development,* 1973, *38* (Serial No. 152).

SIMONS, H.D. *Black dialect and reading interference: A review and analysis of the research evidence.* Berkeley: University of California, School of Education, 1973, mimeographed.

Footnotes

1. The work reported in this chapter was supported by a grant from the Carnegie Corporation of New York.
2. The chapter draws upon work reported in Technical Reports 115, 121, and 125.

Part 2   Implications for Practice

INTRODUCTION

You have just read five articles based on current theory and research from an interactive perspective. Unlike models which are primarily text-based, an interactive orientation stresses the contributions of the reader, text, and context to comprehension.

The articles in this section are organized according to the same three aspects of comprehension as Part 1 but suggest implications for instructional environments. The first two articles consider reader/text interaction by proposing interactive comprehension strategies and comprehension monitoring procedures. Langer's article, based on a theory of memory, schema theory, and metacognition, presents a technique to assess and activate background knowledge before reading. She provides a framework that can help teachers determine whether students possess the necessary knowledge to successfully comprehend a text and how to link what the students already know to the new information in the text. Smith-Burke proposes a sequence of activities including reading, writing, listening, and discussion in order to help students understand the constructive nature of the reading process and develop "independent" comprehension, monitoring, and problem solving strategies for reading by phasing out teacher assistance.

The third article focuses on text structure and how it can influence comprehension. Using text analytic techniques, Ringler and Weber have integrated information on story characteristics and inferencing in order to help teachers better realize the types of inferences children may need to make in order to comprehend a story.

The last two articles explore the contextual factors which influence instruction and learning. Green and Harker describe the nature of the instructional dialogue. They view the act of reading to children as primarily a sociolinguistic process which is both instructional and interactive. They consider story reading a communicative/sociolinguistic process and present instructional implications derived from two studies of story reading to children. Sims stresses cultural aspects within the classroom interaction which may impede comprehension. She suggests that the teacher must be aware of the student's communication and learning abilities, must look beyond linguistic variations, and must focus on factors within the classroom context to improve learning.

We hope our readers will relate their prior knowledge about children and learning to the ideas expressed in this section, and think about how these ideas relate to what they are doing in the classroom.

Facilitating Text Processing:
The Elaboration of Prior Knowledge

Judith A. Langer
University of California at Berkeley

To develop efficient comprehension and promote new learning, teachers are advised to start with what their students know. Sometimes this is interpreted very simply. A teacher introducing a textbook chapter about the nation's capitol, for example, may begin by asking, "Has anyone ever visited Washington, D.C.?" Too often, only one child has actually visited the nation's capitol, and while this child tells about the trip, other class members remain uninvolved.

Such problems have led many teachers to feel that students lack relevant prior knowledge and the ideas in textbooks are so far from their students' experiences that the job of bridge building is almost impossible. The apparent discrepancy between the language and ideas in the text and the prior knowledge and language of the students creates major instructional problems for the teacher and major learning problems for the students.

"Starting with what the students know" is a particularly sophisticated concept and, when understood both theoretically and practically, will permit the teacher to help students read their texts with greater ease. In reality, students have more prior knowledge about a topic than is readily apparent. If this knowledge is effectively tapped, the bridge between reader and text will result in more successful comprehension and recall. *How* one encourages students to use links between their knowledge of the topic and the text's topical content makes the difference.

This chapter begins with a brief presentation of the theory which forms the conceptual base of an instructional activity designed to access prior information and facilitate text processing. The second part of the chapter presents a prereading plan which focuses on the development and organization of conceptual knowledge relevant to major ideas expressed in a text. The link from theory and research to instructional implications is demonstrated throughout the chapter.

Background

In recent years, much research has focused on reader-author interaction in comprehension of text. Some of this research suggests that in and of themselves, the graphic representations in a text do not carry meaning. The reader's prior knowledge permits interpretation of the author's intended message and leads to comprehension of the material. As the reader processes the ideas represented in the text, associations are formed which are perceived in light of their possible integration with new ideas expressed in the text (Adams & Collins, 1979). New ideas and information are learned and retained most efficiently when related ideas are already available within the reader's memory. Prior knowledge serves a subsuming role by furnishing "ideational anchorage" during new learning experiences (Ausubel, 1968). This suggests that for efficient text processing and successful comprehension to take place, a link with some already acquired knowledge is necessary. And it is this writer's contention that almost everyone knows something (however remote) about almost everything.

The assumptions underlying this view of reading comprehension emanate from recent research into 1) how knowledge is organized and retrieved and 2) how knowledge relates to reading comprehension, recall, and text processing. Since the organization of knowledge and retrieval of information form the basis for comprehension and learning, a brief review of the ACT model of memory and of schema theory will provide useful background for an expanded understanding of reader-text interaction.

The ACT model (J. Anderson, 1973, 1976) differentiates between declarative knowledge and procedural knowledge—between knowing that and knowing how. The knowledge of a fact or truth is declarative knowledge while the doing of a skill or task is procedural knowledge. Anderson describes declarative knowledge in terms of a propositional network and procedural knowledge in terms of productions. The propositional network is made up of a set of ideas connected by relationships between those ideas. The interaction of the propositional network and procedural productions represents cognition. Anderson suggests that all ideas, links, and productions are permanent once they have been formed, implying that memory breakdowns are caused by inadequate retrieval rather than by the loss of stored knowledge. In recall, a frequently-used link is more likely to be activated than one which is not often used. Also, the greater the number of links with an idea, the greater the probability of recall.

From this brief description, it can be inferred that memory probes could encourage the activiation of less used links to relevant ideas and this, in turn, may increase the use and strength of a particular set of links (Gagné, 1978). Further, the events occurring during a prereading activity based on memory probes may effect the use of links to a particular idea, and may assist students in accessing more appropriate and more highly elaborated knowledge. Prereading activities, then, may help students approach new reading tasks with more meaningful anticipations, and thus with greater cognitive readiness than had the prereading preparation not occurred.

Another large body of research has shown that the organization and accessing of knowledge influence the manner in which the reader organizes information provided by the author and affects the quality of the organization of that knowledge in recall. Rumelhart and Ortony (1977) postulated that knowledge is incorporated into abstract conceptual frameworks or schemata. A schema is a metaphorical allusion representing generic knowledge based on common subject matter, attributes, or associations. Schema theory suggests that text processing relies on the reader's past experiences and prior knowledge. It also describes the manner in which schemata have idiosyncratically been organized and structured, and explains how different kinds of prior knowledge affect retrieval of information and recall of text. Schemata represent what the reader already knows about a topic and help the reader to structure the interpretation of new messages about a topic (Anderson, Pichert, & Shirey, 1977; Anderson, Reynolds, Schallert, & Goetz, 1977). Readers seem to make inferences consistent with their own schemata, relating the elements in the event or text with the generic characterizations in their own schematic structure. Also, the organizational structure of knowledge facilitates learning and remembering of information (Anderson, Spiro, & Anderson, 1978), and may provide a plan which helps readers retrieve information (Pichert & Anderson, 1977).

Pearson, Hansen, and Gordon (1979) hypothesized that readers who have better developed schemata for a particular topic would understand and remember more than those with weaker schemata. Their findings support the notion of comprehension as a process of integrating new information with preexisting schemata. If the schemata are weakly developed, comprehension requiring the integration of new and known information is difficult.

In a related study, Tannen (1979) found that anticipatory structures are based on past experience and these structures can be seen in the retelling of a passage. Furthermore, expectations which support the processing and comprehension of stories also influence comprehension and recall. If the quality of the input is good, recall may still be poor due to inappropriate memory structures (Bobrow & Norman, 1975).

Readers who make fullest use of background knowledge as it applies to organizing and making sense of text have a conscious awareness of how to organize and use that knowledge in relation to a specific text and its content. Good readers think about their thinking and check themselves when the comprehension process breaks down. Brown (1977) suggests that predicting, planning, checking, and monitoring are the basic characteristics of efficient thinking in learning situations. Executive monitoring involves evaluating and regulating one's own ongoing abilities and strategies. Metacognition (Flavell, 1976) refers to an individual's personal awareness of the cognitive processes or strategies used in learning. In deliberate learning, conscious executive control forms the core of intelligent activity. Metacognition is the more encompassing term under which more specific "meta" activities, such as metamemory and metacomprehension, are subsumed. Metamemory (Flavell, 1970) refers to self-awareness of working memory. Some awareness of the workings of memory is necessary for individuals to supervise the strategies used and to monitor the appropriateness of ideas evoked. Metacomprehension skills permit learners to reflect on their own strategies and, for example, to be aware of what they do and do not know in light of their purpose for reading (Brown, 1977). Executive monitoring through metacognitive awareness can lead the reader toward a deliberate search for and refinement of some ideas, rejection of others, and integration and adoption of still others. From this perspective, teachers who wish to help their students comprehend a text as successfully as possible must create conditions under which appropriately related schemata are likely to be accessed. This accessing of related schemata permits a cognitive link with past experiences and allows the formulation of anticipations about the language and content presented in the text. It is by weighing, evaluating, and comparing the relationships of new and old information that comprehension of the author's message, refinement of ideas, and acquisition of new learning takes place. Sometimes students do lack adequate knowledge about the topic being presented and, therefore, experience difficulty comprehending the text. More often, readers experience difficulty because they have not accessed appropriately related ideas, have not activated all available knowledge related to the topic, have not associated the information being presented in the text with their prior knowledge, or have not sufficiently organized the relevant concepts.

Because of life's experiences, every learner can make some link with a new topic of study. What the original experiences were, how they are organized in memory, how frequently they have been activated, or how they are utilized in new learning situations varies from person to person. To facilitate more efficient comprehension of text, teachers can provide experiences which permit students to access and evaluate as much relevant knowledge as possible. Teachers must provide a climate of inquiry which permits students to activate prior knowledge, and encourage discussion in an environment in which students can evaluate the appropriateness of available ideas.

The PReP

The Pre Reading Plan is a three step instructional/assessment paradigm for teachers to use before assigning textbook reading to their classes. It facilitates the conscious accessing of knowledge related to major concepts presented in a text by giving readers the opportunity to access prior knowledge and to elaborate and evaluate accessed ideas. The assessment aspect of the procedure assists the teacher in: 1) determining the prior knowledge a student possesses about a specific topic, as well as the manner in which this knowledge is organized; 2) becoming aware of the language a student uses to express knowledge about a given topic; and 3) making judgments about how much additional background information must be taught before the student can successfully read the text. The instructional aspect of the procedure reminds students of what they already know about a topic; elicits group elaboration of existing language and concepts; and refines anticipations, in turn facilitating learning from text.

The PReP calls for a group discussion before students read the text. The teacher must review the portion of text to be assigned to select a word, phrase, or picture to stimulate group discussion about a key concept in the text. For example, if the text deals with unions, "featherbedding" or "child labor laws" might be selected. A detailed picture of a political convention might be used for a text about the American system for electing representatives. In a brief introduction, the teacher puts the pre-reading activity in context by introducing the topic to be studied. There are three phases to the PReP.

1. *Initial Associations with the Concept*
   In this first phase the teacher says: "Tell anything that comes to mind when . . . (you hear this word, see this picture, etc.)." As each student freely associates and tells what ideas initially came to mind, the teacher writes these responses on the board. During this phase, students have their first opportunity to make associations between the key concept and what they already know.

2. *Reflections on Initial Associations*
   During the second phase, the students are asked, "What made you think of . . . (the response given by each of the students during phase 1)?" This phase encourages students to become aware of the associations they have made, to listen to each other's responses, and to become aware of their changing ideas. Through this procedure they gain the insight which permits them to evaluate the utility of these ideas in the reading experience.

3. Reformulation of Knowledge

After each student has had an opportunity to think and tell about what triggered their ideas, the teacher asks, "Based on our discussion, have you any new ideas about . . . (the word, the picture, etc.)?" This phase allows students to tell about associations which have been elaborated or changed as a result of the discussion. Because they have had a chance to probe their memories and evaluate their ideas in terms of the text, they will read and reformulate their ideas in light of the reading task. The responses elicited during phase 3 are often more refined than those elicited during phase 1.

This three-phase lesson helps teachers and students assess what students already know about a concept and permits students to refine anticipations about the concepts to be read in the text. Students are encouraged to probe for as many links as possible about a given idea, and to formulate additional links in the group discussion. It is particularly important that the teacher not impede students in accessing ideas which may be in the students' concept structure but not in the teacher's.

Phases 1 and 3 elicit "free association" responses whereas phase 2 elicits a metacognitive explanation.

Levels of Response

There seem to be three levels of verbalization during phase 1 and phase 3, based on the amount and organization of students' prior knowledge. Categorization of knowledge into levels (described in Figure 1) provides teachers with diagnostic information in planning for instruction. Previous studies have shown these levels to be more important than IQ or standardized reading test scores in predicting student recall of a particular passage (Langer, 1980; Langer & Nicolich, 1981).

If the student has *much* prior knowledge about the concept being discussed, responses to "Tell me anything that comes to mind when . . ." generally take the form of superordinate concepts, definitions, analogies, or a linking of that concept with another concept to show evidence of high-level integration of ideas. If the student has *some* knowledge about the concept

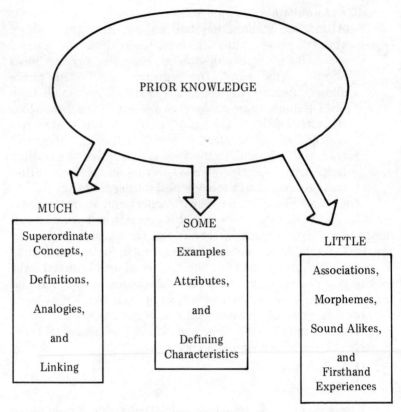

Figure 1. Levels of prior knowledge.

being discussed, responses generally take the form of examples, attributes, or defining characteristics. If the student has *little* prior information about the concept, responses generally focus on low level associations with morphemes (prefixes, suffixes, or root words), words which sound like the stimulus word, or first hand (but not quite relevant) experiences. (A more complete description of the levels or organization of knowledge can be found in Langer, 1981).

An Example

A group of fifth graders were shown a picture of a courtroom scene. Their responses, when asked to tell what came to mind when they saw the picture, are given with their corresponding levels in Figure 2. Phases 1, 2, and 3 are indicated by the

COURTROOM SCENE

STUDENT		RESPONSES	LEVEL
Alice	1	person in court, lawyer, judge and stuff	little—association
	2	someone would be guilty, people can't get out innocent	
	3	person might have to go to jail or pay a fine	little—association
Bob	1	trial and being divorced	little—association
	2	when people get divorced they have to go to court	
	3	court stands for "obey law and don't commit crimes"	much—superordinate
Carol	1	court and judge	little—association
	2	knew judge was in court	
	3	means justice	some—defining characteristic
Ted	1	lawyer, judge and jail	little—association
	2	jury will tell if they're guilty or not	
	3	trust in one another's judgment when you have a jury	some—attribute

Figure 2. Sample responses elicited during phases 1, 2, and 3 of PReP.

appropriate Arabic numerals. Note that levels are assigned only for responses elicited during phases 1 and 3. The levels assigned to each of the responses focus on the type of organization utilized by the student. For example, during phases 1 and 2 Bob seems to rely heavily on associations or possible first hand experiences. As a result of discussion and the metacognitive activity, he developed a more sophisticated concept, as can be seen in his phase 3 response. On the other hand, Alice seems to be working at an association or first hand experience level and has not benefited from the phase 2 discussion; there is no evidence of concept growth from phase 1 to phase 3. Based on this quick analysis, the teacher might expect that Bob can comprehend the social studies chapter dealing with the American judicial system, whereas Alice requires further instruction on specific concepts before reading the text.

It is important that a student who responds at the *little* prior knowledge level during phase 1 be given an opportunity to explain why the response came to mind. Ted, for example, responded with associations during phase 1. However, during the phase 2 metacognitive activity, he said "the jury will tell if you're guilty or not." This awareness, as well as the discussion which took place, may have permitted him to respond at a higher level during phase 3 when he stated a rationale for a trial by one's peers. This student at the *some* level during phase 3 may be ready to successfully engage in textbook reading, but the teacher should keep close watch in case assistance in the form of discussion and concept elaboration becomes necessary.

Responses in the *much* and *some* categories indicate students are likely to read the text with adequate comprehension. However, students at the *some* level may need a bit of teacher guidance, often in the form of probing questions. Students responding at the *little* level usually require direct instruction on relevent concepts before they can successfully comprehend the text. Suggestions for concept instruction procedures can be found in many sources including *Reading and Learning in the Content Classroom* (Estes & Vaughan, 1978); *Teaching Reading in Content Areas* (Herber, 1978); *Learning and Human Abilities* (Klausmeier, 1975); *Facilitating Student Learning* (Klausmeier

PHASE 1 What comes to mind when . . . ?
PHASE 2 What made you think of . . . ?
PHASE 3 Have you any new ideas about . . . ?

STIMULUS ——— (note word, picture, or phrase)

Student Names	MUCH superordinate concepts, definitions, analogies, linking		SOME examples, attributes, defining characteristics		LITTLE morphemes, sound alikes, recent experiences	
	1	3	1	3	1	3
1.						
2.						
3.						
4.						
5.						
6.						
7.						
8.						
9.						
10.						

Figure 3. Prereading Plan response checksheet.

& Goodwin, 1975); and *Teaching Reading Comprehension* (Pearson & Johnson, 1978).

This three part prereading activity gives teachers important diagnostic information about a group's readiness to read a text. Figure 3 will help teachers identify students who are not likely to benefit from textbook reading without first participating in direct concept instruction. The PReP has been most successful when presented as a group (eight to ten students) rather than whole class activity.

Aspects of the prereading plan will be familiar to many teachers. Study guides (Estes & Vaughan, 1978; Herber, 1978), the structured overview (Barron, 1979; Earle, 1976; Herber, 1978; Robinson, 1978), and free association experiences (Estes & Vaughan, 1978; Herber, 1978; Stauffer, 1969) have become frequently used approaches in vocabulary and concept instruction. However, it is the organization of the activities into a structured framework based on recent theory and research which teachers may find new and helpful.

Summary

The prereading plan is an assessment/instructional activity which benefits both teachers and students. Teachers become aware of 1) the levels of concept sophistication possessed by the individuals in the group; 2) the language the students have available to express their knowledge about the topic; and 3) the amount of concept instruction necessary before textbook reading can be assigned. Students are given the opportunity to 1) elaborate relevant prior knowledge; 2) become more aware of their own related knowledge; and 3) anticipate concepts to be presented in the text. Elaboration of prior knowledge, awareness of what is known about a topic, and expectations about content and language to be presented in a text all lead to more efficient processing and recall of subject area text.

References

ADAMS, M.J., & COLLINS, A. A schema theoretic view of reading. In Roy O. Freedle (Ed.), *New directions in discourse processing*, Volume 2. Norwood, New Jersey: Ablex, 1979, 1-21.

ANDERSON, J.R. *Language, memory, and thought*. Hillsdale, New Jersey: Erlbaum, 1976.

ANDERSON, J.R., & BOWER, G.H. *Human associative memory*. Washington, D.C.: Winston, 1973.

ANDERSON, R.C., PICHERT, J.W., & SHIREY, L.L. *Effects of the reader's schemata at different points in time*. Center for the Study of Reading, Technical Report No. 119, April 1979. (ED 169 523)

ANDERSON, R.C., REYNOLDS, R.D., SCHALLERT, D.L. & GOETZ, E.T. Frameworks for comprehending discourse. *American Educational Research Journal*, 1977, *14*, 367-381.

ANDERSON, R.C., SPIRO, R.J., & ANDERSON, M.C. Schemata as scaffolding for the representation of information in connected discourse. *American Educational Research Journal*, 1978, *15*, 3, 433-440.

AUSUBEL, D.P. *Educational psychology: A cognitive view*. New York: Holt, Rinehart & Winston, 1968.

BARRON, R.F. The use of vocabulary as an advance organizer. In H. Herber & P. Sanders (Eds.), *Research in reading in the content areas*. Syracuse, New York: Reading and Language Arts Center, Syracuse University, 1969, 29-39.

BOBROW, D.G., & NORMAN, D.A. Some principles of memory schemata. In D.G. Bobrow and A. Collins (Eds.), *Representation and understanding: Studies in cognitive science*. New York: Academic Press, 1975.

BROWN, A. *Knowing when, where, and how to remember: A problem of metacognition*. Center for the Study of Reading Technical Report No. 47, June 1977.

EARLE, R. *Teaching reading and mathematics*. Newark, Delaware: International Reading Association, 1976.

ESTES, T., & VAUGHAN, J.L. *Reading and learning in the content classroom*. Boston: Allyn & Bacon, 1978.

FLAVELL, J.H. Developmental studies of mediated memory. In H. W. Reese and L.P. Lipsitt (Eds.), *Advances in child development and child behavior* (Volume 5). New York: Academic Press, 1970, 181-211.

FLAVELL, J.H. Metacognitive aspects of problem solving. In L.B. Resnick (Ed.), *The nature of intelligence*. Hillsdale, New Jersey: Erlbaum, 1976.

HERBER, H.L. *Teaching reading in content areas*. Englewood Cliffs, New Jersey: Prentice-Hall, 1978.

KLAUSMEIER, H.J. *Learning and human abilities*. New York: Harper & Row, 1975.

LANGER, J.A. Relation between levels of prior knowledge and the organization of recall. In M.L. Kamil and A.J. Moe (Eds.), *Perspectives in reading research and instruction*. Washington, D.C.: National Reading Conference, 1980, 28-33.

LANGER, J.A. From theory to practice: A prereading plan. *Journal of Reading*, 1981, *25*, 2.

LANGER, J.A., & NICOLICH, M. Prior knowledge and its effect on comprehension. *Journal of Reading Behavior*, 1981, *13*, 4.

PEARSON, P.D., HANSEN, J.D., & GORDON, C. The effect of background knowledge on young children's comprehension of explicit and implicit information. *Journal of Reading Behavior*, 1979, *11*, 201-209.

PEARSON, P.D., & JOHNSON, D. *Teaching reading comprehension.* New York: Macmillan, 1978.

PICHERT, J.W., & ANDERSON, R.C. Taking different perspectives on a story. *Journal of Educational Psychology*, 1977, *69*, 209-315.

ROBINSON, H.A. *Teaching reading and study strategies.* New York: Allyn & Bacon, 1978.

RUMELHART, D.E., & ORTONY, A. The representation of knowledge in memory. In R.C. Anderson, R.J. Spiro, and W.E. Montague (Eds.), *Schooling and the acquisition of knowledge.* Hillsdale, New Jersey: Erlbaum, 1977, 99-135.

STAUFFER, R.G. *Teaching reading as a thinking process.* New York: Harper & Row, 1969.

TANNEN, D. What's in a frame? Surface evidence for underlying expectations. In R.O. Freedle (Ed.), *New directions in discourse processing* (Volume 2). Norwood, New Jersey: Ablex, 1979, 137-181.

Langer

Extending Concepts through Language Activities

M. Trika Smith-Burke
New York University

During the first three years of reading instruction, children read basal materials written in narrative style. These stories function as vehicles for teaching "reading skills." During the intermediate years, teacher expectations begin to change and a shift from narrative to expository text materials begins. By high school, students are expected to comprehend, analyze, study, and retain information on their own—to read and learn about scientific experiments, historical events, and complex math theories. Even the emphasis during story reading changes to the study of literature as content. Reading comprehension is considered a tool, a critical prerequisite for learning. Advanced students must use what they already know to understand and develop new concepts presented in their textbooks, *and* they must study and retain this information for future use.

As students progress through the grades, one important dimension of these changing demands is the shift from teacher imposed structure to student generated structure. In the elementary grades it is the teacher who selects materials to be read, sets purposes for reading, and focuses attention on concepts to be learned. And it is also the teacher who monitors the success or failure of comprehension and learning. By high school, teachers still set objectives and assess student learning, but only in terms of subject matter. Now the students are responsible for *independently* implementing and monitoring comprehension strategies, utilizing study strategies, and monitoring their own learning before teacher assessment occurs.

The many older students who still lack the necessary comprehension and study strategies to cope with academic work are proof that current instructional programs used in the preceding grades need to be reexamined and revised. Students require experiences which not only teach comprehension strategies but also teach *when* and *why* to use them and *how* to monitor the effectiveness of their efforts.

The purpose of this article is to present a new sequence of comprehension activities called *E*xtending *CO*ncepts through *L*anguage *A*ctivities (ECOLA) and the rationale underlying the sequence. Many of the activities will be quite familiar to most teachers. It is the sequencing of the activities and the underlying principles which may be helpful in developing student independence in comprehending. Designed to aid junior and senior high school students in becoming "independent comprehenders" of content materials, ECOLA focuses on comprehension as opposed to study strategies. It is based on an extension of the language experience rationale (Lee & Allen, 1969) and on implications from current research in the areas of comprehension and metacognition.

In this article, a selective review of research on comprehension and metacognition will highlight important concepts on which ECOLA is based; a brief review of other techniques which are consistent with these concepts will be presented; and, finally, the rationale of each step of ECOLA will be described and further explicated with a case study.

Research on Comprehension

Incorporated in many of the current models of the reading process are three major factors which influence comprehension: 1) context, 2) background knowledge, and 3) the constructive nature of comprehension.

Context. Context for reading changes as students become proficient readers. Particularly during first encounters with print, the surroundings in which functional written messages occur provide strong supportive clues to meaning. This context is the real world in which labels and signs are found. As children encounter books, the definition of context changes. In books and other written materials, meaning has been removed from a "real" world situation and represented in print. The author must explicitly create context within the printed material itself, since the author and reader no longer share a real world situation. The author explicitly describes important background and uses writing conventions (Applebee, 1978; Grice, 1975; Halliday & Hasan, 1976; Meher, 1975) and other graphic aids such as pictures, charts, or graphs to clarify the message.

It is a combination of topic, purpose for communicating, and a sense of anticipated audience which determines how the author presents a written message (Flower & Hayes, 1978). In order to reconstruct the author's message, the reader must rely on the contextual cues within the text itself and use them to activate relevant background knowledge. If the author's cues are inadequate, ambiguous, or ignored, readers' interpretations will be highly influenced by the real life context in which they find themselves (Harste & Carey, 1979), and by whatever background knowledge they happen to apply.

Background knowledge. The second major factor which affects comprehension is the reader's background knowledge (Anderson, R.C., 1975; Anderson, Reynolds, Schallert & Goetz, 1977). This knowledge includes facts and concepts, knowledge of how and why people convey different types of messages in oral and written form, and how people relate to one another (Bruce, 1978). Without adequate background the comprehension process may break down, or a partial or idiosyncratic interpretation of a text may occur. It is background knowledge which allows readers to infuse the print with meaning.

Constructive nature of comprehension. The third aspect of comprehension, the constructive nature, involves the constant inferencing which a reader must perform to comprehend a text. As a reader takes in information, sentence by sentence from the printed page, certain experiences and meanings are evoked and must be linked together through inferencing to create an interpretation of the text. Predictions are made concerning what will come next. These are either confirmed or revised (Goodman, 1970). As the reader continues, more information must be integrated into the "constructed whole." Part of this constructive process involves an ongoing self-monitoring or metacognitive process which brings reading to a halt if the reader cannot make sense of the text, and initiates fix-up strategies to regain meaning.

Research on Metacognition

Research suggests that proficient readers have their own highly developed monitoring strategies. When a "triggering event" occurs, the reader becomes aware of comprehension difficulty. Resulting comprehension strategies become planned and conscious (Brown, 1980). A triggering event may consist of any aspect of the text which causes the reader to attend more closely, such as unfamiliar concepts or information which seems inconsistent with either the preceding text or the reader's knowledge base. At this point, the reader uses deliberate problem solving or fix-up strategies such as slowing down, rereading, consciously deciding to continue hoping the meaning will be clarified in the succeeding text, or even rejecting the text as too difficult. Sometimes these strategies include comparing one's own interpretation with those of friends, teachers, or even other authors.

These self-monitoring processes are currently referred to as metacognitive processes (Brown, 1977, 1980; Brown & DeLoache, 1977; Flavell, 1976). Specifically, metacomprehension (the act of monitoring and thinking about how one's own comprehension process is occurring and instituting necessary fix-up strategies) is of particular concern in this article.

Implications for instruction. Current research on the development of comprehension, self-monitoring, and fix-up strategies has important implications for instruction. First, it seems to indicate that elementary children need to experience activities which will help them build an expectation of actively reading for meaning. Monitoring for inadequate information, inconsistencies, false statements, and confusion is an integral part of reading—a skill which must be learned. Students need to develop a repertoire of comprehension, monitoring, and fix-up strategies and the knowledge and awareness of why, how and when to use them. Another implication is that children need to move from external to internal control of comprehension and metacomprehension strategies dealing with explicit and implicit text features. The progression from teacher demonstrations or modeling to concrete experiences grounded in action and then to mental manipulation of text ideas is important. A final point seems to be the need of initially embedding the learning of comprehension and metacomprehension strategies in a familiar, meaningful context in which the strategy being learned is a

Smith-Burke

functional tool, used to accomplish a broader purpose. In this case, the challenge for teachers is to structure classroom environments and language activities so that students must read and write for broader meaningful purposes.

Classrooms for Independent Comprehension

In *How Children Fail*, John Holt (1964) pointed out that many of the children in his school did not realize they did not understand what they had read until they were asked to explain or utilize the information. He poignantly describes the students who felt that "not comprehending" at any level was a form of failure and therefore needed to be hidden or avoided at all cost. Students also felt pressure to produce "*the* correct answer" the teacher wanted.

The irony is that risk-taking—the risk of being different—is necessary to develop and exercise effective comprehension and self-monitoring strategies. Only when students realize what they do not understand, can they begin to generate strategies to extend their own comprehension, and to see the importance of both external monitoring and self-monitoring as they read.

The creation of classroom environments in which students read for meaningful purposes, freely discuss their interpretations and conclusions, risk differing with others, and reflect on how they read is critically important. This is particularly true in subject matter classes, since a portion of the material to be covered in the textbook is, by definition, unfamiliar because it is new. This new content may be the source of comprehension difficulties, particularly when the author has assumed too much knowledge on the part of student readers.

Instruction must focus on helping students become active comprehenders, assuming responsibility for monitoring their own comprehension, and solving comprehension problems when they arise. It must be offered in an environment which will facilitate the development of independent comprehension.

Developing Comprehension and Metacomprehension Strategies: A Review of Techniques

The concept of being an active comprehender in reading, evaluating, monitoring, reinterpreting, and applying information is not new. It dates back to the work of William S. Gray (1919) and Robert Thorndike (1917). However, the parallels with current work in this area are striking. Many teaching techniques developed over the years stress comprehension, self-monitoring, and fix-up strategies. In this section, a selective review will be presented of existing practices which foster the development of these strategies. Then the new instructional sequence, ECOLA, will be described and illustrated with a case study.

One of the oldest, well known reading techniques consistent with the development of active comprehension is the Directed Reading-Thinking Activity (DR-TA; Stauffer, 1969, 1976). Stauffer created this technique to promote active readers who question, think about, and learn from what they read. The first phase of the DR-TA, which includes predicting or defining purposes, reading, and proving, fosters these abilities. Stauffer sees the role of the teacher as that of a facilitator, organizing groups for different projects, pacing activities, promoting thinking and learning through discussion and creative activities. When carried out in its original form, DR-TA helps students learn to set purposes for reading which emanate from different materials, actively predict and question what is read and think about and apply ideas. The teacher helps students become aware of their reading-thinking processes.

Herber's comprehension and reasoning guides (1978) are designed to help students 1) interact with explicit and implicit ideas in the text and 2) relate these ideas to other concepts. These objectives are accomplished through the use of teacher prepared statements to which students must respond. A major strength in this approach is that students interact with one another in small groups, as they complete the guides. Students are expected to support their interpretations with data from the text, other experiences, or reading. Often to explore differences of opinion, students must reread and/or reason with information from the text. These guides provide a nonthreatening structure in which students can take risks and receive feedback from each other. Working in groups deemphasizes the idea of *one* correct answer. Also, students who have less difficulty completing the guides serve as models for others, since they must explain how and why they arrived at their interpretations. The teacher carefully leads the students to realize that information needed to complete the guides is

Smith-Burke

sometimes explicitly stated in the text and sometimes it is implicit. During these lessons the teacher functions as a co-learner modeling the interpreting, clarifying and challenging behaviors which the students are learning.

Manzo's "Request Procedure" (1969) also seems to stress the development of active comprehension and metacomprehension strategies. After reading a selection the teacher and students take turns asking and answering each other's questions. The purpose of this technique is to stimulate an active attitude toward reading and to help students learn to acquire reasonable purposes for reading. The teacher in this case functions as a role model for the students. Another similar but more limited technique is the self-questioning technique, recently developed by T.H. Anderson (1978). In this method, students are taught to formulate integrative questions before reading (such as the main idea of a section). They are given feedback by the teacher who models the questioning when necessary. So far this technique has primarily been used in research situations. However, the results are promising, particularly for the slower students.

Another relatively new technique is Childrey's "Torn to Pieces: Reading a Book in an Hour" (1979). A class is divided into groups, and each group reads one chapter of a book. Then, as a class, the students reconstruct the story. It would seem that by adding careful teacher questioning to this technique, students would both experience and become aware of the constructive nature of the comprehension process. Students who read later chapters would become quite aware of missing or confusing information and must turn to their peers much in the same way that one might have to reread or continue on for clarification. With careful teacher guidance, pointing out analogies, students could learn a lot about comprehension and monitoring strategies as well as enjoy a good story.

In *Reading Strategies: Focus on Comprehension* Goodman and Burke (1980) stress the need to read for meaning, predicting, confirming, or self-correcting when meaning or a sense of syntactic acceptability is violated. By manipulating or selecting certain text characteristics, teachers force students to encounter certain difficulties and to solve problems.

The Language Experience Approach (LEA) is another technique which promotes awareness of the purposes for reading and writing. Allen designed the process of using young children's dictations as their reading material in order to help them realize that what they think can be verbalized orally, and what they verbalize can be written down and read (Lee & Allen, 1963). From their own experiences comes the realization that other people communicate through the printed word which can be read. This technique has been developed and modified by others. Ashton-Warner (1963) used key words stories to teach Maori children, while Stauffer (1970) stressed dictated stories, word banks, and creative writing. Although LEA was designed primarily for use with beginning readers, there are some important concepts in the rationale which have been used in the design of ECOLA.

Extending Concepts through Language Activities

A sequence of activities called Extending Concepts through Language Activities (ECOLA) recently has been developed. It is designed for use in content area classrooms and is based on insights drawn from the research on comprehension and meta-comprehension and an extension of the rationale which underlies LEA. Like LEA all of the language arts (speaking, listening, reading, and writing) are utilized to help students become independent comprehenders.

Initially there are five steps. Some of them may be phased out as students begin to take responsibility for their own comprehension and can selectively use appropriate strategies as criterion tasks and purposes dictate. The steps are 1) setting a communication purpose for reading, 2) silent reading for a purpose and criterion task, 3) crystalizing an interpretation through writing, 4) discussing and clarifying interpretations, and 5) writing and comparing.

Rationale of ECOLA and a case study. In this section, the rationale for each of the five steps of ECOLA will be described and then illustrated with a sample lesson taught to tenth and eleventh graders in an English class (Note 1). Ms. Johnson was teaching a unit on character development and had chosen a short story, "Waiting for Her Train" by Audrey Lee (Note 2). The story is about a day in the life of a woman who had once had a modest income and social position but had become destitute and lonely, forced to live on benches in the train station in Philadelphia. As the episode unfolds, the author uses typical daily incidents to depict the woman's struggle to maintain her pride and sense of self.

Johnson had selected this story because of the vivid images and explicit details which delineate the main character. Also, because her adolescent students were engaged in their own struggle to maintain a sense of self, she hoped they would find Lee's message meaningful. Johnson wished to accomplish several teaching objectives. First, she hoped that students would relate to the human need to maintain a sense of self. She also wanted them to realize that one can vicariously try on life's experiences and emotions through literature. Finally, she planned to help them see how two different authors created their characters by having them compare two story characters and write about a significant person in their own lives.

Step 1. Setting a communication purpose. A purpose for reading needs to be set in relation to the larger context of communication, answering the question, "Why should the reader read this particular piece?" Integrally related is the same question from the author's perspective, "Why did the author write this work?" A communication purpose is not a skill, it is based on a communication need to receive a message from another person. Are students reading to understand and learn, to relax and enjoy a story, or to perform necessary functional tasks?

The communication purpose must be meaningful to students so that reading becomes the necessary tool to receive an important message. Since content materials are usually selected by the teacher, students must learn how the communication purpose emanates from the discipline and the materials. The teacher must lead the students to understand what it means to be a historian, English scholar, mathematician, sociologist, or scientist and how each discipline requires different communication purposes. At first, the teacher models and explains why she/he has set certain purposes. Eventually, the responsibility for setting the purpose is transferred to the students.

Communication purpose setting is influenced by the criterion tasks for the lesson and for the unit. These tasks also influence the reading strategies students must employ. The criterion tasks should be blatantly clear so there are no hidden agendas. Do students have to recognize, recall, or apply the ideas from their readings? The type of criterion or assessment task for learning affects how one must read a passage. With the help of the teacher, students can discuss how effective their purpose setting and reading strategies have been relative to the criterion tasks. Provision for discussion of alternate purposes and/or strategies should be made for occasions on which students fail to succeed on criterion tasks due to either an inappropriate selection of purpose or strategies.

Asking students to read in order to communicate with the author is reminiscent of LEA. Language is written to communicate ideas to others in a more permanent form. The reader interprets the message, trying to reconstruct the original message. However, there is no guarantee the message the author intended will ever be communicated to the reader because of the interactive nature of reading comprehension.

To prepare for a lesson, teachers need to be aware of the types of strategies which may be required by a particular text and/or criterion task. With this awareness, teachers can more effectively elicit and raise to awareness the use of these strategies when students discuss their interpretations and how they arrived at them. By carefully selecting materials, teachers can create a need to read for certain purposes and to utilize certain strategies.

In the lesson on "Waiting for Her Train" Johnson briefly summarized the story for her class and then involved the students in a discussion to set a clear purpose for reading. She asked the following questions:

> Why do authors write about one or two characters?
> What are they trying to tell their readers?
> Has anyone read a story which is primarily about one character?
> How did this character relate to your life?
> How did you feel about the story and the character?
> What might readers gain from reading about a character who is similar to or different from themselves?

As a result of class discussion, the students concluded that they wanted to understand how and why the lady in the story was living this kind of life and how the title related to her life. Johnson added that she would like them to compare how the woman felt about herself to how they felt about themselves.

In leading the students to the purposes of understanding the character's motivations, and the reason for the title and the comparison of the character with their own lives, Johnson had helped them see, at least in part, the role literature can play through vicarious experience, and the role of the author in titling a story.

At this point in the lesson, the teacher explained that they would be reading another story which centered around another main character. The final project (criterion task for the unit) would involve comparing the two characters to each other and to the students' own lives.

Step 2. Silent reading for a purpose and a criterion task. In assigning silent reading, teachers need to remind students of the purposes for which they are reading. By having a clear idea of what the teacher expects, students have a basis for comprehending, self-monitoring, and self-correction, if necessary. Students also are prepared for the next step in ECOLA which is writing their interpretation of the text relative to the purpose. It is important for the teacher to discuss the need for students to clarify and support their interpretations with data from the text, background knowledge, or reasoning.

Johnson asked the following questions to help the students think about how they would read the story. She put them in small groups to discuss the questions.

What information helps you determine why someone does something?

Will everyone agree on the character's reasons for her lifestyle? Why or why not?

What causes the agreement or disagreement?

When you write a story, how do you decide on a title?

Johnson brought the groups together for class discussion. She used an example of a high school student who wouldn't talk to her best friend to elicit all the possible motivations of why this situation might occur. The students offered many explanations, from having a fight with her best friend to the news that the girl's parents were getting divorced.

From the example, Johnson had the perfect opportunity to point out the constructive nature of the comprehension process and how inferences are built from explicit information in the text *and* background knowledge which this information cues. Next, they considered the two questions posed earlier and the reasons why students had come up with different interpretations due to the diversity of background experience and knowledge. In assigning the story, Johnson asked the class to note the details from the story and the background experiences they were using to draw their conclusions about the main character and the title.

Step 3. Crystalizing comprehension through writing. During this step each student and the teacher write about what they have read in relation to the established purpose. The rationale for this step comes from LEA. By writing down thoughts people are forced to commit themselves to an interpretation. To write with a purpose in mind may also give some insight into the demands of expressing ideas from the writer's perspective. Since revealing one's inner thoughts is a risk-taking situation, it is critical to assure the students that these written interpretations are for their eyes alone, unless they choose to share them. Students should also be encouraged to define and write about anything that is confusing. They should be urged to pose questions to the others in class in order to restore clarity. The purpose of this aspect of Step 3 is to direct students to monitor their own comprehension and begin to learn how to define and verbalize what they don't understand in a nonthreatening environment. This monitoring is a necessary prerequisite for knowing which fix-up strategies to use and when to use them. Often when a problem arises, a first strategy is to ask someone else. In ECOLA when a proficient student answers one of these student generated questions (see next step), it is important for that person to explain how she/he constructed the answer from the text—which strategies were used. In this way, not only has a possible comprehension or fix-up strategy been described for the confused student but also when to use the strategy has been clarified. As students are exposed to more strategies, they no longer are forced to turn to others for assistance but have their own inner resources.

Johnson divided the class and half wrote about how and why the lady in "Waiting for Her Train" lived such a lonely life with a facade of respectability and the other half wrote about why the title had been chosen. The teacher joined the latter group and functioned as a cowriter. Everybody related to their lives what they understood about the woman's sense of self.

Step 4. Discussing the lesson. At first it is usually best to let students share their interpretations in small groups of no more than four. This is less threatening and allows for plenty of interaction for each student. Clear directions are essential to make sure everybody explains what led them to their conclusions. Sometimes students prefer to read what they have written to their peers. They may also raise questions about confusing parts of a story. The goals of a group meeting are to understand and discuss each person's interpretation, challenge unclear conclusions which lack support, and note similarities and differences in the interpretations. A time limit must be set for the discussion or it is apt to run on and lack focus.

In one group of four students who were considering the reason for the title, four different perspectives emerged. Steven rather literally assumed the lady was actually waiting for a train because she didn't know where she wanted to go. He added that she wanted to leave the city. Elizabeth challenged that because the lady was so poor, she could never afford a ticket. She cited as evidence the incidents in which the woman had to shoplift and use sample cosmetics. She reasoned that the woman was fooling herself to think she could take a train. Steven realized, as Elizabeth spoke, that maybe this was why the author said she had not decided on her destination.

Barbara stated that she thought the lady was waiting to meet someone coming in on a train to see her. She based her conclusion on the phrase in the story that "she was waiting for her train to come in" and her own experience of waiting for her father's commuter train.

The other students agreed that this might be a possible interpretation but unlikely since the author never mentions another person nor develops this line of thinking. Elizabeth pointed out that the woman seemed very lonely. Everyone concurred.

Brian, a quiet student, commented that maybe the woman had to believe she was waiting for a train to keep her self-respect and her dreams alive. At this point, Barbara excitedly added that was why the author used "Waiting for Her Train" as the title—that the train represented all the possible good things which could happen to her, all the things she wished would happen. Brian continued stating that he thought the lady was very proud and was fighting to keep her pride. He pointed to several incidents in the story as evidence: when she looked down on the vagrant bag lady, when she pretended to shop for food and cosmetics, and when she pretended to buy breakfast at a restaurant. With a puzzled expression, Steven asked the group why the lady was waiting in the station again. He paused thoughtfully and said, as if to convince himself, that maybe she was waiting for someone. At this point, Elizabeth attempted to explain that maybe the woman had nowhere else to go because she was so poor. She hypothesized that maybe the woman lived in the train station. She pointed out that the fact that the author seemed to be describing a daily routine led her to this conclusion. Steven replied it was "kind of sad" that the story was called "Waiting for Her Train" since the lady would probably never change or go anywhere. This comment evoked a lively discussion about whether the lady eventually would or could change.

As students shared interpretations, their ideas changed. Varied background experiences were elicited when they concentrated on different parts of the story. Steven initially was very literal, while Barbara went far beyond the text. Elizabeth and Brian were able to effectively integrate information with background knowledge. From their comments, Barbara was able to form a reason for the title, the purpose for which they were reading. Even Steven eventually saw the irony of the title.

Step 5. Writing and comparing: Before and after. The final step in ECOLA is to have the students, in small groups or individually, write a second interpretation of the text. If done in a group, this activity is similar to writing a group language experience chart. It is very important to allow any individual who prefers to write individually to do so. Initially, students usually find writing together more enjoyable and less threatening. The group setting allows for discussion and resolution of confusing parts of the story. Before making this assignment it is important to review the purposes for which they were reading and the criterion tasks. After the students have completed their second interpretation, through the use of careful questioning and comparison of first and second drafts, the teacher can lead the students to see the constructive, changing nature of comprehension and the relative effectiveness of strategies they used.

The teacher assigned Step 5 as a small group writing project. Barbara, Steven, Elizabeth, and Brian were able to combine their insights into a new written interpretation about the reason for the title. After this task, the teacher asked the students to discuss the following questions in their groups:

How were their first essays similar or different from the group version?

What had led each of them to reinterpret the text? Were there any parts of the new version that they still didn't quite agree with?

What strategies were used to show that certain points were valid, others invalid? What criteria were used to establish validity?

Why can there never be one definitive interpretation of a text?

Two of the four students had changed their interpretations of the text substantially. Steven realized he needed to read beyond the words on the page. He still was not convinced the lady lived in the train station and felt justified since the author never explicitly said this. Barbara expressed a need to focus more closely on the text. She said that listening to the others had helped her consider things she had not thought of before and forced her to reread.

ECOLA is a very detailed process and should not be used on every lesson. Also, after experience with all the steps, in groups, assignments can be made on an individual instead of a group basis. Eventually, lessons can be planned which do not require all steps. The teacher will have to lead students to this conclusion through careful questioning about strategies relative to purpose and criterion task. For example, sometimes the writing steps can be phased out. Finally the decisions of how to read and monitor relative to purpose are left entirely up to the students. The teacher is still responsible for discussions, giving feedback and modeling for students who are not succeeding in comprehending the materials. Particularly for these students, the integration of reading, writing, and discussion with others in ECOLA focuses students on the constructive nature of reading and the need to monitor to be sure the interpretation one constructs makes sense. In the words of Bartholomae and Petrosky (Note 3):

When students focus their attention on their own attempts to elaborate meaning in prose, they come better to understand the conventions governing such elaboration in ways that can make them better readers. They learn how to raise questions, see problems, infer intentions, and predict the direction a discussion might take. When students focus their attention on their experience as readers and on the concept of a reader's response, they learn to see their essays as texts (written interpretation)—an important lesson about writing. "Meaning," as Shaughnessy (1977, p. 223) argues, "resides not in the page nor in the reader but in the encounter between the two."

It is when this encounter occurs actively and thoughtfully that students can be called independent comprehenders.

Reference Notes

Note 1.   Based on a discussion which was part of the course *Content Area Teaching: Reading Problems and Strategies* on Sunrise Semester, CBS-TV, shown in Spring 1979.
Note 2.   The original version of *Waiting for Her Train* was sent to the author by Audrey Lee. A shortened version is included in the *Tactics* series published by Scott, Foresman.
Note 3.   Bartholomae, D., and Petrosky, A. Facts, artifacts, and counterfacts: A basic reading and writing course for the college curriculum. A paper in preparation at the University of Pittsburgh.

References

ANDERSON, R.C. The notion of schemata and the educational enterprise: General discussion of the conference. In R.C. Anderson, R.J. Spiro, & W.E. Montague (Eds.), *Schooling and the acquisition of knowledge.* Hillsdale, New Jersey: Erlbaum, 1977.
ANDERSON, T.H. *Another look at the self-questioning study techniques* (Reading Education Report No. 6). Champaign, Illinois: Center for the Study of Reading, 1978. (ED 163 441)
ANDERSON, R.C., REYNOLDS, R.E., SCHALLERT, D.L., & GOETZ, E.T. Frameworks for comprehending discourse. *American Educational Research Journal,* 1977, *14* (4), 367–382.
APPLEBEE, A.N. *The child's concept of story.* Chicago: University of Chicago Press, 1978.
ASHTON-WARNER, S. *Teacher.* New York: Simon and Schuster, 1963.
BROWN, A.L. *Knowing when, where, and how to remember: A problem of metacognition* (Technical Report No. 47). University of Illinois at Urbana-Champaign, July 1977. (ED 146 562)
BROWN, A.L. Metacognitive development and reading. In R.L. Spiro, B. Bruce, & W.F. Brewer (Eds.), *Theoretical issues in reading comprehension.* Hillsdale, New Jersey: Erlbaum, 1980.
BROWN, A.L., & DELOACHE, J.S. *Skills, plans, and self-regulation* (Technical Report No. 48). University of Illinois at Urbana-Champaign, July 1977. (ED 144 040)

BRUCE, B., & NEWMAN, D. *Interacting plans* (Technical Report No. 88). Cambridge, Massachusetts: Bolt, Beranek and Newman, 1978. (ED 157 038)

CHILDREY, J. Torn to pieces: Reading a book in an hour. In M.T. Smith-Burke (Ed.), *Newsletter, No. 3,* Sunrise Semester. New York: New York University, 1979.

FLAVELL, J.H. Metacognitive aspects of problem solving. In L. B. Resnick (Ed.), *The nature of intelligence.* Hillsdale, New Jersey: Erlbaum, 1976.

FLOWER, L.S., & HAYES, J.R. Problem solving strategies and the writing process. *College English,* 1977, *39* (4), 449–461.

GOODMAN, K. Reading: A psycholinguistic guessing game. In H. Singer & R.B. Ruddell (Eds.), *Theoretical models and processes of reading.* Newark, Delaware: International Reading Association, 1970.

GOODMAN, Y., & BURKE, C. *Reading strategies: Focus on comprehension.* New York: Holt, Rinehart & Winston, 1980.

GRAY, W.S. Principles of method in teaching reading as derived from scientific investigations. *National Society for the Study of Education yearbook, 18,* part 2. Bloomington, Illinois: Public School Book Company, 1919.

GRICE, H.P. Logic and conversation. In P. Cole & J.L. Morgan (Eds.), *Studies in syntax* (Volume 3). New York: Academic Press, 1975.

HARSTE, J.C., & CAREY, R.F. Comprehension as setting. In R.F. Carey & J.C. Harste (Eds.), *New perspectives on comprehension,* monograph in language and reading series. Bloomington: Indiana University Press, 1979.

HERBER, H. *Teaching reading in the content areas* (2nd ed.). Englewood Cliffs, New Jersey: Prentice-Hall, 1978.

HOLT, J.H. *How children fail.* New York: Dell, 1964.

MANZO, A.V. The ReQuest procedure. *Journal of Reading,* 1969, *13,* 123–126.

MEYER, B.J.F. *The organization of prose and its effect on memory.* New York: North Holland American Elsevier, 1975.

SHAUGHNESSY, M. *Errors and expectations.* New York: Oxford University Press, 1977.

STAUFFER, R.G. *Teaching reading as a thinking process.* New York: Harper & Row, 1976.

STAUFFER, R.G. *The language experience approach to the teaching of reading.* New York: Harper & Row, 1970.

STAUFFER, R.G. *Directing reading maturity as a cognitive process.* New York: Harper & Row, 1969.

THORNDIKE, E.L. Reading as reasoning. A study of mistakes in paragraph reading. *Journal of Educational Psychology,* 1917, *8,* 323–332.

Comprehending Narrative Discourse: Implications for Instruction

Lenore H. Ringler
New York University
Carol K. Weber
York College
City University of New York

Comprehension of narrative discourse is initiated with the first story ever read to a young child and continues as the developing child listens to and then reads increasingly more complex materials. To comprehend, the child must infer the author's message by using the child's own available language knowledge sources. As the author and the listener/reader are active participants in constructing meaning, it is essential that teachers be cognizant of both characteristics of listeners/readers and characteristics of the author's written text. That is, teacher knowledge of both of these factors is crucial to understanding observed reader-text interactions. While characteristics of readers vary, depending upon their conceptual knowledge and experiential background, language, and affective base, written material has permanence. It is this permanence that allows the teacher to analyze a selected text and use the information gained from text analysis as a base for working with a variety of readers. This knowledge base provides a guide for planning teaching strategies to facilitate the interaction between author and reader.

Recent theoretical work on text analysis can be useful to teachers as they attempt to understand the interaction of reader and author. Researchers are studying the ways in which reader knowledge interacts with text characteristics and this analysis is presently taking many forms. Text is being studied through the analysis of semantic structures and logical relations between ideas at the propositional and passage levels (Frederiksen, 1975a, 1975b, in press; Kintsch, 1974; Kintsch & van Dijk,

1978; Meyer 1975; van Dijk, 1977). Another approach involves the formulation of story grammars which are assumed to be representations of readers' schemata for story structures and organizations (Mandler & Johnson, 1977; Rumelhart, 1975; Stein & Glenn, 1979; Thorndyke, 1977). Other researchers have focused on the importance of drawing inferences to comprehending written discourse (Schank, 1975; Clark & Haviland, 1976). Recently, Warren, Nicholas, and Trabasso (1979) developed a set of categories to describe the requisite inferences to understand event chains which formulate story relations available to readers in text rather than presuming to model the readers' story schemata.[Note 1].

While all of this work is theoretically important, at this time direct application for instructional purposes is limited. There is no empirical evidence to support instructional programs or the construction of materials based on any one method of text analysis. Rather, at this point in our knowledge, insights gained from the theoretical work in this area can increase teacher understanding of the demands of texts on readers. They can also serve as a basis for guiding teacher observation, as readers interact with text as well as when teachers and readers interact after a text has been read. Thus, teacher analysis of texts should not be limited to the work of any one theorist. Rather, analysis should sample from the many different approaches to text analysis to develop sensitivity to the variations inherent in readers and in texts.

In planning a lesson, teachers need to consider both the material to be read and the background of the reader. The level of the material cannot be determined solely by publisher designations which are based on traditional readability formulas, as these formulas are limited. Neither semantic properties of the text, nor background knowledge and experience of the reader are adequately weighted in these formulas. Rather, teachers need to be aware that texts of varying levels of difficulty can be selected for the same reader as the quality of interaction will differ in different reading situations (Weber, 1979).

Examination of text involves an analysis of the characteristics of the selected text and careful study of questions provided by the author. Preparation of additional structured questions may also be needed. In analyzing the characteristics of the text, the teacher notes the type of text, the author's view of audience, the author's background, and the author's purpose. Further, the teacher focuses on the organizational structure and the language used by the author to construct the message. Through this analysis the teacher may become aware of information that is *explicitly* stated by the author (which the reader may gain from the text) and information that is *implied* by the author (which the reader must supply or infer). This teacher knowledge is an important base for understanding reader responses as they interact with text.

Texts may evoke responses that directly replicate the information presented in text, or the reader may apply prior knowledge and background experiences to infer relations among ideas and bring needed information to the text. In addition, the text may evoke other responses that are unique but appropriate, based on the prior knowledge of the reader as the reader expands upon the text. Additional responses to the text may involve judgments in regard to "the goodness, suitability, or workability" (Guilford, 1959, p. 476) of materials read. This form of higher level thinking, in which the reader either spontaneously or through specific questioning evaluates text, is often referred to as critical thinking. It involves reader reaction to what is read.

Replicative responses are only a minor part of processing text; the major part of constructing meaning from text is inferencing. Therefore, teacher analysis of text requires consideration of some of the types of inferences needed to construct meaning from text. The work of Warren, Nicholas, and Trabasso (1979) provides one taxonomy for text analysis in which they distinguish among three general categories of inferences: logical inferences, informational inferences, and value inferences. This taxonomy provided a base for developing a framework in which the characteristics generally associated with story type text could be related to specific inferences required for understanding narrative text. Viewing inferences within this framework provides a flexible guide from which teachers can analyze narrative text.

The relations between the categories of inferences and story characteristics will be illustrated initially by considering the three types of inferences implicit in characterization and plot (Warren, Nicholas, Trabasso, 1979).

Ringler and Weber

In characterization, authors present characters through behavior attitudes, feelings, thoughts, language, and the reaction of others toward them. Some techniques an author may use to describe a character include 1) telling about the character, 2) describing the character and surroundings, 3) showing the character in action, 4) letting the character talk, 5) revealing the character's thoughts, 6) showing what others say to the character, 7) showing what others say about the character, 8) showing the reactions of others to the character, and 9) showing the character's reaction to others (Hook, 1963).

Understanding characterization is dependent primarily upon the construction of two of the specific types of inferences within the general category of logical inferences—motivational and psychological causation. Generally, logical inferences include causes and conditions under which characters behave and events occur. Motivational inferences include inferring the reasons for a character's voluntary thoughts, actions or goals or reciprocally predicting thoughts, actions or goals based upon stated causes. On the other hand, psychological causation includes inferring the reasons for involuntary behavior, attitudes, feelings, or thoughts of a character.

Plot development is most closely related to two other subcategories of logical inferences: physical causation and enabling inferences. In plot development, the significant actions or related events unfold in a specific order and lead to a story outcome. That is, plot usually involves a developing problem (conflict), climax, and the conflict solution in which efforts of the protagonist(s) lead to a resolution of the problem. Physical causation involves inferences about the mechanical or nonhuman reasons for the unfolding of actions or events in a story. Enabling inferences determine the physical or environmental conditions that are necessary but not sufficient for an event to occur.

The logical inferences required to understand characterization and plot can be elicited by "how" and "why" questioning which is either reader generated or, if necessary, teacher imposed. Characterization and plot may also involve the second category of inferences, informational inferences. This second source involves the specific people, instruments, objects, times, places, and contexts of events, and are made in answer to the questions, Who? What? When? and Where? These inferences yield details and add elaborative information about the characters or situations which may not be required for comprehension.

Informational inferences are also involved in understanding setting and mood. Setting includes the place, time, customs, and practices of people as revealed through the language of the characters, character descriptions, and the accompanying illustrations. Mood refers to the impression created by the setting, atmosphere, situation, and language. Spatial and temporal inferences, which are additional subcategories of informational inferences, are used to locate a specific event or series of events in place and time and determine their duration. Familiarity with events similar to those in the story would provide a context of place or general activity leading to further understanding of story events.

The last category of inferences, value inferences, involves intentions of the author, judgments about the thoughts and actions of the characters, and concern for the validity of the events of the story. Thus, this category of inferences is involved in reacting critically to all of the story characteristics inherent in narrative text. These inferences are based on the reader's value system, prior knowledge of similar situations, and general knowledge of literature. For example, construction of evaluative inferences is prerequisite to understanding story theme, style, and genre. The theme of the story reflects the author's intentions, while the structure and organization reflect the author's style and use of genre. More specifically, theme may be described as a generalization about people and/or the world that emerges from the story. Theme reveals the significance of the actions and is consistent with the plot and characters. The type of story and the point of view or perspective from which the action is observed, is generally referred to as style and genre. In developing a point of view, an author may serve as a narrator in two ways: as participant or as observer. Authors who use the third person "stand outside" of the narrative and look at the characters and situations. Some authors shift the point of view from the first person to third person as different events in the story occur. It is in this last category of inferences that the reader applies evaluative judgments to react to story content and structure.

Figure 1 summarizes the major relations between the categories of inferences and story characteristics.

Inference Taxonomy	Story Characteristics
Logical Inferences	Characterization
	Plot
Informational Inferences	Characterization
	Plot
	Setting and Mood
Value Inferences	Characterization
	Plot
	Theme
	Style and Genre

Figure 1. Summary of illustrative relations between categories of inferences and story characteristics.

As noted, the categories of inferences and related story characteristics are a suggested framework for examining narrative discourse and for analyzing readers' spontaneous responses to text and readers' responses to more structured questioning.

Following the selection and analysis of appropriate text, the teacher is ready to observe the reader as text is comprehended. Observation of this interaction between reader and text should occur initially without interference from the teacher. This procedure is suggested as discourse recall is natural for children and does not necessarily bias a learner to process text in a particular way. It provides the teacher with information about how the learner is constructing meaning from text without external influence (Frederiksen, in press). For this purpose, reader's preliminary responses to the reading of written discourse should be based on the reader's free recall of silently read text. This free recall of text is initiated with questions like:

— Tell me what you have read using your own words.
— What is this story all about?
— Tell me as much information as you can about what you have just read.

As noted, reader response to such questions is not interrupted by the teacher until the reader has completed responding. In this way, the reader expresses what has been reconstructed during reading without any external cuing, thus providing the teacher with initial insight into how the reader processed the text.

Following free recall, *probe questions* are used to elicit further recall of text. These questions *minimally cue* the reader to recall additional information, thus adding to the teacher's understanding of reader-text interaction. This technique has been found to elicit additional meaning from both good and poor readers (Tierney, Bridge, & Cera, 1977). Probe questions are constructed by the teacher immediately following recall and are *based directly on the recall.* Examples of the probe questions are:

—Tell me more about what you have read.
—Tell me more about what happened.
—Tell me more about the people that you just read about.
—Tell me more about where this happened.

More specific reference to the text may be included in probe questions to extend the information included by the reader in free recall.

In addition to free recall and probe questions the teacher may also use author constructed questions if available, teacher constructed questions, or a combination of both. Since structured questions impose the author's or teacher's view of what is important in the text, it is necessary to avoid use of structured questions until all possible information has been elicited during free recall and probe. In this way the teacher is able to distinguish between that information generated freely, information elicited with minimal cuing, and information generated through direct cuing. At times when a reader demonstrates sufficient depth of inferencing through freely recalling text information and by responding to nondirective or very general probe-type questions, teacher imposed structure questions are not required.

Reader responses during free recall, probe recall, and structured questioning are examined with reference both to the passage and to the reader in order to understand how the reader reconstructed the author's message(s). As previously described, reader responses may be based on information that is directly stated in the text or the reader may infer relationships based on textually given information. In addition, the teacher may observe other responses that are idiosyncratic but relevant, based upon the previous experiences and knowledge of the reader as it relates to the information in the text. Teacher understanding of the depth and scope of reader processing of text is dependent upon integrating the knowledge obtained from reader-text interaction within the framework of the demands of the text and purposes for reading.

To illustrate some aspects of text selection, text analysis and reader-text interaction a first-grade story has been chosen. The selected story comes from folklore and is a fable which has been transmitted from generation to generation through the tradition of story telling and has been transcribed into written form. This type of story evolved as people tried to socialize children into their culture's value system. The particular fable selected uses talking animals to point up a moral which is directly stated at the end.

The selection of this story implies reader knowledge of some of the characteristics of turtles, ducks, and geese. Knowledge of the physical attributes and habits of each character, and the relatedness of ducks and geese, are crucial to understanding this story. If such knowledge is not part of the prior background and experience of the reader, the teacher would need to build the necessary concepts prior to reader-text interaction, so that the reader would be more likely to infer relevant information.

Following selection of the story and analysis of important background concepts, the teacher analyzes the text to note specific story characteristics and related inferences that may be recalled by the reader. For this story, the following are characteristics that would be noted:

Style and Genre

Fable told by the author using the third person point of view in which animals take on human characteristics.

Characterization

Turtle—likes to splash and swim in pond; likes to talk to his friends; does not want to live alone; is unable to keep quiet when necessary.

Too Much Talk
A Jataka Tale

Turtle lived in a small pond.
He liked to splash.
He liked to swim.

"We will carry you," said Goose.
"Just hold onto this stick with
 your mouth."

"You must hold on tightly," said Duck.
"You can't talk when we fly."

Turtle wanted to go very much.
So he said, "I won't talk."

Goose took hold of one end of the stick.
Duck took hold of the other end.
Turtle took hold of the middle.
Then the three went up.

Soon Turtle looked down.
He saw a big lake.

Goose and Duck—are good friends and are friends of
the turtle; want to move to a new pond; help turtle to go with
them; leave turtle to live alone in a new home.

Plot

Turtle, Duck, and Goose were friends. Turtle was happy in
his home when Duck and Goose decide to move to a new home
over the mountain. Turtle wants to go with them but he cannot

"Let's stop here," said Turtle.

Down went Turtle.
He landed in the lake.
Duck and Goose just flew on.

Turtle had a new home.
But he had lost two friends.
Turtle had learned a lesson.

**Sometimes even a little talk
is too much.**

From Scott, Foresman Basics in Reading, *Calico Caper* by Ira E. Aaron
et al. Copyright © 1978, Scott, Foresman and Company. Reprinted by
permission.

fly. Duck and Goose decide to carry Turtle on a stick so he
can go with them. Turtle has to hold onto the stick with his
mouth and therefore cannot talk. Turtle talks as they are flying
over a lake, falls, and lands in the water. Turtle has a new home
but loses his friends.

Setting and Mood

A country area with mountains, ponds, and lakes. The
mood changes from happy to sad as the plot develops.

Theme

Sometimes even a little talk is too much.

To illustrate some of the inferences required to construct meaning from this text the first fourteen propositional units will be analyzed as suggested by the work on event chains (Warren et al., 1979). In this type of analysis each proposition is an event that often contains one predicate relation.

1. Turtle lived in a small pond.
2. He liked to splash.
3. He liked to swim.
4. Best of all, Turtle liked talking to his friends.
5. One friend was Duck.
6. The other friend was Goose.
7. One day Goose said, "There is a little pond over the mountain.
8. Duck and I want to live there."
9. "Please don't leave," said Turtle.
10. "Goose wishes you could go
11. and I do too," said Duck.
12. "But I can't go," said Turtle,
13. "You will be flying.
14. I don't have wings."

As only part of the text is presented, it is important to recognize the focal event around which these propositions are organized. At this point in plot development, the focal event or moving point in the unfolding narrative is located in proposition eight in which the major character is presented with a problem that needs to be resolved. If reader-text interaction was stopped at this point in the narrative, the reader could make inferences based upon information already presented in the text or could predict events to come based upon past story information and prior knowledge of similar situations.

If, on the other hand, the entire narrative is read without interruption, free recall may be organized around a number of focal events. Inferences in this case could be based on retrospective knowledge of the entire narrative. Dependent upon the reader and the text, it may be facilitative to plan reading experiences around particular focal events rather than have readers process the entire story without reader-teacher interaction.

In examining the propositions listed above, some of the inferences which could be made by the reader are presented in Figure 2 according to major inference category. For each inference, there is noted the specific type of inference, the

	Inference	Specific Type	Proposition	Related Story Characteristic
Logical Inferences	Turtle didn't want to live alone	Motivational	9	Plot
	Turtle became sad	Psychological	8, 9, 12	Characterization Mood
	Turtle couldn't go over the mountains with his friends	Physical	7, 13, 14	Plot
	Duck and Goose had flown over the mountain before	Enabling	7	Plot
Informational Inferences	Duck and Goose wished Turtle could go with them	Pronomial	9, 10, 11	Plot
	Turtle liked to splash and swim in the pond	Referential; Anaphoric relation	1, 2, 3	Characterization
	Turtle, Duck and Goose live in the country	Spatial	1, 7	Setting
Value Inferences	Duck and Goose didn't like Turtle as much as he liked them	Evaluative	8, 9, 10, 11	Characterization

Figure 2. Sample inferences based on "Too Much Talk"

proposition or propositions that it is dependent upon, and the related story characteristic(s).

If the reader does not spontaneously infer important story information during free recall, the teacher may probe to elicit additional inferences or if necessary further cue the reader through the use of structured questions. Examples of structured questions to elicit logical inferences, informational inferences, and value inferences based on the total narrative are presented below. The questions are categorized by story characteristics, and the type of inferences expected in response to the question is noted.

Characterization

Why did Turtle want to go with his friends? (motivational)

How did Turtle feel when Goose and Duck said they wanted to live over the mountain? (psychological)

Why could Goose and Duck fly over the mountain and Turtle couldn't? (physical)

Why does Turtle have to use his mouth to hold onto the stick? (physical)

*Why did Turtle fall into the lake? (physical or psychological)

How did Turtle feel in his new home? (psychological)

What friends did Turtle like to talk to? (referential)

Why do you think Duck and Goose flew on? (evaluative, actions of characters)

Plot

How did Duck and Goose know that there was a little pond over the mountain? (enabling)

*Why did Duck and Goose get a stick? (motivational or physical)

Why did they pick a long stick? (enabling)

Who wants to live over the mountain? (pronomial)

Where did Turtle want to stop? (referential)

When did Turtle get a new home? (temporal)

Ringler and Weber

Setting and Mood

Where do Turtle, Duck and Goose live? (spatial)
Where was Turtle when he saw the lake? (spatial)

Style and Genre

Could this story really have happened? Why? (evaluative, validity of story events)

Theme

What did the author want us to learn from this story? (evaluative, author's intention)

Some questions that most probably would yield more than one relevant response, dependent upon reader-text interaction, are starred. The type of inference that may be elicited by these questions may vary. To illustrate, a reader's response to the question, "Why did Duck and Goose get a stick?" may be, "They wanted to help Turtle go with them," or "Turtle didn't have wings and can't fly with them." Both responses are appropriate; in the first case the reader has made a motivational inference whereas in the second case the reader has made a physical inference.

It is important for teachers to remember that while they may expect a certain response to a particular question, other responses may be just as relevant. The work of Pearson and Johnson (1978) addresses this issue when they discuss the relation between questions and reader responses. This relation between questions and responses is based upon the interaction of the knowledge sources of readers with text. They emphasize that when readers make inferences they either connect textually given information that is not directly related by the author or they create plausible responses that are based on the text but require additional reader-based information. As the reader is an active participant when constructing meaning from print it would be expected that reader responses would differ and that different but relevant responses could be made to the same story.

"Too Much Talk" was analyzed in detail to illustrate one framework that uses narrative discourse analysis as a base for instruction. Implicit in this approach is that reading necessitates active involvement of the reader through self-initiated questioning and self-monitoring of interaction with text. Also implicit is that reader characteristics will guide the teacher in planning for instruction and in choosing what to emphasize when guiding a particular reader-text interaction. For example, dependent upon reader needs the teacher may choose to emphasize only one or two of the characteristics of stories and the related inferences or only one focal event of a story with its related inferences. Readers' spontaneous responses to the selected text and teacher's focus would then determine the amount of structured intervention required. This approach requires that teachers be able to spontaneously modify their planned actions to meet the immediate needs of readers. Thus, individual readers or groups of readers, specific story demands, and teacher focus all guide the teacher in selectively determining the type and amount of external structure to be brought to reader-text interaction.

A reading environment in which readers and teachers have interacted actively with each other and the text means that both readers and teachers will bring expanded and/or restructured knowledge to the next reading experience. That is, every reading experience leaves readers and teachers somewhat changed. As readers' concepts, background knowledge, and interests expand, teacher selection of narrative discourse will expand to include different types of stories with different content and structure. These varied materials may be analyzed by applying the illustrated framework or by using different theoretical perspectives. Recognition that the relations among readers, texts, and teachers are continually modified by experience is basic to meeting situational needs of readers and guiding reader development.

Reference Note

Note 1. For theoretical background, see the chapter in this volume by R.J. Tierney and J. Mosenthal, *Discourse comprehension and production: Analyzing text structure and cohesion.*

References

CLARK, H.H., & HAVILAND, S.E. Comprehension and the given—new contrast. In R.O. Freedle (Ed.), *Discourse production and comprehension*. Hillsdale, New Jersey: Erlbaum, 1976.

FREDERIKSEN, C.H. Discourse comprehension and early reading. In L. Resnick and P. Weaver (Eds.), *Theory and practice in early reading*. Hillsdale, New Jersey: Erlbaum, in press.

FREDERIKSEN, C.H. Representing logical and semantic structure of knowledge acquired from discourse. *Cognitive Psychology*, 1975, *1*, 371–458 (a).

FREDERIKSEN, C.H. The effects of context-induced processing operating on semantic information acquired from discourse. *Cognitive Psychology*, 1975, *7*, 139–166 (b).

GUILFORD, J.P. Three faces of intellect. *American Psychologist*, 1959, *14*, 469–479.

HOLLAND, N.N. *Poems in persons: An introduction to the psychoanalysis of literature*. New York: W.W. Norton, 1973.

HOOK, J.N. *Writing creatively*. Boston: Heath, 1963.

KINTSCH, W., and VAN DIJK, T.A. Toward a model of text comprehension and production. *Psychological Review*, 1978, *85*, 363–394.

KINTSCH, W. *The representation of meaning in memory*. Hillsdale, New Jersey: Erlbaum, 1974.

KINTSCH, W. On comprehending stories. In M. Just & P. Carpenter (Eds.), *Cognitive processes in comprehension*. Hillsdale, New Jersey: Erlbaum, 1977.

MANDLER, J.M., & JOHNSON, N.S. Remembrance of things parsed: Story structure and recall. *Cognitive Psychology*, 1977, *9*, 111–151.

MEYER, B.J.F. *The organization of prose and its effect on recall*. Amsterdam: North Holland, 1975.

PEARSON, P.D. *Scripts, texts, and questions*. Paper presented at the National Reading Conference, Atlanta, Georgia, December 1976.

PEARSON, P.D., & JOHNSON, D.C. *Teaching reading comprehension*. New York: Holt, Rinehart & Winston, 1978.

RUMELHART, D.E. Notes on a schema for stories. In D.G. Bobrow & A.M. Collins (Eds.), *Representation and understanding: Studies in cognitive science*. New York: Academic Press, 1975.

SHANK, R.C. The role of memory in language processing. In C.N. Cofer & R. Atkinson (Eds.), *The nature of human memory*. San Francisco: Freeman, 1975.

STEIN, N.L., & GLENN, C.G. An analysis of story comprehension in elementary school children. In R.O. Freedle (Ed.), *New directions in discourse processing* (Volume 2). Norwood, New Jersey: Ablex, 1979.

THORNDYKE, P.W. Cognitive structures in comprehension and memory of narrative discourse. *Cognitive Psychology*, 1977, *9*, 77–110.

TIERNEY, R.J., BRIDGE, C., & CERA, M.J. *The discourse processing operations of children*. Paper presented at the National Reading Conference, New Orleans, Louisiana, December 1977.

Too much talk. In R.E. Jenning & D.E. Prince, *Calico caper*. Glenview, Illinois: Scott, Foresman, 1978, 101–108.

WARREN, W.H., NICHOLAS, D.W., & TRABASSO, T. Event chains and inferences in understanding narratives. In R. Freedle (Ed.), *Discourse processing: Multidisciplinary approaches*. Hillsdale, New Jersey: Erlbaum, 1979.

Reading to Children:
A Communicative Process

Judith L. Green
University of Delaware
Judith O. Harker
Pepperdine University

A tiger went for a walk in the jungle. The fur on his back was smooth and rich, as golden as a kingly crown, as black as a raven's wing. There wasn't a sound, the way the tiger walked.

From *The Way the Tiger Walked*
(Chacones, 1970)

Stories such as *The Way the Tiger Walked* (1970) are read in classrooms and homes across the nation. Educators engage children in story reading activities with the expectation that reading to children will help extend such language skills as vocabulary and syntax (Bougere, 1973; Chambers, 1971; Cohen, 1968; Cullinan, 1977; Chomsky, 1972; Huck, 1973; McCormick, 1977; Sims, 1977), aesthetic and literature appreciation skills (Groff, 1977; Huck, 1976; Lamme, 1976; McCormick, 1977; Sims, 1977; Stewig, 1978), as well as children's knowledge of the world (Bougere, 1973; Huck, 1976). Evidence of the effect of reading to children on their subsequent growth in the language skills described above is inconclusive. A major reason for this may be that reading to children is seen primarily as a literary, interpretive, or pedagogical process. We will argue that it is primarily a sociolinguistic process.

The purpose of the present paper is twofold: first, to explore the nature of story reading as a communicative process and, second, to present findings from two studies of reading to children for comprehension purposes which help us raise questions about the nature of the process and point to areas for further consideration.

Reading to Children: Some Instructional Considerations

Reading to children, when used to develop and extend listening comprehension skills, requires more of the adult reader than simply reading the story and asking questions. What more is involved concerns both researchers and practitioners interested in effective teaching practices. By more, we mean the strategies and techniques, the communicative processes, that enable the reader to bridge the gap between the author and the listener.

In the past, the search for instructional strategies that enable teachers to effectively present stories for young children to comprehend, produced a series of conflicting results. For every study that suggested the teacher engage in one type of behavior (Tutolo, 1978; Vukelich, 1979; Tutolo, 1979; Brophy & Evertson, 1976), another study existed to suggest that that particular type of behavior was not effective (Coody, 1973; Brophy & Evertson, 1976; Huck, 1976).

Results of this nature may appear contradictory and confusing to those who are seeking the strategy or set of strategies that will insure effectiveness in all story reading situations. However, for those who understand reading to children as a communicative process, the results are not surprising and do not necessarily negate one another. They suggest that in some situations one strategy might be appropriate and effective and in other situations that same strategy might not be useful. Factors such as developmental differences, teacher's goals, the nature of the text, as well as skills and abilities of students, all influence the instructional process and potentially influence the effectiveness of a given set of strategies.

The problem is more complex than which strategy to use in which context. Brophy and Evertson (1976) capture the complexity when they state:

Effective teaching is not simply a matter of implementing a small number of "basic" teaching skills. Instead . . . effective teaching involves *orchestration* of a large number of factors, continually shifting teaching behaviors to respond to continually shifting needs (p. 139).

In the remainder of this paper, a series of conversational factors that influence a teacher's orchestration of instructional strategies will be discussed. To build on the orchestration analogy, just as the conductor of an orchestra must understand music and conducting theory to produce a harmonious symphony, so must the teacher understand the conversational and instructional process to produce, with the students, a coherent entity called a lesson. We will argue that knowledge of conversational factors in concert with instructional factors provides a framework which can be used to guide the orchestration and lead to more systematic goal attainment in teaching.

Two Aspects of the Process: Planning and Implementation

Instructionally and interactively, the process of reading to children involves three components: the student, the teacher, and the story (text). Each of these components can be understood in the abstract as separate entities: the student has developmental characteristics, reading/listening abilities, interests in various topics, and social expectations; the teacher has interests, beliefs, cognitive knowledge about subjects, and goals and objectives for lessons; and the text has content and structural characteristics which can be formally represented and described, as well as graphic features such as illustrations. As separate entities, each can be used to guide the planning stage of lesson formation. These components can also be understood as the bases of teacher decision-making in the interactions that are an integral part of lesson implementation.

As a framework for lesson planning. The three components (the student, the teacher, and the text) can be seen as separate factors that must be considered when planning a story reading lesson. That is, the three components can act as a framework to limit what can occur instructionally in a particular lesson. This aspect of the process is represented in Figure 1.

The components, viewed this way, are seen as influencing the lesson primarily at the planning phase. They act to guide or frame the teacher's decision-making, not only about *what* to teach but *how* to teach it. Decision-making about what will occur and how it will occur is determined or planned in advance. At this level, questions to be addressed by the teacher include: 1) What are the needs of my students that must be considered? 2) What goals do I want to achieve and how will I achieve them? 3) How can I most effectively present the text? 4) What kinds of behaviors or interactions do I want to allow during each phase of the lesson?

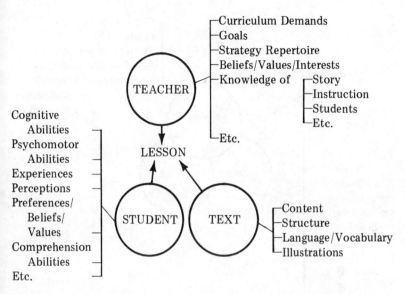

Figure 1. Components involved in planning story reading lessons.

Once these decisions have been made, the components are then relegated to a background position and the teacher is ready to present the lesson in accordance with these plans. We consider this a somewhat static view of teaching as a decision-making and communicative process.

As a framework for implementing lessons. Although advance planning is necessary and cannot be ignored, decision-making does not stop with this phase of the lesson. For example, if a teacher asks a question during a story and receives a response, the teacher must then decide whether to ask another question, make a comment, or continue with the story. The children, on the other hand, must also decide if they will respond or take another course of action, such as ask their own question or make a spontaneous comment. The teacher and student, therefore, are interactors and decision makers who play an active part in what happens in a lesson.

The components, when viewed dynamically, are seen as interacting. Figure 2 presents this view.

To understand how these components interact, we must understand teaching as a communicative process. That is, teaching as a process in which teachers and children interact with and build on objects in the environment (texts, audiovisuals, mani-

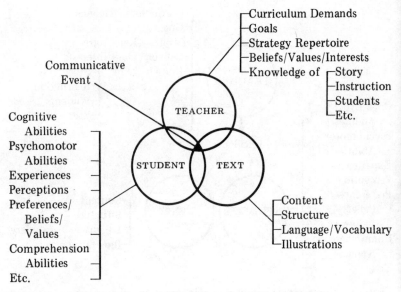

Figure 2. An interactive/communicative view of components involved in story reading.

pulatives) and behaviors of others, as well as their own behaviors, to construct the lessons and activities of the classroom (Gumperz, 1976; Green, 1977).

Summary. This section and Figures 1 and 2 show that bridging the gap between the student, the teacher, and the text is a multistep process. The first step is basically a planning stage whose outcome is a structure for a lesson—a lesson plan. This plan is based on the teacher's consideration, prior to lesson implementation, of each of the three components and selection of the subcomponents which apply to the lesson being planned.

The second step is more complex. It is an interactive stage and involves instructional dialogue between teacher and student around the text. Step one acts as the framework for the interactions in step two. The three components of the first step are now viewed dynamically as interacting in the production of the actual lesson event. It is this interactive process that is the "more" referred to at the beginning of this section. Teachers who understand the basic elements of the communicative process as it is realized in instructional dialogues can be more effective decision-makers as they orchestrate the event phase of the lesson. In the next section, we will discuss aspects of the communicative process that teachers need to consider when planning and implementing instructional activities.

Understanding the Communicative Process

All communication, and especially communication as it occurs in the teaching process does not occur randomly. Conversation is a rule governed process (both linguistically and socially) whose operation can be reliably observed and described in actual teaching situations (Green, 1977; Green & Wallat, 1979; Mehan, Cazden, Coles, Fisher & Maroules, 1976; Sinclair & Coulthard, 1975). However, before proceeding with the discussion of components and features of the communicative process, a word of qualification is necessary. The field research on face-to-face interaction is still in its infancy. What is involved in the communicative process and how these factors vary within and across communicative situations is still being explored. Therefore, readers must use their own knowledge and observations of communication in the classroom as a framework to determine how the aspects of conversational structure apply to the various lessons and activities in their classrooms.

Communicative competence. When people engage in conversations, they bring with them not only cognitive experiences and knowledge about the world and how it functions, but communicative experiences and knowledge about conversations and how they function. This knowledge has been defined by Hymes (1974) as "communicative competence." Hymes pointed out that the child, in acquiring communicative competence,

> acquires competence as to when to speak, when not, and as to what to talk about with whom, when, where, and in what manner. In short, a child becomes able to accomplish a repertoire of speech acts, to take part in speech events and to evaluate their accomplishment by others (p. 277).

Not all children in classrooms have reached the same developmental level or have had the same set of communicative experiences in the home, in the community, or in educational settings and, therefore, enter school with varying degrees of communicative knowledge and abilities (Halliday, 1973; Tough, 1974). Since the degree to which participants in a communicative situation share rules which influence the effectiveness of the conversational endeavor, the teacher must account for these differences when planning for instruction. Given that the purpose of classroom conversation is to promote learning, the degree to which these rules are shared can directly effect learning outcomes.

Two examples will be used to illustrate the value of understanding communicative competence as related to classrooms. The first example will illustrate broad issues that influence communication in an interethnic situation. The second example will illustrate communicative requirements within a specific lesson. In her study of communication among the Warm Springs Indians, Philips (1974) found that a conflict existed between the communicative expectations of the school and those of the community. In school, children were expected to read or speak in front of other class members, to compete with other students, and to interact directly with the adults in the classroom. In contrast, Philips found that at home and in the community these same children were not expected to interact directly with adults beyond the immediate family. They were expected to learn how to do tasks by observing adults engaged in the task, not by asking questions. Children were also expected to work together to problem solve, not to compete with each other. Finally, individual members of the community did not perform in front of others in competitive ways.

When these students entered the classroom, they did not have strategies in their repertoire that would permit them to participate fully in classroom events. Instead, the classroom communicative structures worked against them. Had the teachers understood the difference between the communicative competence required in the community and that required in the school, they would have had a basis for building a communicatively effective environment that would have been more consonant with their expectations and might thereby have eliminated the conflict suggested in this example.

Once students and teacher have developed a series of communicative contexts in the classroom, the students' repertoires can be expanded to include the more traditional types of communicative expectations of the school. This latter step is necessary at some point in the students' educations if they are to communicate with other groups in the broader society. The teachers' task then is twofold: first, they must understand and account for communicative background experiences of their students and second, they must teach communication strategies to students to enable them to gain access to the broader community.

Communicative conflict can also occur on a microlevel, the level of the individual message. Within any given lesson, students may not read the teacher's communicative expectations correctly. That is, they may not read the situational demands correctly and, therefore, the selected strategies might not be effective. The following example is a description of a segment from a videotape lesson of reading to children, discussed later in this paper. The teacher in this example is questioning six children about the story that has just been read to them, *The Way the Tiger Walked*.

The teacher begins the sequence by asking a child at the end of the row, "If you could be any animal you wanted, what would you be?" The child provides an appropriate answer, "A great, big gorilla." The teacher asks, "Why?" The child provides the "because" answer and the teacher proceeds to ask the next child in the row a similar question. This child also provides an appropriate short answer, and the teacher asks this child "Why?" This pattern is repeated with the next child but not with the fourth child. The fourth child spontaneously provides the short answer plus the answer to the why question. The teacher does not ask this child any other questions but proceeds to the next child. The fifth child responds only with the short answer and the teacher proceeds to ask the child the "Why?" question. The sixth child, like child four, answers with the short answer and spontaneously answers the "Why?" question. As with child four, the teacher does not ask for any further information.

This sequence demonstrates that this teacher wanted the more elaborate answer. Each time the answer to the why question was not received spontaneously, the teacher asked the question. The teacher's intent can be verified by considering the behavior with child four and child six. Both of these children read the intent of the question and answered the "Why?" question spontaneously. Neither child was then queried further.

This suggests that children must use their communicative competence on a message-by-message basis. The children in this segment had to read the teacher's intended meaning by considering the chain of questions asked, the way other children responded to the questions, and the teacher's behavior when other children responded to the questions. The implication is that teachers need to be aware of how they are asking questions, what effect the way they ask questions might have on student performance, and what the communicative demands are for each type of classroom interaction.

The need to account for differences such as those above was formalized in a court case (U.S. District Court, Eastern District, Michigan, Civil Action No. 7-71861). On behalf of their children who speak black English, a group of parents filed a suit against one school in Ann Arbor, Michigan, for failure to teach standard English. The court ruled that the existence of a difference in language use between black English and standard English did not, in itself, constitute a language barrier. Rather, the teacher's lack of knowledge of and lack of accounting for the difference between the language of the home and the language of the school, especially in the area of reading, constituted a language barrier.

The court case and the first example point to the discontinuity for some children in the communicative competence developed in these children's homes and community with that required in the school. Although the children have little trouble communicating effectively in their community, a problem arises in formal instructional situations. What the court stated was that the teachers did not have adequate knowledge of the language the children spoke in the home, nor did they understand how to bridge the gap between the language of the home and the standard English of the school and the society as a whole. One implication of this case is that the teacher must know how to extend the communicative competence of the child so the child can effectively participate in the academic and social activities of the school and become socially and economically competitive in the wider society.

Knowledge of the communicative competence construct provides a framework for understanding what is involved in communication in general. We will now consider specific factors involved in the communicative process when used for instructional purposes.

Conversational coherence. The concept of coherence refers to the existence of thematic relations within and across messages leading to a specific goal. As Frederiksen (1977) pointed out, "The property that makes the discourse more than a collection of unrelated simple sentences is coherence." Coherence, therefore, means that the instructional text has unity of topic. However, this unity does not happen accidentally but results from the participants' adherence to the rules for conversational topics. As Gumperz (1976) states, "Rules for interaction are seen as instrumental and goal directed and only topics relatable to these goals are admissible" (p. 28). In instructional terms this means that if the purpose of the lesson is to explore how apples grow, then talking about playing baseball would not be appropriate.

Classroom conversations, especially those for instructional purposes, vary from free conversations in specific ways. In free conversations, topics are negotiated by the participants (Gumperz, 1976; Sinclair & Coulthard, 1975). However, in instructional conversations, the teacher maintains the veto right over topic. This does not mean that students cannot introduce topics, but that the teacher reserves the right to accept a topic or to veto it.

The acceptance or rejection of a topic by a teacher depends on a variety of factors (Wallat & Green, 1979). How the teacher sees the topic as relating to the goals of the lesson, what effect the topic will have on obtaining instructional goals, what the long term goals are for the children, and what the teacher believes to be good educational practice are some of the factors that influence whether a teacher will accept a student's topic. The example in Table 1 will help illustrate several of the factors that influence topic occurrence in a conversation.

The general topic in this segment is story related—the tiger and what he will teach the elephant. The topic is introduced by the teacher's extension of a student comment (line 327), "he gonna do them all." The teacher's question, "How Does an Elephant Walk?" (line 328), legitimizes the topic for general discussion. Since the teacher does not direct the question either verbally or nonverbally to any student in particular, all students may answer until the teacher indicates closure. Closure for this topic does not occur when the teacher returns to the text, but rather with line 335, when student "m" responds to the question,"How Does an Elephant Walk?" Observation of nonverbal

Table 1

Structural Map of
Conversational Coherence and Divergence: Teacher W

Transcript Line	Source	Potentially Divergent Messages	Thematically Tied Messages
327	j		he gonna do them all
328	TE		HOW DOES AN ELEPHANT WALK?
329	c		boom
330	j		he sinks, he sinks the ground in about that much when he walks.
331	j(nv)		(uses hands to indicate depth)
332	Text		THE TIGER STALKED UP TO THE ELEPHANT. THEN, SUDDENLY, HE SPREAD OUT HIS EARS.
333	all		ears!
334	Text		UNTIL THEY LOOKED LIKE SMALL GOLDEN WINGS. HE WALKED WITH HEAVY STEPS. AND THE GROUND SHOOK UNDER HIS FEET. RUMBLE-SWAY! RUMBLE-SWAY! RUMBLE-SWAY! "WHAT A POWERFUL WAY TO WALK!" HE THOUGHT.
335	m		earthquake
336	j	is this school quake proof?	
337	TE	I DON'T KNOW.	
338	TE	WHAT WOULD YOU DO IF THERE WERE AN EARTHQUAKE?	
339	f	I'd get out of here real quick.	
340	c	I'd jump right out.	
341	c	I'd climb on that table.	

TOPIC CONTINUES FOR 10 MORE TRANSCRIPT LINES

352	TE	OK	
353			LET'S FINISH THE STORY, OK?
354	allnv		(students stop talking)
355	Text		AND THEN THE ELEPHANT SLOWLY RAISED . . .

behavior showed that the teacher accepted the student's comment as topic related.

What occurs next show one special feature of instructional conversations. In line 336, student "j" asks whether the school is earthquake proof. This topic, while triggered by the previous student's comment, is not topic related. The question of whether the student meant this as a topic to be discussed at this time or simply wanted an answer is not relevant. What occurred is that the teacher turned the question into a formal topic for discussion by all students. This action produced an extended interchange not focused on the general lesson goal.

As shown on lines 352–353, the teacher had to refocus the students' attention on the purpose of the lesson, the story, after the divergence. The teacher's actions and not the students' produced the divergence.

There is a popular notion in the pedagogical literature that suggests teachers need to capitalize on students' interests when they are expressed. This is called the "teachable moment." Observation of teacher W's actions throughout the lesson lead to the interpretation that this teacher valued building on students' comments and capturing the teachable moment. What is not clear in the teaching literature is that the teachable moment must occur at the actual moment of stated interest. A digression of this type, within a lesson, pulls the children's attention away from the main purpose of the lesson. A divergence, therefore, can be viewed as interrupting the coherence of the lesson. The effect of divergence on student performance is an area of needed research. Some tentative findings on this topic are presented in the last section of this paper.

Contextualization Cues. Conversations unfold message-by-message. Thematic coherence, therefore, is the product of a series of tied messages. To return to the orchestra analogy, just as we must listen to groups of notes played in particular ways before we can identify a melody, so we must listen to groups of messages before we can identify a theme or thematic change. Participants in a conversation, just like listeners of a symphony, must process bits of information and from these bits interpret what is meant.

Meaning viewed this way is context bound. As Gumperz and Herasimchuk (1973) have shown:

A major important analytic principle to emerge from recent work in this area is that it is impossible to interpret situated meanings apart from the total context of what has been said before and what is said afterwards. The interpretation of a message is not a constant; it depends on what it is in response to and how it is received. What is said at one point in a conversation may change the interpretation of everything that has gone before (p. 103).

What this means in pedagogical terms is that children who are participating in a lesson do not know what to expect, except on the broadest level, in advance of the lesson's implementation. Meanings of words and events are determined by what occurs in the process of making a lesson happen. The fact that today is Wednesday, and on Wednesdays at 11:30 a.m. we have a story, does not tell the children how the story will be presented, what role they are to play in the lesson, or what they must do with the story after it has been told. These questions only can be answered by interpreting messages and behaviors in the actual lesson.

What participants read in order to interpret messages and groups of messages are contextualization cues (Gumperz & Herasimchuk, 1973). Corsaro (1981) defines contextualization cues as specific communicative elements including

> linguistic communicative functions containing phonemic, syntactic, and semantic elements; paralinguistic features (intonation, stress and pitch); gesture and proxemic features; and the manipulation of physical objects in the ecological setting.

Orchestration of a lesson, therefore, includes verbal, nonverbal, and paralinguistic elements of a conversation. To gain a clearer picture of the way these cues function let's consider the segment from teacher G's story reading of *The Way the Tiger Walked* (Chacones, 1979), presented in Table 2.

The contextualization cues for the story reading indicate how the teacher segmented the story for the children, where the teacher placed the stress (on words and events), and what the bits for input were for the listener. In addition, the nonverbal aspect of the cues indicate that the teacher used eye gaze and body language throughout the presentation.

On a conversational level, this segment is interesting. The teacher did not automatically receive a response to the question, but had to orchestrate the answer. When the teacher received a low informative answer (line 074), ummm hmmmm, to the first question, a second question was asked. The second question provided the students with further input into the nature of the answer the teacher desired. However, the teacher still did not receive an answer to the second question (line 075), so the question was restated in different ways two more times (line 077, 079). In line 081, "As gold as a," the teacher changes strategy and rather than asking a question, provides a part of the answer. This strategy is rewarded by a response from student *b*. After this sequence, when the teacher asks a question

Table 2

Transcript and Contextualization Cues: Teacher G Story Reading

Transcript Lines	Source	Message	Contextualization Cues
068	Text	A TIGER WENT FOR A WALK IN THE JUNGLE	1. Stress on *tiger* 2. Rhythm different from 068 3. 1.0 second pause after message 4. Pitch in *jungle* drops off
069	Text	THE FUR ON HIS BACK WAS SMOOTH AND RICH AS GOLDEN AS A KINGLY CROWN	1. Stress on *smooth, rich, golden* 2. .5 second pause after message
069	Text	AS BLACK AS A RAVEN'S WING	1. Stress on *black* 2. Slight pause after black 3. 2.0 second pause after wing 4. Looks up at children
070	Text	THERE WASN'T A SOUND	1. Lower volume, whisper 2. Halting rhythm 3. .5 second pause 4. Scans children 5. Moves body in toward children
071	Text	THE WAY THE TIGER WALKED	1. Increase speed 2. Still in whisper 3. 1.7 second pause 4. Teacher's body position shifts 5. Her head turns toward students,

Table 2 (Continued)

Transcript Lines	Source	Message	Contextualization Cues
072	TE	CAN YOU SEE HOW BEAUTIFUL THE COLORS WERE	1. Looking toward students, teacher leans forward 2. Eyes scan group 3. Increase in volume 4. Increase in speed 5. Stress on *were*—no stress on other words
073	TE	IN YOUR MIND?	1. Returns to former stress pattern 2. Rising intonation at end 3. .8 second pause
074	b	ummm hummm	1. *b* shakes head up and down 2. One student closes eyes/leans back 3. No response from other students
075	TE	CAN YOU REMEMBER THE WORDS THAT TOLD YOU HOW GOLDEN AND HOW BLACK THE COLORS WERE?	1. Stress on *how, golden* 2. Pause after *you* 3. Drop intonation at end 4. Scans children/leans forward 5. 1.0 second pause at end of message
076	allnv	(no response)	
077	TE	WHAT WERE THEY?	1. Stress on *were* 2. No rise or fall on *they*

078	allnv	(no response)	

079 TE — WHAT DID THE WRITER SAY?
1. Increase in speed
2. Lower volume
3. *b*'s hand raises/looks at TE
4. 1.0 second pause

080 allnv — (no response)

081 TE — AS GOLD AS A...
1. Stress on *gold*
2. Elongates *A*
3. *b*'s hand lowers at beginning
4. *b* during elongation of *A* looks at TE and opens and raises hand

082 b — as gold as a crown and as black as a raven's wing
1. *b* makes eye contact with TE
2. Pause between *a* and *raven*
3. Drops head with *raven*
4. Raises head with end of message
5. 1.0 second pause
6. *b* smiles during pause
7. Maintains eye contact with TE

083 TE — B, YOU'RE A GOOD LISTENER
1. Gaze on *b*
2. Extremely low volume
3. Stress on *good*

084 TE — COULD YOU HEAR HIM AS HE WALKED?
1. Stress on *could*
2. Increase in volume
3. Rising tone at end/speed increase
4. .5 second pause

there is a response. Observation of the remainder of the lesson showed that the teacher rarely had to repeat a question; children disagreed with one another; children would evaluate each others answers; no divergences occurred; and student involvement, while teacher directed, was plentiful.

Without consideration of the contextualization cues, the messages that formed the input for participants on a microlevel would not have been possible. By considering the orchestration of Teacher G and contrasting it with that of Teacher W, we can see that, while the teachers had similar goals, they had different ways of orchestrating the interactions. The example of Teacher G also demonstrates that rights and obligations of students for participation are negotiated and not preset. That the children waited to find out what was required before participating can be seen in the fact that the teacher had to ask four questions and then provide a prompt. These actions alerted the children to the type of participation required in this part of the lesson. Contextualization does not occur only on a microlevel. Messages tie hierarchical levels together to form interaction units. In Table 2, the teacher reads a section of the text without interruption. Her nonverbal (proxemic/distance; kinesics/body language) and paralinguistic cues indicate that student comments are not expected. After frame-by-frame microanalysis, of nonverbal (proxemic and kinesic cues) aspects of teacher-student interaction during a reading lesson, McDermott (1976), found that different types of groups' positionings existed for different aspects of the general activity. For example, when children were in reading positions, they were seated in their chairs, their bodies and heads were leaning in and down, and their eyes were on the text. Consideration of position between teacher and students provides information to participants as well as researchers about the requirements for participation.

While sequences of discourse (text) like the one in the example do form an interaction unit, the majority of interaction units are not of this type. What occurs next may make the meaning of this unit clearer. In lines 073-074, the teacher asks a question and receives a response (ummmm, hmmmm). This response, while low informative, does meet the conversational expectation that when a question is asked, the listener will provide a response. However, what occurs next is indicative of how classroom conversations differ in terms of units of interaction from free conversations.

In a free conversation, if a question is asked the responder assumes the questioner does not already know the answer. In the classroom, Mehan (1979) suggests this assumption does not hold. Teachers ask questions to which they already know answers and students are to determine what is required. Another way to view this aspect of conversations is to understand the pedagogical nature of classroom questions. Teachers use questions for a variety of pedagogical and social purposes—to involve children in lessons and to assess children's knowledge as well as to provide information. However, teachers are not the only ones to act in unexpected ways in free conversations. In lines 076, 078, and 080, the teacher receives no response to questions. This action in a free conversation would be a serious breech in conversational rules. However, in the classroom, the no response is neither socially nor pedagogically inappropriate but can occur for a variety of reasons—a student may not know an answer, may be uncertain of the requirements for participation, or may not choose to participate for personal reasons. Only by observing the contextualization cues and the teacher's actions can the meaning of these actions be determined.

A question followed by either a response or no response can be considered a unit of completed interaction. As these two examples show, interaction units are negotiated and are not decided by a predetermined commitment about what ought to occur or any preplanned structure. Interaction is a cooperative effort.

The interaction units in this example tie together. When both topic and pedagogical purpose are considered, units larger than interaction units can be identified. These units are instructional sequence units. For example, the segment of text presentation has a single topic and a single pedagogical intent. These units, therefore, represent an instructional sequence. A new instructional sequence in this example begins with the question on line 072-073, "Can you see how beautiful the colors were in your mind?" In this sequence, which extends from 072 to 084, the teacher indicates through her actions that the children are expected to ask and respond to questions during the story reading and the topic for discussion is how the author said the tiger looked. When the teacher shifts the topic to how the tiger walked with the question on line 084, "Could you hear him as he walked?" another instructional sequence begins.

It is interesting to note that, while the topic shifts, the pedagogical intent does not shift. The pedagogical intent, or the rights and obligations established for participation, are the glue that tie instructional sequences together to form the phase unit of a lesson. As the illustrations from Teachers G and W show, different teachers have different expectations for participation. These expectations are not overtly stated but are flagged by the manner in which the teacher orchestrates the lesson. Each phase of a lesson has a different right and obligation for participation—an introduction, a story presentation, and a discussion.

Summary. Lessons are not predetermined entities except in the most global sense. Lesson plans, therefore, are guides that limit options and establish goals. Lessons are constructed bit-by-bit, from the bottom up, by the cooperative actions of teachers and students *cooperating with each other* to achieve the goals of the teacher. The complexity of the process was captured by Erickson and Shultz (1977) who described what is involved in establishing contexts for communication:

> Contexts are not simply given in the physical setting . . . or in combinations of personnel. Rather, contexts are constituted by what people are doing where and when they are doing it. . . . Ultimately, social contexts consist of mutually shared and ratified definitions of situations and in the social actions persons take on the basis of those definitions (pp. 5–6).

Lessons viewed in this manner form specific types of contexts; lessons are complex entities. They are neither scripts to be followed strictly nor unitary communicative wholes. Different expectations for participation exist for different parts of a lesson; therefore, different communicative contexts exist within a lesson (Green & Wallat, 1979). In addition to acquiring cognitive knowledge in a lesson, children must also learn about the expectations for participation that exist for different parts of a lesson.

In this paper, we have shown that children learn about rules for conversation by observing and participating in conversations. Their past experiences help them "read" the requirements for the present situation. What they read helps them select strategies from their repertoire to use in the new situation. Therein lies the "Catch 22." Children can be misled about a situation if they focus on the most global level, e.g. the teacher's statements that the lesson is storytelling. Florio and Shultz (1979) recently explored the question of context equivalence between home and school. They found that just because two situations look alike on the surface (e.g. reading to children, at home and at school), does not mean the requirements for participation are the same. This means that children could read participation requirements incorrectly or they could be misled by surface features of the situation.

If teachers are to help children extend their communicative competence, they must become more aware of students' knowledge of communicative requirements, become more sensitive to the effects that different ways of orchestrating instructional events have on student participation and learning, and become more aware of how demands for participation vary across the contexts and lessons in the classroom. With this knowledge, teachers can help children bridge the requirements from one context to the next and can help children learn to read the cues to contextualization.

Research Findings: Story Reading and Comprehension

Does looking at teaching in this way make a difference? Tentative findings from communicative research indicate that this is a fruitful way to approach not only the study of reading to children but the study of peer-peer interactions (Cherry-Wilkinson & Dallaghan, 1979; Steinberg & Gazen, 1979), the construction of social norms in the classroom (Wallat & Green, 1979), teacher-child interactions (Gumperz, 1981; McDermott, 1976; Mehan, 1979; Merritt & Humphrey, 1979), language of the home (Arnold, 1979; Cook-Gumperz, 1979; Cook-Gumperz, 1981) and the study of context in the classroom (Erickson & Shultz, 1977; Florio & Shultz, 1979). While the list is not all inclusive, it does indicate that the exploration of communication used for educational and instructional purposes and the acquisition of communicative skills are growing areas of study.

A concrete example of the importance of the approach presented in this paper is to be found in the results of two studies concerned with exploring reading to children for comprehension purposes. The first study (Green, 1977) explored a methodology for capturing and describing the teaching-learning process as it unfolds on a variety of conversational and pedagogical levels. Description of this system has been reported elsewhere (Green, 1977, Green & Wallat, 1979; Green & Wallat, 1981). One set of findings is relevant to this topic and will be presented.

Green explored the effect of conversational/pedagogical practices on students' performances on story retelling. In this study, ten teachers read and discussed the same story, *The Way the Tiger Walked* (Chacones, 1970), with six children from their classrooms (grades 1-3). After the presentation of the lesson, the children were interviewed individually to obtain their retelling of the story. The retellings were then analyzed using a protocol designed by Green (1977) and based on Ruddell's definition (1974) of levels of comprehension (factual, interpretive, applicative) and skills of comprehension (events recalled, sequence of events, facts recalled, details recalled).

The findings reported in this section are those which relate to the effect of differences in orchestration strategies on student performance. The two teachers referred to in this paper were participants in this study. Teacher G's students performed in the top 25 percent of all students and Teacher W's students in the lowest 25 percent. One finding related to the amount of language used by different teachers. The analysis was based on description of types of interaction units. When the total occurrence of the various types of interaction units was measured globally across the total lesson, no difference was found across the ten teachers of the study. Regardless of how much talk occurred, the teachers tended to use the same types of interactions strategies and the percentage of occurrence in each teacher's lesson was similar for all teachers.

Differences in language use did emerge, however, when the lesson was divided into its phases (Bales & Strodtbeck, 1967) and when the orchestration of the units within these phases was considered. The three teachers with the highest student performances showed similar patterns of use and distribution. The three teachers with the lowest rated student performances also showed a similar pattern of language use and distribution. The patterns for these two groups were very different.

Teachers who received high ratings based on student performance on story retelling tended to provide some introduction and then present and discuss the story simultaneously. These teachers did not have a separate discussion phase. In contrast, teachers who were rated in the lowest 25 percent tended to present some introduction, a separate story presentation phase, and a separate discussion phase. Teachers who were ranked between these two groups tended to have a pattern that showed more equal distribution across the three phases of the lesson. This finding suggest that, even if teachers have the same goal, they may take different routes to reach that goal and, if the goal of the lesson is story retelling, then the way in which the lesson is structured affects the retelling. Using simultaneous discussion and story presentation appears to produce better retellings than does a structure in which the story is presented and then discussed.

When the question of divergence from task was explored one interesting pattern was observed. Teacher W, the teacher in the example presented in Table 1, had the most divergences. She also had students who performed in the lowest 25 percent. While it is not possible to make a definitive statement, the data suggest this strategy or method of orchestration does have a negative influence on student performance on story retelling.

While these findings point out differences in orchestration, further research is necessary in this area. Green's study raises questions regarding teaching practices which can be answered empirically. Stephenson (1979) attempted to answer one of these questions. In an effort to determine the effect of different lesson structures on children's comprehension of text, she undertook a naturalistic, small-scale study in her own classroom. She randomly selected two groups of six children and presented five stories to them over a five-week period. Group A received discussion after the story presentation for the first four stories; Group B received discussion during the presentation for the first four stories. The conditions for both groups were reversed on the fifth story.

While no statistical differences were found between the two groups on recall on the five stories, a microanalysis of student performance produced some trends which appear to have educational significance. Group A and Group B, while randomly selected, were not equally rated in terms of readiness to read and cognitive ability. Group A was rated considerably higher on an average than Group B. In addition, Group A's lesson structure (discussion after the story) was more consonant with the naturally occurring pattern for storytelling in Stephenson's class prior to the study. In light of these findings, the no difference finding is interesting. The academically slower Group B, with the new lesson structure, performed as well as the more advanced Group A. Stephenson's field notes support the interpretation that structuring the questioning during the lesson helped the slower group of children. She also noted that the group who had discussion during the telling of the story was more attentive, more responsive, and needed less prompting during retelling. In addition, Stephenson suggested the group that had the retelling after the story may have remembered the story from the discussion and not from the actual presentation.

When Stephenson altered the conditions for presentation on the fifth story, Group A's score (the group that now had discussion during the story) increased, while Group B's scores decreased. This pattern further supports the interpretation that discussing the story during story presentation influences students' retelling performance in a positive way.

Conclusion

This paper focused on the nature of teaching as a communicative process and the different effects of orchestration on student participation and learning outcomes. Three directions are suggested: 1) reading to children needs to be considered in its broader social context, 2) children's comprehension of text can be enhanced by considering organizational structure of the lesson, and 3) teaching needs to be viewed as an ongoing decision-making process in which teacher and students work together to construct the lesson. The framework we presented and the definition of concepts provide a structure to guide thinking and planning.

Stephenson's study shows that the classroom teacher can research the questions raised by researchers external to the classroom. We would like to suggest that a cooperative effort between external researchers and teacher/researchers can produce a sensitive description of the processes involved in teaching reading for comprehension of questions based on instructional needs of teachers. The two studies cited above show that descriptive and empirical studies complement each other and are not mutually exclusive.

One final note about communicative development. Cazden (1972) has suggested a language continuum:

language   language
universals ←——————————————→ specifics (p. 103).

Language universals (syntax, phonology) are acquired by all native speakers of a language. Language specifics, on the other hand, need specific exposure and experiences and are not acquired by all speakers of a language. Communicative competence, as discussed in this paper, is a language specific. Therefore, teachers must take special care to structure situations so children may acquire the competence required in school situations as well as in the broader society. In doing this, they may eliminate one source of interference in communication in general, and in story comprehension in particular.

References

ARNOLD, M. Early child-child communication. In J. Green (Ed.), *Communicating with young children. Theory into Practice*, 1979, *18*(4).

BALES, R., & STRODTBECK, R. Phases in group problem-solving. In E.J. Amidon and J.E. Hough (Eds.), *Interaction analysis: Theory, research, and application*. Reading, Massachusetts: Addison-Wesley, 1967.

BOUGERE, M. Oral language and literacy: A psycholinguistic view. In M. King, R. Emmans, and P. Cianciolo (Eds.), *A forum for focus*. Urbana, Illinois: National Council of Teachers of English, 1973.

BROPHY, J., & EVERSTON, C. *Learning from teaching: A developmental perspective*. Boston: Allyn & Bacon, 1976.

CAZDEN, C. *Child language and education*. New York: Holt, Rinehart & Winston, 1972.

CHACONES, D. *The way the tiger walked*. New York: Simon and Schuster, 1970.

CHAMBERS, D.W. *Children's literature in the curriculum*. Chicago: Rand McNally, 1971.

CHERRY-WILKINSON, L., & DALLAGHAN, C. Peer communication in first grade reading groups. In J. Green (Ed.), *Communicating with young children. Theory into Practice*, 1979, *18*(4).

CHOMSKY, C. Stages in language development and reading exposure. *Harvard Educational Review*, February 1972, *42*.

COHEN, D. The effects of literature on vocabulary and reading achievement. *Elementary English*, February 1968, *45*.

COODY, B. *Using literature with young children.* Dubuque, Iowa: W.C. Brown, 1973.

COOK-GUMPERZ, J. Communicating with young children in the home. In J. Green (Ed.), *Communicating with young children. Theory into Practice*, 1979, *18*(4).

COOK-GUMPERZ, J. Persuasive talk: The social organization of children's talk. In J. Green and C. Wallat (Eds.), *Ethnographic approaches to face-to-face interactions in educational settings.* Norwood, New Jersey: Ablex, 1981.

CORSARO, W. Entering the child's world: Research strategies for field entry and data collection. In J. Green and C. Wallat (Eds.), *Ethnographic approaches to face-to-face interaction in educational settings.* Norwood, New Jersey: Ablex, 1981.

CULLINAN, B. Books in the life of young children. In B. Cullinan and C. Carmichael (Eds.), *Literature and young children.* Urbana, Illinois: National Council of Teachers of English, 1977.

ERICKSON, F., & SHULTZ, J. When is a context? Some issues and methods in the analysis of social competence. *Quarterly Newsletter of the Institute for Comparative Human Development*, February 1977, *1*(2).

FLORIO, S., & SHULTZ, J. Social competence at home and at school. In J. Green (Ed.), *Communicating with young children. Theory into Practice*, 1979, *18*(4).

FREDERIKSEN, C. Structure and process in discourse production and comprehension. In M.A. Just & P.A. Carpenter (Eds.), *Cognitive processes in comprehension.* Hillside, New Jersey: Erlbaum, 1977.

GREEN, J.L. Pedagogical style differences as related to comprehension: Grades one through three. Unpublished dissertation, University of California at Berkeley, 1977.

GREEN, J.L., & WALLAT, C. When is an instructional context? An exploratory analysis of conversational shifts across time. In O. Garnica and M. King (Eds.), *Children, language, and society.* Pergamon, New Jersey, 1979.

GREEN, J.L., & WALLAT, C. Mapping instructional conversations: A sociolinguistic ethnography. In J. Green and C. Wallat (Eds.), *Ethnographic approaches to face-to-face interaction in educational settings.* Norwood, New Jersey: Ablex, 1981.

GROFF, P. Let's update storytelling. *Language Arts*, 1977, *54*(3).

GUMPERZ, J.J. Teaching as a linguistic process. Unpublished position paper, National Institute of Education Conference, 1975.

GUMPERZ, J.J. Language, communication, and public negotiation. In P. Sanday (Ed.), *Anthropology and the public interest.* New York: Academic, 1976.

GUMPERZ, J.J. Conversational inference and classroom learning. In J. Green and C. Wallat (Eds.), *Ethnographic approaches to face-to-face interaction in educational settings.* Norwood, New Jersey: Ablex, 1981.

GUMPERZ, J.J., & HERASIMCHUK, E. The conversational analysis of social meaning: A study of classroom interaction. In R. Shuy (Ed.), *Monograph series on language and linguistics.* Georgetown: Georgetown University Press, 1973.

HALLIDAY, M.A.K. *Explorations in the functions of language.* London, England: Edward Arnold, 1973.

HUCK, C. Meeting the challenge of literacy. In M. King, R. Emmans, and P. Cianciolo (Eds.), *A forum for focus*. Urbana, Illinois: National Council of Teachers of English, 1973.

HUCK, C. *Children's literature in the elementary school*. New York: Holt, Rinehart & Winston, 1976.

HYMES, D. *Foundations in sociolinguistics: An ethnographic approach*. Philadelphia: University of Pennsylvania Press, 1974.

LAMME, L.L. Reading aloud to young children. *Language Arts*, November/December 1976, *53*(8).

McCORMICK, S. Should you read aloud to your children? *Language Arts*, February 1977, *54*(2).

McDERMOTT, R. *Social contexts for ethnic borders and school failure*. Paper delivered to the First International Conference on Nonverbal Behavior, Toronto, 1976.

MEHAN, CAZDEN, COLES, FISHER, & MAROULES. *The social organization of classroom lessons*. San Diego: Center for Human Information Processing, University of California, 1976.

MEHAN, H. What time is it, Denise? Some observations on the organization and consequences of asking known information questions in classroom discourse. In J. Green (Ed.), *Communicating with young children. Theory into Practice*, 1979, *18*(4).

MERRITT, M., & HUMPHREY, F. Teacher, talk, and task: Communicative demands during individual instruction time. In J. Green (Ed.), *Communicating with young children. Theory into Practice*, 1979, *18*(4).

PHILIPS, S. The invisible culture: Communication in classroom and community on the Warm Springs Reservation. Unpublished doctoral dissertation, University of Pennsylvania, 1974.

RUDDELL, R. *Reading-language instruction: Innovative practices*. Englewood Cliffs, New Jersey: Prentice-Hall, 1974.

SIMS, R. Reading literature aloud. In B. Cullinan & C. Carmichael (Eds.), *Literature and young children*. Urbana, Illinois: National Council of Teachers of English, 1977.

SINCLAIR, J., & COULTHARD, R. *Toward an analysis of discourse: The English used by teachers and pupils*. Oxford, England: Oxford University Press, 1975.

STEINBERG, Z., & CAZDEN, C. Children as teachers—of peers and ourselves. In J. Green (Ed.), *Communicating with young children. Theory into Practice*, 1979, *18*(4).

STEPHENSON, G. The effects of discussion time in story reading on listening comprehension. Unpublished master's thesis, Kent State University, 1979.

STEWIG, J.W. Storyteller: Endangered species. *Language Arts*, March 1978, *55*(3).

TOUGH, J. Talking, thinking, and growing. New York: Schocken, 1974.

TUTOLO, D.J. A cognitive approach to teaching listening. *Language Arts*, 1977, *54*, 278–282.

TUTOLO, D.J. Attention: Necessary aspect of listening. *Language Arts*, January 1979, *56*(1).

VUKELITCH, C. The development of listening comprehension through storytime. *Language Arts*, 1976, *53*, 889–891.

WALLAT, C., & GREEN, J. In J. Green (Ed.), *Communicating with young children. Theory into Practice*, 1979, *18*(4).

Dialect and Reading: Toward Redefining the Issues

Rudine Sims
University of Masachusetts

It is the premise of this paper that speaking black dialect (or any dialect of American English) does not, in and of itself, interfere with learning to read (i.e. comprehend) written American English. What follows is a rationale for that position, some possible alternative explanations for reading problems among black children, and some suggestions and implications for teachers.

A Rationale

Research evidence does not support the assertion that dialect interferes with learning to read. Reviews of the literature Baratz (1971); Harber and Beatty (1978); Harber and Bryen (1976) reveal surprisingly few studies which involve black dialect speakers in actual reading. The influence of *Teaching Black Children to Read* is reflected in the fact that much of the research that does involve reading relates to the proposition strongly advocated in that volume, particularly by Joan Baratz and William Stewart, that speakers of black dialect should be taught to read with materials written to reflect the syntactic features of that dialect, i.e. "dialect readers." In such studies (Bartell & Axelrod, 1973; Hockman, 1973; Rosen & Ames, 1972) children typically are presented with reading or listening comprehension tasks in which the subjects read or listen to one passage in black dialect and one in standard English. The hypothesis is that if difficulty is caused by a mismatch between the language of the reader and the language of the written material, then reading should be easier (the readers should perform better) if the mismatch is eliminated. The contradictory results of such studies indicate some problems in interpreting the research.

One such problem is in the very creation of the "dialect materials." Whether the writer merely translates from one dialect to another syntactic/morphological features such as word order or verb forms, or also incorporates stylistic and vocabulary changes, can make a difference in the degree to which the dialect material differs from the standard material, and possibly in the relative comprehensibility of the material. Another problem is in the measuring of comprehension. Some researchers use typical informal reading inventory error counts, with no indication in the published research report of whether dialect differences in pronunciation or grammar count as errors. Others correlate the quantity of dialect features displayed in oral reading which scores on standardized reading tests, or use dialect versions of the tests as one of the reading tasks. When such correlations are statistically significant, the researcher reports a relationship between dialect and reading, not always being careful to point out that that relationship may not be causal.

An even more basic problem is one of definition. Researchers are not consistent in their definitions of "speakers of black dialect." Some are identified through the use of a sentence repetition task, others are apparently defined as speakers of black dialect by virtue of their being black and having low income, or by the common sense of researchers and their familiarity with the dialect. Even the critical term "interference" is not consistently defined across studies. Some researchers are willing to define interference as any use of the reader's dialect while reading standard English, e.g. pronouncing "they" as "dey," and to suggest there is evidence that dialect interferes with oral reading, but that the question of whether that interference has a negative effect is still open. Others define interference as intrusion with negative effects, and therefore find no dialect interference. It is not surprising, then, that reviewers of the research tend to suggest that evidence is inconclusive.

One group of studies involving the oral reading of speakers of black dialect (Goodman, 1978; Goodman and Burke, 1973;

Liu, 1973; Rigg, 1974; Simons and Johnson, 1974; Sims, 1972) is consistent in finding that dialect does not interfere with reading comprehension. These studies involve readers from grades two to ten, and have certain characteristics in common. In all of the studies, readers were asked to read whole selections, rather than sentences or excerpts, permitting them to make use of the redundancy and cohesiveness of a full text. Dialect was presumed not to be interfering unless it caused some change in the meaning of a passage or sentence, i.e. surface changes in grammar or vocabulary were considered not to be changes in meaning. Readers' miscues were examined, in the context of the sentences in which they occurred, as an assessment of ongoing comprehension during the reading of the text. Retellings were assessed as a post reading measure of comprehension. While the researchers were not all asking the same questions, and some used measures and procedures in addition to the ones cited, some findings were consistent across studies. Speakers of black dialect showed evidence of receptive control of standard English, and were able to accommodate in their reading to the styles of written English. There was great variability both within and across speakers in the use of dialect features in oral reading and retelling, i.e. individual readers did not use individual features of black dialect with 100 percent consistency. As is true for all readers, regardless of dialect, ease or difficulty of comprehension was related to factors other than the dialect of the reader, such as the readers' familiarity with story concepts, the obscurity of the theme, unfamiliarity with vocabulary, or the complexity of the sentence structure. Where studies involved material written in black dialect and other material in standard English, no differences in performances could be attributed to differences in the dialect of the materials.

Since none of those studies involved children at the very beginning of their school careers, or children without enough proficiency to sustain themselves through the reading of a short story, it has been suggested that they may have eliminated the very children for whom dialect does interfere with learning to read, the so-called nonreaders. The fact is that these studies do provide evidence that speakers of black dialect *can* and *do* learn to read, and that when they are unsuccessful, the cause of that failure must be sought outside the dialect per se.

A second basis for the premise that dialect does not interfere with reading comprehension is the proposition that currently most speakers of black dialect are at least receptively bidialectal. While it is probably true that social and economic isolation of blacks has aided in the survival of black English, it is also true that today's black children, particularly with the availability of television, are not isolated from varieties of English other than their own. For example, television commercials, Saturday cartoons, "Sesame Street," and the "Incredible Hulk" are not presented in black English, yet teachers can attest to the fact that black English speaking children understand and enjoy them and many other features of television. Black children and their parents in their roles as workers and consumers also have contact with speakers of other varieties of English. Teachers and researchers also have observed many instances in which both child and adult speakers of black dialect provide, in conversations or in play, convincing imitations of "proper" speakers, such as teachers or social workers, giving evidence of selective productive control of standard English. Actually, it is not surprising that black English speakers can understand other varieties of English, since, as native speakers of English, they share with other speakers most of the features of American English. In fact, many, though not all, of the structural and phonological features of black English are found in other regional and social dialects of English, the difference being a matter of frequency or of distribution in different linguistic contexts. Speakers of black dialect are not speakers of a foreign language. If dialect interference is measured on the basis of the productive language of the reader, then an important language strength of black dialect may go unrecognized. It is the ability to understand written language that is important in reading, not the ability to produce it, and to the extent that written English reflects standard spoken dialects of English, the ability to understand those spoken dialects is an important asset in learning to read.

A third basis for the rejection of an assumption of dialect interference is that the nature of written English and the nature of the reading process permit written English to be functional across dialects. In some sense, written English, particularly that of school texts, does not accurately reflect anyone's oral dialect. Spelling remains constant across dialects, so that, even though Bostonians, Atlantans, and Detroiters may pronounce it differently, "park" is always spelled p-a-r-k. Speakers of various dialects of English have different sets of homophones (e.g. are hairy and Harry pronounced the same way?), different patterns of sound-letter correspondence (e.g. does root rhyme with boot?), and different grammatical features (e.g. Do you wait *for* Jane or wait *on* Jane? Does one have two *pair* of shoes or two *pairs*? Is this *as far as* you go or *all the farther* you go?). In addition, written English has stylistic features which make it easily distinguishable from spoken English. Reading it is not simply a matter of "translating" written symbols into oral language, which then can be understood if it matches the reader's language, though such a view seems to underly some of the assertions that dialect interferes with learning to read. Reading is a much more complex process than that view admits, but it is not necessarily more complex for speakers of black dialects than for speakers of other dialects of English.

The process involves using printed symbols to construct a message which has been encoded in those symbols. It is not a serial, linear, letter by letter, word by word processing of the print, but involves sampling print and predicting meanings on the basis of that sampling and the reader's knowledge of his/her language, and of the concepts involved. The message is not in the surface features of the print (Goodman, 1978). The process allows speakers of black dialect, as well as any other speakers of English, to use their extensive language knowledge, including receptive knowledge of standard English, to understand written English. *All* readers show the influence of their own language in their reading. When that influence is seen as erroneous and unacceptable, initiate readers may experience confusion and may be cut off from one of the major resources they must use in learning to read—their language. Under those circumstances, learning to read may indeed become difficult, but it is not the dialect that has made it so.

Possible Alternative Explanations

If not "dialect interference," then what can account for the relatively poor performance of black children and others of similar status on tests of school achievement in general and reading achievement especially? In reality, findings of statistical relationships between black dialect and low reading scores should not be surprising. Black dialect is a social marker. It identifies an individual as a member of a group with low prestige in this society—a group whose members are not expected to achieve, whose achieving members are considered exceptions to the norm. This is a problem that is pervasive in American society, and is reflected in the institutional policies of our schools as well as in the day to day interactions in our classrooms. In addition, there is the possibility that the problem is at least partly a pedagogical one. There is not an intention here to lay blame at the feet of teachers, but an assertion that it is time to recognize the problem as something other than or more than a linguistic one.

Pedagogically, it is possible that the reading instruction received by speakers of black dialect is ineffective and inadequate to their needs. For instance, part of the mischief that remains from the deficit theories of the sixties is the notion that black children from inadequate material circumstances need more "structure" and more "concrete" experiences than other children. Where that dictum has been applied to reading instructional programs and materials, the results have been inane, programed, drill-the-skills packages—divorced from the language and experiences the children bring with them to school and force-fed to them bit by boring bit. Such programs are sometimes promoted as being especially appropriate for "disadvantaged" children, on the assumption that the materials compensate for the children's deficiences—of attention span, of structure and discipline in the home, of language, of contact with books. Programs tend to focus at the beginning levels on sound-letter correspondences, on the assumption that speakers of "different" dialects must develop improved auditory discrimination skills before they can learn to read. It is unlikely, however, that the reading process and the cognitive processing involved in learning to read English differ across social groups, so it is hard to see how an instructional program for the "disadvantaged" should differ qualitatively from one for "advantaged" children. The basic overarching pedagogical principles should remain constant. An effective management system cannot be equated with effective reading instruction.

It is possible, too, that reading instruction may focus so heavily on skills that attention to whole language and to comprehension is sacrificed. This writer recently observed for

90 minutes in a second grade class during a reading instructional period. In the entire one and one-half hours, the reading groups did nothing more than complete skills pages from various workbooks, all of which involved phonics. Not once did either the children or the teacher read anything except the unconnected sentences and phrases on those workbook pages. Since the principal indicated that this was a good teacher, and since my visit to observe her reading instruction was planned, it is probable that this teacher was not atypical, at least in her district. This heavy focus on paper and pencil exercises and lack of attention to comprehension instruction is apparently part of a general problem that is not limited to speakers of black dialect. Durkin (1979), in a study that may have far-reaching influence, reports on 299.95 hours of observing reading and social studies classes in central Illinois in order to discover whether elementary schools provide instruction in reading comprehension. She found 1) practically no comprehension instruction; 2) very little reading instruction of any other kind; and 3) considerable time spent on assignment giving and checking, on teacher interrogation as an assessment of comprehension, and on transitions and noninstructional activities. To the extent that Durkin's findings are representative of instructional practices nationally, inadequate instruction in reading comprehension may be a serious problem in many school settings. Where those school settings include large numbers of children who are black and poor and speakers of black dialect, it is possible that the combination of ill-conceived reading programs and poor instructional strategies may account, in part, for the relative difficulty these children appear to have in developing literacy.

However, as Durkin points out, many children learn to read, evidently in spite of their teachers' lack of attention to comprehension instruction. Apparently, the negative consequences of inadequate instruction are not distributed evenly among the school population. One possible explanation for this differentiation is that instructional programs and practices are administered in a social context, and their effects are not unrelated to the sociocultural factors which affect children's lives outside the school as well as within it. Sociocultural factors determine, for example, which societies are literate and which are not. Groups and individuals develop literacy as they develop and perceive needs which can be served through the use of written language, or through the fact of becoming literate. In the United States, irrespective of dialects, when children come to school having lived for five years in a family and community where books, other written material, and reading itself are highly valued; when they have been read to almost daily; and when they have been encouraged to try to read and write for themselves; they will probably learn to read, regardless of the quality of the instruction they receive in school. Reading is for the most part self-taught, and the role of instructors is to create a learning environment—to provide appropriate materials, to introduce problems which can be solved through written language, to provide information and feedback, to answer questions. That instructional role is an essential one, and its importance cannot be underestimated; but it *can* be carried out in the home and community by nonprofessionals. When children come to school having lived in material circumstances that preclude the purchase of books and the luxury of reading time; or when their families and others in their community place higher value on oral communication than on written documents; then the instructional role must be carried out by the school. In such circumstances, the teacher becomes responsible for making certain that the children discover from the beginning of their schooling that reading is *for* something, that it is another way to use language, that learning to read is worth the effort. To the extent that the latter group of children includes speakers of black dialect, the failure of the schools' instructional programs to take into account some of the sociocultural factors involved in the development of literacy may account for some of the inverse correlations between black dialect and reading achievements.

Further explanations for the apparent reading problems of many black children may be sought in the situational contexts in which reading instruction takes place—in individual classrooms, in the school as an institution, and in the society at large. Black dialect signifies membership in a low status group in American society, and that status is often perpetuated in schools and classrooms. In recent years, researchers have begun applying ethnographic methods to the study of classroom interactions. Ethnographic researchers attempt to understand behavior in a social context, and to describe what it is that people know that enables them to behave appropriately in a given social situation. In instructional settings, ethnographic studies enable researchers to discover among other things, patterns of miscommunication between teachers and students, differential structuring of reading groups and their activities, differences in the ways teachers respond to the initiatives of various children, and differences in the ways teachers evaluate the responses of different children. Byers and Byers (1972) reported on a filmed observation of a white teacher and four children in a nursery school setting. The teacher and one of the black children tried repeatedly to establish communication through eye contact and touch, but more often than not, they failed to do so. The teacher and one of the white children were much more successful at establishing and maintaining communication. Byers and Byers suggest that attempts to communicate failed because the teacher and the black child did not share the same nonverbal communicative codes. They further imply that this difference in nonverbal codes can account for the school problems of children who do not share their teachers' cultural background and therefore cannot easily interpret the subtle communications which permit full participation in the learning experiences of the classroom. McDermott and Gospodinoff (in press), on the other hand, assert that the miscommunication argument is too simple. They suggest that "different communicative codes represent political adaptations. . . . [They are] the accomplishments of people trying to get the most out of political and economic contexts for their being together." They describe one first grade classroom in which five of its six minority members were in the bottom reading group. The reading time allotted for all three groups was the same, but the bottom group spent only one third as much time as the top group in actual reading activity. The rest of the time was spent on children's attempts to capture the teacher's attention. The net result was that the bottom group fell farther and farther behind. McDermott and Gospodinoff suggest that both the teacher and the children make adjustments to each other's problems, and that, while the adjustments are not positive in terms of the children's educational needs, they are sensible and functional in the setting in which they occur. Studies like those of Byers and Byers and McDermott and Gospodinoff have the potential to help educators understand what happens in classrooms where black children and others learn to read, and in classrooms where they do not.

Earlier studies have documented the phenomenon of the self-fulfilling prophecy. "Dialect speaker" is just one more of the alliterative labels—i.e. deprived, deficient, disadvantaged, disabled, different—which function to sort children into self-perpetuating nonachieving groups. Harber and Beatty (1978) report studies which indicate that black dialect triggers for many teachers lower expectations, lower estimates of intelligence, and lower ratings of performance than for children who are speakers of higher status dialects. Given that kind of "head start," it is no wonder speakers of black dialect appear to have difficulty learning to read.

The interactions between teachers and students, however, must also be viewed in the larger school context in which they occur. Teachers sort children into groups because they feel pressured to do so. Teachers are held "accountable" for students' performance on standardized tests, which are themselves sorting mechanisms. Educators tenaciously cling to the test-related myth that all children should be reading "on grade level." Relatively modest federal funds are distributed where incomes are low and minority children are abundant, though the bulk of federal aid to education is distributed elsewhere. But federal aid carries no incentive for administrators to provide support for teachers to substantially improve reading achievement. Outside the school itself, inadequate housing, discriminatory housing policies, and extremely high unemployment work together to ensure the perpetuation of urban ghettos, and the social and psychological problems they spawn. In that context, the inverse correlations between black dialect and reading achievement must be understood as part of the problem of the larger American society, and the schools which are a reflection of that society.

A discussion of what might explain a lack of reading achievement among black children should not be closed without some mention of the possibility that reports of such lack of achievement are, like those premature reports of Mark Twain's death, greatly exaggerated. Readers who are proficient, who understand and are willing to play the tester's games, will score high on standardized tests. Those who do not make high scores, however, can only be said to have made low scores. They cannot be shown, on the basis of the quantity of "right answers" they produce on typical standardized tests, to have achieved a certain specifiably lesser degree of literacy. I do not mean to suggest that a problem does not exist, only that while we are searching for its causes, we need also to examine the uses, abuses, and misuses of the tests and test scores which are the data used to identify the problem, and which will be used to show the public that the problem is being solved.

Implications for Teachers

Where, then, do we go from here? Improving the overall quality of education, and in particular the development of literacy, for blacks and others with inadequate material resources in this country will require a major commitment of resources and major changes in educational, social, and economic policies. In the meantime, change can begin with individual teachers in individual classrooms.

Individual teachers can, first of all, learn to recognize and respect the legitimacy of language and cultural variation. What is needed is not a linguist's knowledge and ability to describe the features of a dialect or the ability to speak the same dialects as the children in a given classroom. What is needed is a linguist's knowledge of the cognitive and linguistic adequacy and validity of all dialects, and a linguist's acceptance of the legitimacy of language differences. What is needed is a sensitivity to the language of the children in a given class, a tuning in to the ways that have, in the terminology of M.A.K. Halliday, learned how to mean. Though knowledge in and of itself will not change attitudes, it is a first step. In the case of black English, one beginning place is Smitherman's book *Talking and Testifying* (1977), which describes both the linguistic features of black English, and its stylistic attributes, which are often ignored in discussions of black dialect. When teachers understand the language of their children, they can build on that understanding to expand children's language proficiencies, including their abilities to read and write.

As teachers learn more about language variation, they will need to help children learn to respect language differences, too. Differing dialects carry more or less social prestige, and children do learn which ones are more highly valued than others. One way to begin to help children recognize and respect the validity of language variation is to introduce them to library books which make use of a variety of dialects, styles, and registers. Books are available which contain regional and social dialects, such as that of the Old West or the South or the Appalachian Mountains, as well as black dialects as found, for example, in some of the books of Lucille Clifton and John Steptoe. Finding language variation in print lends a certain validity somehow makes the language legitimate.

A second consideration for teachers is to recognize the essentially normal and healthy nature of the children being discussed here. Schools and reading teachers need to abandon the medical pathology metaphor they have adopted in dealing with children who do not conform to their expectations. Children are not patients, they are learners. They have survived for six years; they have come to school having learned a language. Those facts provide ample evidence of their intelligence and their capacity to learn. Schools must, therefore, stop examining, diagnosing, and prescribing remedies and start creating environments that encourage children to continue learning in school settings as they have been learning in other settings. In creating such environments, teachers must consider that the social and psychological characteristics of an environment are as important as the physical characteristics. It is not enough, for example, to supply an attractive reading corner if only the "good" children or the "high achievers" get to use it. Children learn early, for another example, whether it is *what* they say or write that is important to the teacher, or *how* they say or write it. A learning environment must be one in which the learner is respected.

A third consideration for teachers is the quality of the reading instruction that takes place in their classrooms. To be effective, reading instruction must be based on a reliable theoretical base. Teachers should have some clear notion of the model of the reading process underlying their instructional practices, and be able to make decisions about materials and programs based on that model and their knowledge of the learners. When a teacher's manual contains assertions that contradict what a teacher knows about reading or about children as learners, that manual, and possibly that set of materials, should be rejected. The answer to reading difficulties does not lie at the end of the packaged program rainbow. Children can learn to read using various kinds of materials if those materials are meaningful and appropriate to the experiences and language proficiency of the children using them.

To be effective, reading instruction must not be divorced from the rest of the school curriculum and from the lives of the readers. It cannot be something that happens exclusively during "reading group" time. What is read cannot be exclusively stories unrelated to readers and their lives—stories that exclude them and their experiences or even insult them or their intelligence. Reading needs to be connected to writing and both need to be connected to purposeful activities. Children can use written language to learn about and to tell others about themselves and their worlds. To the extent that reading and writing remain purposeful, and to the extent that reading and writing activities build on what learners already know, comprehension will be made relatively easy.

Teachers must recognize that, in both reading and writing activities, the influence of children's oral language will be evident. That influence must be considered natural and normal, not pathological. The major focus must be on the process of writing, on the content of the written product, and on understanding of material that is read. On that foundation, teachers can help children expand the varieties and styles and forms of language they can use effectively and appropriately.

Conclusion

The issue of "dialect" will likely remain an issue for as long as language functions as a marker of social status. However, the issue of "dialect and reading" should be resolved long before the general one. Learning to read English cannot be considered the exclusive province of speakers of high prestige dialects of English. When schools fail to help speakers of low prestige dialects achieve what is considered an adequate level of literacy, the schools must recognize that they, and the society they reflect, own the failure, not the children. Some children who are speakers of black dialect, as well as other black children who are not, *are* learning to read in our classrooms. Perhaps it is time to focus on the positive—to discover what happens in successful classrooms by examining them through a grid that takes into account the entire situational context in which children do learn to read. However, schools are notoriously slow to change. It is likely they will continue to embrace the medical pathology metaphor. Perhaps then, it is time to examine the schools and the society, to diagnose the problems to be found there, and to prescribe remedies for their failures.

References

BAILEY, B. Toward a new perspective in Negro English dialectology. *American Speech*, October 1965, *40*(3), 171–177.

BARATZ, J. A review of research on the relationship of black English to reading. Paper presented at the annual convention of the International Reading Association, Atlantic City, 1971.

BARATZ, J., & SHUY, R. *Teaching black children to read.* Washington, D.C.: Center for Applied Linguistics, 1969.

BARTELL, N., & AXELROD, J. Nonstandard English usage and reading ability in black junior high students. *Exceptional Children*, 1973, *39*, 653–655.

BYERS, P., & BYERS, H. Nonverbal communication and the education of children. In C. Cazden, V. John, & Hymes (Eds.), *Functions of language in the classroom.* New York: Teachers College Press, 1972.

DURKIN, D. What classroom observations reveal about reading comprehension instruction. *Reading Research Quarterly*, 1978–1979, *14*(4), 481–533.

GOODMAN, K.S. *Reading of American children whose language is a stable rural dialect of English or a language other than English.* Final Report, NIE 0-00-3-0087, U.S. Department of Health, Education and Welfare. National Institute of Education, August 1978.

GOODMAN, K.S., & BURKE, C.L. *Theoretically based studies of patterns of miscues in oral reading performance.* Final Report, Project No. 9-0375. U.S. Department of Health, Education and Welfare, Office of Education, Bureau of Research, April 1973.

HARBER, J., & BEATTY, J. (Compilers). *Reading and the black English speaking child.* Newark, Delaware: International Reading Association, 1978.

HOCKMAN, C. Black dialect reading tests in the urban elementary school. *Reading Teacher,* 1973, *26,* 581-583.

LIU, S. An investigation of oral reading miscues made by nonstandard dialect speaking black children. Unpublished doctoral dissertation, University of California, 1973.

McDERMOTT, R., & GOSPODINOFF, K. Social contexts for ethnic borders and school failure. In A. Wolfgang (Ed.), *Nonverbal behavior.* New York: Academic, in press.

RIGG, P. A psycholinguistic analysis of the oral reading miscues generated by speakers of rural black dialect compared to the miscues of speakers of an urban black dialect. Unpublished doctoral dissertation, Wayne State University, 1974.

ROSEN, C., & AMES, W. Influence of nonstandard dialect on the oral reading behavior of fourth grade black children under two stimuli conditions. In J.A. Figurel (Ed.), *Better reading in urban schools.* Newark, Delaware: International Reading Association, 1972.

SIMONS, H., & JOHNSON, K. Black English syntax and reading interference. *Research in the Teaching of English,* Winter 1974, *8,* 339-358.

SIMS, R. A psycholinguistic description of miscues generated by selected young readers during the reading of text material in black dialect and standard English. Unpublished doctoral dissertation, Wayne State University, 1972.

SMITHERMAN, G. *Talkin and testifying: The language of black America.* Boston: Houghton Mifflin, 1977.

TURNER, L. *Africanisms in the Gullah dialect.* Chicago: University of Chicago Press, 1949.

A PUBLISHING PROGRAM
TO SERVE YOUR NEEDS...

The development of professional publications that uniquely meet the current needs and expectations of reading teachers, researchers, librarians, and other educators is a major goal of the International Reading Association. Your brief responses to the questions below will help us plan for the future.

Reader Meets Author/Bridging the Gap

Judith A. Langer and M. Trika Smith-Burke

This book came to my attention through

_____ my membership in IRA

_____ my school library

_____ a colleague

_____ my child's interests in reading

_____ other (*please specify:* _____)

Chapters which interested me most were

_____   _____

_____   _____

Least helpful portions of the book were

_____   _____

_____   _____

Topics that I wanted to know more about were

_____   _____

_____   _____

My needs would best be served through

_____ interpretations of research

_____ practical suggestions for classroom use

_____ help for parents

_____ other (*please specify:* _____)

Use reverse side for additional comments and free samples.

Reactions to this volume...(*continued*)